Praise for *How to Talk Finance*

'A fundamental understanding of finance is crucial for anyone wanting to progress in business. Ted explains the basic concepts well using clear language and helpful examples. This book is a great starting point for anyone looking to be able to "talk numbers" credibly.'

Steve Wilkinson, UK Managing Partner, Ernst & Young

'Absolutely essential reading for every candidate, past, present and future on *The Apprentice* – and a most useful, plain-speaking, down to earth book on finance for anybody planning to enter business and everybody who is already there.'

Nick Hewer, one time advisor to Lord Sugar on *The Apprentice*

'An essential read for those who wish to increase their understanding of the fundamentals of finance.'

Lee Johnson, Global HR Director, Coroda

'Finance books don't normally "grip" me but this one is a great tool for quick clarifications of finance terms as well as more detailed illustrations to help demystify the world of finance – definitely a book to have on the desk!'

Rachel Kay, Managing Director, Thales Training & Consultancy

HOW TO TALK FINANCE

PEARSON

At Pearson, we believe in learning – all kinds of learning for all kinds of people. Whether it's at home, in the classroom or in the workplace, learning is the key to improving our life chances.

That's why we're working with leading authors to bring you the latest thinking and best practices, so you can get better at the things that are important to you. You can learn on the page or on the move, and with content that's always crafted to help you understand quickly and apply what you've learned.

If you want to upgrade your personal skills or accelerate your career, become a more effective leader or more powerful communicator, discover new opportunities or simply find more inspiration, we can help you make progress in your work and life.

Pearson is the world's leading learning company. Our portfolio includes the Financial Times and our education business, Pearson International.

Every day our work helps learning flourish, and wherever learning flourishes, so do people.

To learn more, please visit us at **www.pearson.com/uk**

How to Talk Finance

Getting to grips with the numbers in business

Ted Wainman

Harlow, England • London • New York • Boston • San Francisco • Toronto • Sydney • Auckland • Singapore • Hong Kong
Tokyo • Seoul • Taipei • New Delhi • Cape Town • São Paulo • Mexico City • Madrid • Amsterdam • Munich • Paris • Milan

Pearson Education Limited
Edinburgh Gate
Harlow CM20 2JE
United Kingdom
Tel: +44 (0)1279 623623
Web: www.pearson.com/uk

First edition published in Great Britain 2015 (print and electronic)

ISBN: 978-1-292-07438-2 (print)
       978-1-292-07440-5 (PDF)
       978-1-292-07441-2 (ePub)
       978-1-292-07439-9 (eText)

British Library Cataloguing-in-Publication Data
A catalogue record for the print edition is available from the British Library

Library of Congress Cataloging-in-Publication Data
Wainman, Ted.
  How to talk finance : getting to grips with the numbers in business / Ted Wainman. -- 1st Edition.
    pages cm
  ISBN 978-1-292-07438-2
  1. Business enterprises--Finance. 2. Corporations--Finance. I. Title.
  HG4026.W336 2015
  658.15--dc23
                          2015004045

10 9 8 7 6 5 4
19

Cover design by Two Associates
Print edition typeset in 9.5pt ITC Giovanni by 3
Print edition printed by Ashford Colour Press Ltd, Gosport

NOTE THAT ANY PAGE CROSS REFERENCES REFER TO THE PRINT EDITION

Contents

Acknowledgements

We are grateful to the following for permission to use copyright material:

Image on page xiii Syda Productions/ Shutterstock.com; image on page xvi maradonna 8888/ Shutterstock.com; image on page 7 Andrey Popov/ Shutterstock.com; image on page 32 the Everett Collection/ Shutterstock.com; image on page 34 Marina Sun/ Shutterstock.com; image on page 37 studio 55/ Shutterstock.com; image on page 45 ekkstock/ Shutterstock.com; image on page 99 Stuart Mikes/ Shutterstock.com; image on page 118 anigoweb/ Shutterstock.com; left hand image on pages 120/121 Tiplyashina Evgeniya/ Shutterstock.com; right hand image on pages 120/ 121 AMA/ Shutterstock.com; image on page 126 talitha_it/ Shutterstock.com; image on page 150 Maksim Kabakou/ Shutterstock.com; first image on page 181, and on page 262, Javier Brosch/ Shutterstock.com; image on page 190 Rawpixel/ Shutterstock.com; image on page 197 PhotographyByMK/ Shutterstock.com; image on page 207 davidelliotphotos/ Shutterstock.com; image on page 226 Slavoljub Pantelic/ Shutterstock.com; image on page 253 koya979/ Shuterstock.com; image on page 281 Khen Guan Toh/ Shutterstock.com; image on page 283 kurkhan/ Shutterstock.com; image on page 292 Tom Saga/ Shutterstock.com

The publisher would like to thank British Telecommunications plc, National Grid and Tesco plc for their permission to use the financial data in this book.

In some instances we have been unable to trace the owners of copyright material, and we would appreciate any information that would enable us to do so.

About the author

Ted Wainman started out with Ernst & Young (EY), where he trained and qualified as an Associate Chartered Accountant (ACA). After six years with EY working with a wide variety of clients, Ted joined JPMorgan and spent a further six years working in investment management. Whilst at JPMorgan, he undertook a company-sponsored MBA in the International Management of Financial Services, from which he graduated with merit at the top of his class.

Since 2003 Ted has been designing, developing and delivering programmes for private sector companies (including blue chips and financial services) across a wide range of business needs. Whether focused on programmes to build awareness and detailed understanding around financial drivers of their business, addressing new operational initiatives or supporting business change, Ted is experienced in working with key stakeholders within the business to construct training programmes that deliver sustained change.

Ted has worked extensively across the UK, as well as mainland Europe, the Middle East and Africa, with a wide range of companies – primarily private or listed – from large blue chips to small family-run outfits, in manufacturing, services and financial services and is experienced in addressing the needs of programmes across varying cultural backgrounds.

Ted has drawn on his experiences of working with over 170 clients in more than 25 countries to write this book. Finding the common questions that are always asked, Ted has written a book that provides the building blocks to allow managers to fully understand the finances of their business and to develop their commercial acumen.

Not sure about the difference between gross and net margin? Confused between margin and mark up? Muddled between the balance sheet and P&L account? Getting your accruals and prepayments the wrong way round? Not sure what EBTIDA, IRR or the WACC is, or why they are important? Then this book is for you – written in easy-to-understand plain English with practical examples, this book will give you the confidence to talk finance.

Introduction

'Finance is very simple but it is made to look complicated to justify the fees.'

www.fool.com

Have you ever been in a business meeting and, when the person from the finance team starts talking, you can see everyone's eyes glaze over (and a few start to lose the will to live)?

Welcome to *How To Talk Finance: Getting to grips with the numbers in business.*

The fact that you are reading this suggests that:

▶ you have picked this book off the shelf at a bookshop and are wondering whether it really is possible to learn finance – a dry subject at the best of times – from a book

▶ you have purchased the book online and are wondering whether you have just made a big mistake – maybe you should open it in a few places to make it look like it has been read and then put on a shelf to gather dust

▶ you have found it lying around and have picked it up just to see how boring a book really can be

▶ or (maybe) you think that this will be the next 'number 1 best seller holiday must-read of the year' and want to get ahead of the crowd.

Whatever your reason, I somehow doubt that the latter will score very highly.

Why are you reading this book?

As we have discovered from the likes of Enron, WorldCom and the banking crisis of 2007–8, a sound financial control lies at the heart of a successful business. And yet, many managers in business have a poor understanding of the subject and not only find it difficult to contribute to discussions when financial issues are being addressed, but also they actually feel prevented from doing so due to their lack of confidence in the subject. Understanding finance is, therefore, a crucial skill for managers and anyone looking to progress in the modern workplace.

As we travel through corporate life – from someone who works as a sole trader (for him or herself) to the person who works in a multinational corporation – an understanding of the finances of the business becomes increasingly important as we move up the corporate ladder.

It is possible to leave marketing to the marketers, manufacturing to the manufacturers, buying to procurement, compliance to the legal team and sales to the sellers. But every role will have a direct impact on the finances of the business and understanding this impact is a crucial skill in being able to advance up an organisation.

Managers often will have their first encounter with finance when budget responsibility is thrust upon them – What is a budget? What is the difference between a budget and a forecast? How do I do it? – often with very little formal training or help.

There are many books in the FT Pearson range that will deal with the topics covered in this book in greater detail – from budgeting and forecasting to analysis of accounts. You can see the full list of available titles at **www.pearsoned.co.uk/bookshop**. But, while other books may deal with specific topics in greater detail, this book aims to give the broad brush big picture of finance.

This book aims to deliver a 'Ronseal' promise (you may remember the Ronseal advertisements – 'It does exactly what it says on the tin' – well, this book aims to give you 'exactly what it says on the cover') an overall big picture of the world of business finance and how companies work financially. You should treat this book as the first building block in your financial education. If, then, you need a greater understanding of any specific element (how to build a budget from scratch, drawing up a business plan or pricing a derivative), you can be comfortable that the basics are in place.

It is probably worth mentioning the scope of this book. This book aims to deal with the finances of a normal company – from a small trading company to a large blue chip. The accounts of banks and insurance companies are considerably more complex and, while many of the concepts contained in this book will be relevant, almost all of the ratios and analysis will not.

In addition, this book focuses on for profit companies with shareholders. Thus while, again, there will be parts that are relevant, it is not focused on the not for profit companies (such as charities) or government sector organisations.

What is accounting?

Let us start this book by defining finance and accounting:

'Accounting is the process of identifying, measuring and communicating financial information to permit informed decisions by users of that information.'

Now, let us be clear here – it is the bean counters (as the finance team are sometimes affectionately known) who are responsible for identifying, measuring and communicating. If you are training to become an accountant – ACA or CIMA or the equivalent – then this book may be useful, but you are probably not the target audience.

It is the managers in the business, who are expected to make informed decisions. They can only make informed decisions if they can read and understand the information that they are being provided with by the finance team.

Don't know your P&L from your gross profit? Keep getting your accruals and prepayments muddled up? Still not sure how a company can make a profit and still go bust? Then this book is for you. It will start managers on the road to financial literacy by:

▶ helping managers understand the financial implications of their operational decisions

▶ helping managers read and interpret the financial information provided in the management information reports produced by the finance team

▶ giving managers the confidence to take the appropriate, informed action, where necessary.

Can you learn finance from a book?

Good question. And the answer is definitely 'yes', but it is hard work.

Have another look at the earlier definition of finance and accounting. Learning finance is a bit like learning a foreign language. It is very difficult to become fluent in Spanish, Italian or Arabic by rote, learning phrases from a book – just as it is very difficult to learn finance from a book; but the books are there to help.

So what is the best way to learn a new language? To immerse yourself in the culture – go to Spain and live there, make sure you speak only Spanish and read Spanish newspapers. You will pick up the language quickly. Do you feel embarrassed speaking to a Spanish child who clearly has a greater grasp of the language than you? Of course not – they have been speaking the language for much longer.

Now, you should approach finance in exactly the same way. The members of the finance team have been 'speaking' finance for many years. The concept of accruals and prepayments is second nature to them because they are 'fluent' in finance. Just as the notes on a sheet of music will 'sing' to a competent musician who can read music, so the figures on a balance sheet will 'sing' to an accountant (a sad analogy, I know, but bear with me).

So, use this book as a starting point – not an end in itself. Read each chapter slowly – making sure you understand fully the points being made. Try not to bite off more than you can chew – it is not an Agatha Christie novel – racing to the last page will not tell you who dunnit. Then return to each chapter as necessary – use it as a reference guide to gain, consolidate and retain your knowledge (the Key learning points at the end of each chapter are there to assist you when you revisit the topic). Remember – your undivided attention will pay dividends; it will be worth the time and effort in the long run.

And a final piece of advice: if you are in Spain (learning Spanish) and you hear an unfamiliar word or phrase – what should you do? Ask the person who said it to translate – that way you will learn. In exactly the same way, have the confidence to challenge anyone (particularly from the finance team) who uses terminology with which you are not familiar. Ask them to continue to explain the term or phrase until you **fully** get it! Remember – they are meant to be fluent, but you are not. Don't let them pull the wool over your eyes!

Additional resources

 In writing this book, I have tried to make everything as simple and as interesting (can finance be interesting?) as possible. Rather than using fictional 'Sam Smith and his Shipyard' accounts, I have used the accounts of companies that I hope you have heard of. All of the information in this book is publicly available on websites or at Companies House.

All the accounts of the companies refer to prior years and, in some cases, may appear a little dated. The concepts covered and the learning points will remain the same, but do try to obtain the most recent accounts (try typing '[company name] annual report and accounts' into Google) and see how the figures have changed and what this means for the business.

I have also put together some videos to explain some of the concepts covered. At the time of writing, those listed at the beginning of each chapter are available on YouTube, but others will be added in the future. I hope that you find them useful. They can be found on my website at **www.wainman. net** (links to the videos can be found at **www.wainman.net/wainman.net/ resources.html**). If you can't find something you are looking for, then please do visit the website; alternatively, you are welcome to drop me a line (my email is at the end of this chapter).

Further questions

During each chapter there are additional questions. There are no right answers to these questions – these are merely further areas for research or questions to provide you with a focus on where to apply your knowledge or increase your understanding of the topic.

Key learning points

 A summary of the Key learning points for each chapter is provided at the end of that chapter. This should assist you, should you need to refer back to the contents of a particular chapter.

Next steps

 At the end of each chapter there is a short paragraph on next steps. This will contain suggestions on what you should do to consolidate and embed the knowledge that you have gained from reading the chapter.

The next steps, together with your thoughts on the Further questions should help you to apply your newly gained knowledge in a practical way and so improve your financial thinking skills.

Test yourself

 At the end of each chapter you will find some multiple choice (or, in some cases, multiple guess) questions – designed to assess your understanding of the topics covered in that chapter. You can find the answers to these questions at the back of the book.

Glossary

Probably the best place for a glossary of financial terms is the Internet (such as **http://en.wikipedia.org/wiki/Finance** or **www.investopedia.com**). However, I have included a glossary of the terms used in this book that may not appear familiar.

And finally… I do not expect that this book will become the next Harry Potter and fly off the bookshelves, but I do hope that you find the topics covered useful, engaging and interesting. Please do feel free to get in touch regarding any topics covered in this book.

Ted Wainman
ted@wainman.net
www.wainman.net
March 2015

Test yourself

0.1 Finance is:

   (a) not important in a business ☐

   (b) the domain of the finance team only ☐

   (c) crucial to managing a business effectively ☐

   (d) the only thing that managers should consider when running a ☐
business

0.2 Accounting is about:

   (a) making sure that the business is profitable ☐

   (b) providing financial information to assist with running the business ☐

   (c) keeping the finance department busy ☐

   (d) telling sales people what they cannot do ☐

CHAPTER ONE

How a company is financially structured and how it trades

'Watch your finances like a hawk.'

H. Jackson Brown Jr

 ## Aim

The aim of this chapter is to understand how a company is financially structured and how a company trades.

 ## Outcomes

By the end of this chapter you will understand:

▶ the difference between a sole trader, a partnership and a limited liability company

▶ how the accounting equation describes the balance sheet

▶ how the balance sheet and profit & loss account interact

▶ how a company accounts for transactions in the balance sheet and profit & loss account

▶ that profit is not the same as cash generated

▶ what 'accrual' accounting means.

1

Additional resources

▶ Links to videos are available at: **www.wainman.net/wainman.net/resources.html**

Is it plus or minus?

One of the most common questions when looking at financial figures is: 'is it a plus or a minus?'. A key skill in being able to 'read' financial information is to be able to change the question to 'is it an asset or liability?' (if you are looking at the balance sheet) or 'is it an income or expense?' (if you are looking at the P&L).

Let's look at an example. In the profit and loss account of a business, you will find income and expenses. These may be presented like this:

Sales	£ 100
Costs	−£ 60
Profit	£ 40

Sometimes brackets are used instead of the minus sign (they are easier to spot):

Sales	£ 100
Costs	(£ 60)
Profit	£ 40

However, a company may ignore the use of a minus sign or brackets, assuming that costs are obviously costs and do not need a minus sign at all:

Sales	£ 100
Costs	£ 60
Profit	£ 40

All of the above are 'correct' if (cosmetically) presented differently. Now look at the following figures:

Sales	£ 100
Cost of Sales	£ 60
Gross Profit	£ 40
Operating Costs	£ 20
Other income	(£ 5)
Operating Profit	£ 25

In this example, 'other income' has brackets around it – presenting the number as a negative. The £20 on the line above is a cost, so 'other income' is presented as a 'negative cost' – in effect, an income. Your ability to spot these concepts will improve with practice.

When looking at the balance sheet, the same concept applies. Sometimes in the 'assets' section of a balance sheet, you will be presented with a 'negative asset' – which is, in fact, a liability. Similarly, a negative liability must be an asset.

The first chapter of this book will introduce the concepts of income, costs, assets and liabilities, so if the above does not make total sense at this point, don't worry too much. But you might like to revisit this section as you read through the book. The key is to try to start thinking in terms of income and costs or assets and liabilities, not in terms of plus and minus.

What is a sole trader?

Let us first consider an individual who works for himself and who we shall call Arthur. Irrespective of what he actually does, whether it is manufacturing goods, buying and selling or providing a service, he is known as a sole trader.

Arthur

SOLE TRADER

? What sort of businesses do you think are sole traders?

What is a partnership?

Now let us assume that Arthur decides to go into business with Becky. Becky also works for herself as a sole trader. They agree to pool the income that they receive, deduct any costs incurred, and share anything left over on an equitable or pre-agreed basis. They have formed what is known as a partnership.

Arthur   Becky

PARTNERSHIP

? Accountancy and law firms are often partnerships. Why do you think this is?

? What other businesses can you think of that are partnerships?

What is a limited company?

Rather than forming a partnership with Becky, Arthur might choose to set up a separate company with Ben, which they will decide to call A&B Ltd. The main difference between Arthur and Becky working together in a partnership and Arthur and Ben working together for the company is that the company is a separate legal entity. What is the effect of separating the owners from the business? There is a 'veil of incorporation' that separates Arthur and Ben, as the owners, from the company itself. Ltd means 'Limited' – as in 'limited liability'. This refers to the limited liability of Arthur and Ben as the shareholders.

For example, if A&B Ltd was to borrow £10,000 and not be able to repay the loan, then Arthur and Ben – as the shareholders – would not be personally liable for that debt. Their liability would be limited to the amount of their original investment, perhaps as little as £100 each.

? What other advantages can you think of for creating a limited company?

What is the role of the directors?

So, Arthur and Ben have set up A&B Ltd. They need someone to run the company, so they appoint a board of directors. Initially, they appoint themselves as directors, and thus A&B Ltd becomes an owner-managed business. In effect, Arthur and Ben, as the **directors**, are now running the business on behalf of Arthur and Ben as the **owners**.

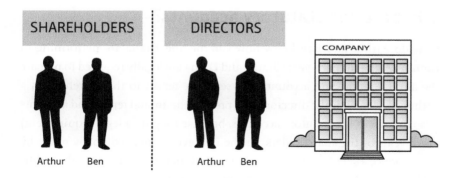

? Every company must have at least one director as a minimum. What limits the maximum, do you think?

Are the directors always the owners of a company?

As the company grows, Arthur and Ben may need additional help in running the business. In this case they might ask Charlie and Diana to join them on the board.

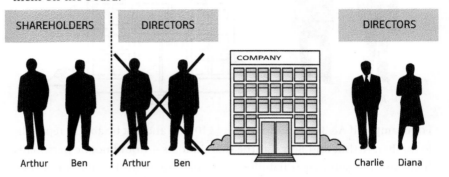

The company continues to grow, and becomes so successful that Arthur and Ben decide to retire from the day-to-day running of the business. They remain as the shareholders but are no longer directors. We now have a situation where the owners of the business (Arthur and Ben) are different from the managers of the business (Charlie and Diana).

? What sort of companies do you think will have the shareholders and the directors as the same people?

? For what sort of companies will the directors and the shareholders be different people?

What are the statutory accounts?

How do Arthur and Ben know how Charlie and Diana are performing in running A&B Ltd? Each year Charlie and Diana are legally required to prepare the annual report and accounts and send the report to the shareholders – Arthur and Ben. It is the directors who prepare the annual report and accounts (also known as the statutory accounts, because they are a legal requirement) every year for the shareholders. In the UK, every single company must, by law, produce a set of statutory accounts – and they are available to the public at Companies House (see **www.companieshouse.gov.uk**).

? What would be the implication of not having to prepare financial statements?

What is the role of the auditors?

Each year Arthur and Ben receive the annual report and accounts from Charlie and Diana, detailing how A&B Ltd has performed financially over the previous 12 months. How do Arthur and Ben rely on the figures contained in the report and ensure that Charlie and Diana are telling the truth? The answer is that the shareholders (Arthur and Ben) will appoint an independent auditor to check the figures on their behalf. The auditor is appointed by the shareholders to check the figures that are prepared by the directors. Note – the auditors are not responsible for preparing the accounts, only checking them!

? What might be the impact if it was the directors who appointed the auditors?

What is the difference between the executive and the non-executive directors?

Ella and Fiona have joined Charlie and Diana on the board of A&B Ltd. Charlie and Diana are executive directors, whereas Ella and Fiona are non-executive directors. So, what is the difference between the two roles?

As the board of directors, together they determine the overall strategic direction of the company. Charlie and Diana, as executive directors, are responsible for executing that strategy. They have day-to-day responsibility for the running of the business. Ella and Fiona, as the non-executive directors, are responsible for holding Charlie and Diana to account. Non-executive directors usually are individuals who have a wealth of business experience, work for a number of different companies on a part-time basis, and can act as a mentor for the full-time directors. But they are also there to ensure that the executives, Charlie and Diana, are running the business in the best interests of the shareholders, Arthur and Ben (who by now have retired to a private island). Corporate governance states that companies must also be run in the interests of the employees and suppliers, but the primary interests are those of the shareholders.

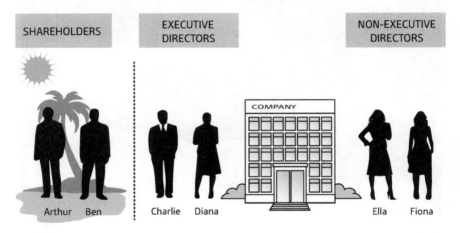

As shareholders, Arthur and Ben do not have right of access to the boardroom (if you buy a share in BP then you cannot attend board meetings!). So, the non-executive directors are appointed by the shareholders to hold the executive directors to account and to ensure that the business is being run in the best interests of the shareholders. This is a little bit like your local school – the head teacher and his or her senior leadership team (head of English, head of Maths, etc.) are the executive and have day-to-day responsibility for running the school and they sit on the governing body. The representatives from the local community – perhaps the local church, representatives from the parent teachers association and others with an interest – are also on the governing body;

they do not run the school, but act as friendly advisors to the executive, providing feedback and guidance, but, ultimately, ensuring that the school is run in the best interests of the children (and no one else, including pushy parents!).

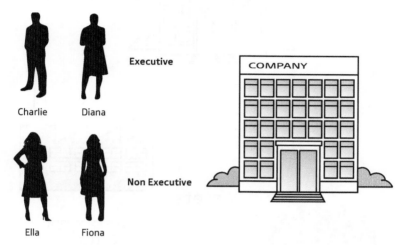

? What sort of companies have non-executive directors?

? What sort of companies do not have non-executive directors? Why not?

What are assets?

A&B Ltd has assets. These are things that are owned by the company, such as tables, chairs, computer equipment, cash and stock in the warehouse. Despite what you might have been told, members of staff are not assets. This is because members of staff are not owned by the business; they are, in fact, contracted to undertake work and are therefore treated as an expense.

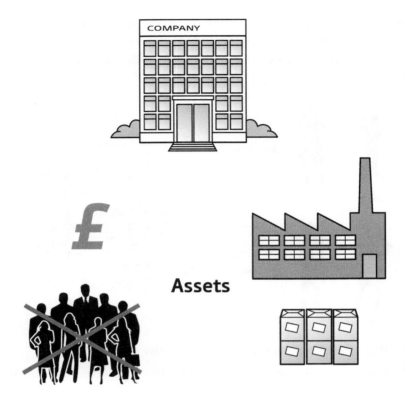

Assets

? What sort of assets does your business have?

What are liabilities?

A&B Ltd also has liabilities. These are amounts owed by the company to third parties. Typically, the largest liabilities of a company will be any debts that it has and any amounts owed to suppliers that have not yet been paid.

? What sort of liabilities does your business have?

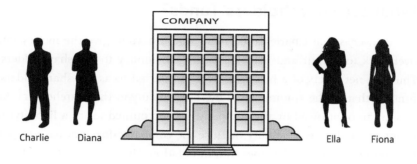

Charlie   Diana   Ella   Fiona

Liabilities

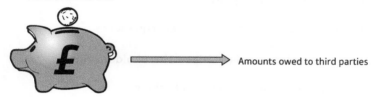

Amounts owed to third parties

What is liquidation?

If A&B Ltd was put into liquidation, the assets would be sold off and turned into cash. The first thing that the directors must do with that cash is pay off their liabilities – the debts, suppliers, staff and any other amounts owing. Any money left over is known as the net assets. That is, the assets, net of (or less) the liabilities of the business. What would the directors do with this money that is left over?

? When a company is put into receivership, it continues to trade. When a company is put into liquidation, it ceases to trade. Why do you think this distinction exists?

? Can you think of a company that has been put into administration, but not into liquidation (often referred to as pre-pack in the UK or Chapter 11 in the USA)?

What are shareholders' funds?

The answer is that Charles and Diana would have to give the money left over back to Arthur and Ben, i.e. return the money to the shareholders. Thus the net assets of a business are also referred to as the shareholders' funds – that is, the amount owed by the company to the shareholders. As it is an amount owed by the company, it is accounted for as a liability; it is not referred to as a liability because the company does not have to pay the amount back unless it goes into liquidation. However, it is treated as a liability in the accounts.

What is the accounting equation?

We are now introduced to the accounting equation:

assets less liabilities = shareholders' funds

We can rearrange the above equation to show:

assets = shareholders' funds plus liabilities

or

assets less shareholders' funds less liabilities = zero

It is a zero-sum game. The assets of a business are always equal to the liabilities of the business. Thus, we are introduced to the balance sheet. The balance sheet is so known because it always balances. One side is always equal to the other.

? What do you think the accounting equation will look like for your business?

What will we find in shareholders' funds?

We have shown that the shareholders' funds is the amount that is left over after deducting liabilities owed to third parties from the assets of a business. However, it is not just the balancing figure, all transactions are specifically accounted for. So what are the two main things that make up the shareholders' funds? What are the two main things that a company owes back to its shareholders?

How is investment accounted for in shareholders' funds?

The first element of the shareholders' funds of a business is the investment made by the shareholders. Because, if Arthur and Ben were to invest £50 each into A&B Ltd, the business would show assets of £100 (i.e. the cash) and shareholders' funds of £100 (i.e. the amount owed back to Arthur and Ben) and thus the balance sheet would continue to balance.

How is retained profit accounted for in shareholders' funds?

The second element of the shareholders' funds (of a business) is any profit that it has made and that has been reinvested back into the business on behalf of the shareholders. So, if A&B Ltd took the £100 that was originally invested by Arthur and Ben, started trading and generated a profit of £50, it could do one of two things with that profit. The directors could decide to pay a dividend (which is a distribution of profit) to Arthur and Ben, or they could decide to reinvest it back into the business, or a combination of both.

So, if A&B Ltd generated a profit of £50 and paid £20 back to Arthur and Ben in the form of a dividend, then it would still owe the shareholders (Arthur and Ben) the £30 that was not paid back to them – this is in effect the retained profits (sometimes referred to as retained earnings) and would, therefore, appear as part of the shareholders' funds on the balance sheet.

= Shareholders' Funds

Investment   Retained Profit

? What do you think is the mix between these two elements of share-holders' funds for your business?

How do the profit & loss account and balance sheet interact?

Now that Arthur and Ben have set up A&B Ltd, let us see how the company actually trades.

Imagine that Arthur and Ben each invest £50 into A&B Ltd. The assets of the business would be £100 in cash. At this point the company does not have any liabilities (amount that it owes to third parties) so the net assets of the company are £100. This £100 of net assets is represented by the shareholders' funds, that is, the original investment of £100, plus any retained profits. As the company has not undertaken any trading activities as yet, there are no retained profits to reinvest back into the business.

What is the balance sheet?

The balance sheet is a snapshot in time. It is an 'as at' position. It shows the assets and the liabilities of the company at a particular point in time. The only two things that you will find on the balance sheet are the assets and the liabilities of the company.

Balance sheet	End of day 0
Assets	£ 100
Liabilities	£ 0
Net assets	£ 100
Shareholder funds	
Investment	£ 100
Retained profits	£ 000
	£ 100

What is the profit & loss account?

The income statement, also known as the profit & loss account (P&L), is the company's trading account. This is where a company will show its sales (also known as turnover, revenue, or income) and its costs or outgoings (including such things as wages and salaries). While the balance sheet is a snapshot in time, the profit & loss account is a journey between two points in time (each point being represented by the balance sheet); the profit & loss account shows the trading for a particular period of time, such as a day, a week, a month, or a year.

How do we account for trade in cash?

Arthur and Ben take the £100 cash and head off down to the local market where they meet George, who is selling apples for £1 each. Arthur and Ben agree to buy 100 apples from George. They hand over the £100 cash and George hands over the apples.

Who owns the apples?

Obviously it is Arthur and Ben (or, to be exact, A&B Ltd). And, if they own the apples, they can do whatever they want with them. And they want to sell. So they meet Harry who agrees to buy the 100 apples for £500 (they are either very high-quality apples or Arthur and Ben are very persuasive). Harry hands over the £500 cash and Arthur and Ben hand over the 100 apples. Now who owns the apples? Again it is pretty obvious that Harry owns the apples and, if Harry owns the apples, then Arthur and Ben can record the trade in the books of A&B Ltd.

They have made sales of £500, their costs were £100, leaving a profit of £400.

What does the balance sheet now look like?

Now they can update the balance sheet. Having started the day with £100 in cash, turned that cash into apples and sold the apples for £500 cash, Arthur and Ben now have £500 in cash. They don't have any other assets (remember, they have sold the apples). For the sake of this example, we will ignore tax, and so A&B Ltd has no liabilities (remember they paid cash when they bought the apples from George). The net assets of A&B are, therefore, £500.

The net assets of £500 are represented by the shareholders' funds of A&B Ltd. That is, the original investment of £100 and the £400, which is the total profit the company has made ever since it started trading and is not yet given back to the shareholders; it has been reinvested back into the business by the directors on behalf of the shareholders.

Profit & loss account		During day				
Sales		£	500			
Costs		(£	100)			
Profits		£	400			
Balance sheet	End of day 0			End of day 1		
Assets	£	100	cash	£	500	cash
Liabilities	£	0		£	0	
Net assets	£	100		£	500	
Shareholders' funds						
Investment	£	100		£	100	
Retained profits	£	0		£	400	
	£	100		£	500	

Arthur and Ben could now choose to put A&B Ltd into liquidation. In this case, the £500 cash would be divided between Arthur and Ben. The £250 that each receives would be their £50 original investment plus half (because each owns half of the company) of the retained profit of £400. But they don't want to put the company into liquidation, they want to continue trading.

How do we account for trading on credit?

Arthur and Ben head back out to meet up with George, who is still selling apples for £1 each. Once again, George agrees to sell 100 apples for £100 to Arthur and Ben. Unfortunately, Arthur and Ben forgot to bring the cash with them.

What is a creditor?

So George agrees to sell the apples on credit; Arthur and Ben take ownership of the apples and agree to pay George the £100 the following day. George is a 'creditor' (sometimes referred to as a 'payable') to the business – someone to whom the business owes money.

Who owns the apples?

Now who owns the apples? The answer is Arthur and Ben because, even though they may not have paid for the apples, they have taken legal ownership – the title of the goods has changed hands. So, if Arthur and Ben own the apples, they can do with them whatever they want. And they want to sell them. So they go and meet Harry who again agrees to buy all of the apples for £5 each.

What is a debtor?

Unfortunately, Harry has also forgotten to bring any cash with him. So Arthur and Ben agree to sell the apples to Harry on condition that Harry agrees to pay for them the following day. So who owns the apples now? Harry, because even though he has not yet paid for them, the legal title has been transferred. Harry is a "debtor" (sometimes referred to as a "receivable") to the business – someone who owes the business money. And so if Harry owns the apples Arthur and Ben can record the transaction in the books of A&B Ltd.

What does the P&L look like?

Sales were £500 and the costs were £100, leaving a profit for day two of £400. At the end of day two, Arthur and Ben can prepare the balance sheet of A&B Ltd.

What does the balance sheet look like?

They started the day with £500 cash and, because none of the transactions involved cash, they finished the day with £500 cash. Do they have any other assets? Yes, the £500 that they are owed by Harry is treated as an asset. Harry is known as a debtor. Do they have any liabilities? Yes, the amount that they owe George for the purchase of the apples is a liability, in this case £100. George is known as a creditor. Thus, £500 of cash plus £500 owed by Harry less £100 owed to George results in net assets of £900.

This is represented by the shareholders' funds. The investment remains at £100. A&B Ltd started the day with £400 of retained profits, generated an additional £400 profit during day two and so now finishes with £800 of retained profit. £800 of retained profit plus the £100 of investments equals £900 in total, equal to the net assets of the business; the balance sheet continues to balance.

Profit & loss account	During day 1	During day 2	
Sales	£ 500	£ 500	
Costs	(£ 100)	(£ 100)	
Profits	£ 400	£ 400	

Balance sheet	End of day 0		End of day 1	End of day 2	
Assets	£ 100	cash	£ 500 cash	£ 500	cash
				£ 500	debtors
Liabilities	£ 0		£ 0	(£ 100)	creditors
Net assets	£ 100		£ 500	£ 900	
Shareholders' funds					
Investment	£ 100		£ 100	£ 100	
Retained/profits	£ 0		£ 400	£ 800	
	£ 100		£ 500	£ 900	

What if there is no trading?

Day three and all this trading is very tiring for Arthur and Ben. So all they do is go and visit Harry, who pays them the £500 cash that he owes them and then they visit George and pay him the £100 that they owe. The balance of £400 cash they take home and add to the original £500 of cash. And, at the end of day three, they prepare their accounts.

Total cash is now £900. They are not owed any money because Harry has paid them. They do not owe any money because George has been paid. And so net assets are still £900. The shareholders' funds are also £900 – made up of the original £100 investment plus the £800 of retained profit, that is the total profit made ever since A&B Ltd started trading, but not yet given back to shareholders.

Profit & loss account		During day 1		During day 2		During day 3	
Sales		£ 500		£ 500		£ 0	
Costs		(£ 100)		(£ 100)		(£ 0)	
Profits		£ 400		£ 400		£ 0	
Balance sheet	End of day 0		End of day 1		End of day 2		End of day 3
Assets	£ 100 cash		£ 500 cash		£ 500 cash		£ 900 cash
					£ 500 debtors		
Liabilities	£ 0		£ 0		(£ 100) creditors		
Net assets	£ 100		£ 500		£ 900		£ 900
Shareholders' funds							
Investment	£ 100		£ 100		£ 100		£ 100
Retained/ profits	£ 0		£ 400		£ 800		£ 800
	£ 100		£ 500		£ 900		£ 900

We have now learnt how a company is financially structured and how a company trades. But there is something else that is also very important to notice here.

Are profit and cash the same thing?

Look closely at the above accounts. The company started day one with £100 cash and finished day one with £500 cash – an increase of £400. It made a profit during day one of £400. During day one cash generated and profit were the same.

In day two the company also made a £400 profit; but what about the amount of cash in the business? The company started with £500 cash and finished the day with £500 cash, in effect there was no increase in cash.

During day three the company did not make a profit, as it was not trading. However, it started the day with £500 cash and finished the day with £900 cash, a total increase of £400 cash.

And thus we see that profit and cash generated are not the same thing. You can make a profit without generating cash (as in day two) and you can also generate cash without making a profit (as in day three).

? Does your business make a profit?

? Does your business generate cash?

? Are the two figures (profit and cash) similar or very different?

? Why do you think this is?

What is accrual accounting?

The profit made by a company is different from the cash generated due to **accrual accounting** or the **matching concept**. Under the accrual accounting concept we recognise income when we earn it, not when we physically receive the cash. We recognise costs when we incur them, not when we physically pay for them. And that is why profit and cash generated are not the same thing.

? Small companies are allowed to account on a cash basis. Why do you think this is?

? Large companies must, by law, account on an accrual basis. Why do you think this is?

Chapter summary

In this chapter we have looked at how a company is structured financially and how the accounting equation describes the balance sheet of a company. We also looked at how a company trades through the profit & loss account – using the accrual or matching concept – to recognise income when it is earned and costs when they are incurred. The profit & loss account reflects the trading during a period, whereas the balance sheet reflects the position of the company at a snapshot in time. Sales and costs are found in the profit & loss account, whilst assets and liabilities are found in the balance sheet.

	Dr	Cr
Balance sheet	Assets	Liabilities
Profit & loss account	Costs	Sales

 Next steps

▶ Think about your business:

   ▶ How much income do you think it generates?

   ▶ How big are the costs?

   ▶ What sort of assets do you have on the balance sheet?

   ▶ And what sort of liabilities?

   ▶ How big do you think those numbers are?

▶ We are going to have a look at the financial statements later on in this book, but this is an opportunity to think about what those numbers might look like.

▶ Now consider the accrual accounting concept:

   ▶ When does your business recognise a sale?

   ▶ If you work for a retailer (such as Marks & Spencer Plc) then this should be a pretty easy question – it will be at the point of sale (i.e. the checkout).

> ▶ But what if you are building an aircraft carrier? Do you show the sale in your accounts on the day that it is sold? Or is it the day that the contract is signed?
>
> ▶ How much flexibility do you think the finance team have as to when they can call a sale a sale?

 Key learning points

▶ The accounting equation states that 'assets less liabilities is equal to shareholder's funds'

▶ The balance sheet contains the assets and liabilities of a business – it describes the financial position of a business at a particular point in time

▶ The profit & loss account contains the sales and costs of a business – it describes the trading results between two points in time

▶ Any profit not paid to the shareholders as a dividend is reinvested back into the business and will appear on the balance sheet

▶ Income is recognised when it is earned, not when the cash is received; costs are recognised when they are incurred, not when the cash is paid.

 Test yourself

1.1 A sole trader is someone who:
  (a) works for themselves ☐
  (b) buys and sells fish – specialising in Dover Sole ☐
  (c) is the sole owner of a company ☐
  (d) trades goods but not services ☐

1.2 A partnership is one where:
  (a) profits are shared equally between the partners ☐
  (b) profits are shared equitably between the partners ☐
  (c) profits are distributed to the shareholders before the partners get paid ☐
  (d) the company cannot make a loss ☐

1.3 A company is best described as:
(a) the same as a sole trader ☐
(b) the same as a partnership ☐
(c) a separate legal entity ☐
(d) an organisation with employees ☐

1.4 The veil of incorporation:
(a) limits the liabilities of the shareholders to their investment ☐
(b) limits the liabilities of the debt providers to their investment ☐
(c) separates the executive from the non-executive ☐
(d) separates assets and liabilities ☐

1.5 The role of the executive board is to:
(a) work on a part-time basis ☐
(b) maximise their share options ☐
(c) formulate and implement strategy ☐
(d) formulate strategy and hold the non-executive to account ☐

1.6 The role of the non-executive board is to:
(a) work on a part-time basis ☐
(b) maximise their share options ☐
(c) formulate and implement strategy ☐
(d) formulate strategy and hold the executive to account ☐

1.7 The statutory accounts:
(a) show only the balance sheet ☐
(b) show only the profit & loss account ☐
(c) show only the cash flow statement ☐
(d) are a legal requirement of all limited companies ☐

1.8 The role of the auditors is to:
(a) do what the directors ask them to do ☐
(b) prepare the accounts ☐
(c) check the accounts and sign them off as true and fair ☐
(d) minimise the tax of the company ☐

1.9 The accounting equation states that:
(a) assets must be greater than liabilities ☐
(b) assets will always be equal to liabilities ☐
(c) the difference between assets and liabilities is profit ☐
(d) shareholders' funds will always be an asset ☐

1.10 The balance sheet contains:

(a) assets and liabilities ☐

(b) assets and expenses ☐

(c) income and liabilities ☐

(d) income and expenses ☐

1.11 If a company makes a profit it can either:

(a) spend it or reinvest it ☐

(b) reinvest it or return it to shareholders ☐

(c) return it to shareholders or pay a dividend ☐

(d) pay a dividend or spend it ☐

1.12 Who appoints the auditors of a company?

(a) The directors ☐

(b) The non-executive directors ☐

(c) The shareholders ☐

(d) The bankers ☐

1.13 Shareholders' funds are:

(a) an asset ☐

(b) a liability ☐

(c) an income ☐

(d) an expense ☐

1.14 The matching concept ensures that:

(a) income and expenses are recognised in the period ordered ☐

(b) income and expenses are recognised in the period invoiced ☐

(c) income and expenses are recognised in the period paid ☐

(d) income and expenses are recognised in the period earned/ ☐
incurred

1.15 Profit and cash are:

(a) always the same ☐

(b) sometimes the same ☐

(c) never the same ☐

(d) inversely related ☐

CHAPTER 2
How a company is funded

'If you owe your bank a hundred pounds, you have a problem. But if you owe a million, it has.'

John Maynard Keynes

 ## Aim

The aim of this chapter is to understand the business cycle of a company, how a company is funded and the advantages and disadvantages of the two primary sources of that funding. We will also touch on the world of derivatives.

 ## Outcomes

By the end of this chapter you will understand:

▶ the business cycle

▶ the difference between debt and equity as a means of funding the business

▶ the advantages and disadvantages of each of the two methods of funding

▶ what a derivative is and how it is used to manage risk.

Additional resources

▶ Links to videos are all available at: **www.wainman.net/wainman.net/resources.html**

What is the business cycle?

Every company starts off by raising cash. A company – as a separate legal entity (defined in Chapter 1) – must issue at least one share that must have a value; the company must also appoint at least one director to run it.

The company uses the invested cash to buy assets, which in turn are used to trade and to generate a profit, which is then turned into cash. You will remember from Chapter 1 that profit is not the same as cash. What can a company do with that cash? It can either reinvest to buy more assets and therefore generate greater profits in the future or it can return the cash to the shareholders.

? What sort of investments does your business undertake to generate future profits?

? Does your business return profits to investors? Or is the profit reinvested?

How does this relate to Arthur and Ben?

In the last chapter, Arthur and Ben set up A&B Ltd and then raised £100 (from themselves!). They used the money to purchase apples (i.e. to buy assets) and then to sell them for a profit. Once they had collected the money owed to them (and paid any outstanding liabilities), they were left with a (in our example rather small) pile of cash.

What did they do with that cash?

Well, as they did not pay any dividends to themselves, they must have (by definition) reinvested the cash back into the business. In fact, on day two, they could have bought many more apples, especially if they had remembered to take the cash with them.

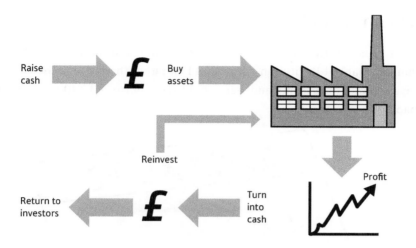

From where does a company obtain investment?

In the last chapter, Arthur and Ben set up a company (A&B Ltd) by investing £50 each. This type of investment is known as equity. However, there are two primary sources of finance available to a business – debt and equity.

Let us look at debt first.

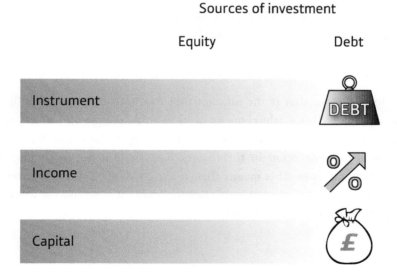

What is debt?

Debt comes in the form of a loan to the business, usually by a bank or similar financial institution. Thus A&B Ltd, rather than raising the equity investment from Arthur and Ben, could have borrowed £100 – from a bank.

What reward does the debt provider receive?

The income or reward to the provider of debt (i.e. the bank) is in the form of **interest**. This interest is fixed, which means that it is compulsory and must be paid by the borrower (A&B Ltd). If you are not sure of this point – consider what the reaction of your bank might be if you decided to stop paying the interest on your mortgage…!

The loan capital, that is the amount that has been borrowed (£100), is also repayable (this might come as news to some people on interest-only mortgages but, yes, they are going to have to repay the original amount borrowed at some point in the future). The amount borrowed may be secured on an asset. This means that, if the company that has borrowed the money cannot repay that loan, then the lender will receive the asset on which the loan has been secured.

What is the relationship between risk and return?

So, if a bank lends some money to A&B Ltd, and secures their loan on an asset, then the loan becomes a **lower** risk to the bank; as a result, they will accept a **lower** rate of interest. This introduces us to the relationship between **risk** and **return**.

If a lender makes a loan, which is secured on asset (such as a mortgage) then they will accept a lower rate of interest. If a lender makes a loan which is unsecured (such as a credit card) then they will require a much higher rate of interest, to compensate them for the additional amount of risk that they are taking on. 'Payday lenders' in the UK make highly risky loans and therefore felt the need to charge in excess of 5,000% interest before this rate was deemed excessive and was capped by the UK government.

Did you know that if you had borrowed £100 from a 'payday lender' in the UK and did not make any repayments for 10 years, you would end up owing more than the debt of the United States of America (which, in 2014, owed over $17 trillion). In fact, you would end up owing approximately £55,000,000,000,000,000,000 (that is £55 quintillion or 18 zeros). Of course, payday lenders do not make loans at these rates for 10 years – their business model is based on loans of up to 30 days (a typical loan of £100 at 5% for 30 days would result in a final payment of just under £170). Either way, it is best to repay on time.

Thus, the primary concerns to a lender are:

(a) Can you afford to pay the interest or 'service' the debt?

(b) Will you be able to repay the capital when it falls due?

Which of these do you think is the most important?

The answer is (a). Why? Well, let us consider a large company such as National Grid. It is quite possible that they will have to repay a $1 billion loan next month. From where do you think National Grid will get $1 billion? Not from income, as this is needed to pay for the day-to-day running costs of the business; nor from selling assets, as it needs these to provide its services. In fact, National Grid is most likely to borrow $1 billion to repay the original $1 billion loan. This is known as rolling over or refinancing. A financial institution will lend $1 billion to National Grid only if it believes that National Grid can service that debt.

? How much debt is used to fund your business?

? Do you think this is a lot or a little?

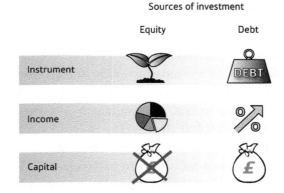

Sources of investment

What is equity?

The other source of finance available to a business is equity. An equity investor buys a share of the business and becomes a part owner. In our example, in Chapter 1, Arthur and Ben are equity owners of A&B Ltd.

What is the reward to the equity provider?

The income that a shareholder receives comes in the form of a **dividend**. Who sets the dividend? It is the directors who set the dividend, and not the shareholders. The directors can choose to increase the dividend, reduce the dividend or cancel the dividend altogether. This form of income is, therefore, variable in the eyes of the equity investor (whereas the debt investor sees the interest as fixed , even though it may vary with interest rates).

For A&B Ltd, the shareholders – Arthur and Ben – were the directors, so this distinction was blurred; but if you were to buy a share in National Grid, for example, then you would have to accept whatever dividend the directors decided to pay. If you were unhappy with the dividend, then you could always sell your share to someone else. If everyone is unhappy, then they could band together and demand the directors rethink their dividend policy.

The equity capital that has been invested is non-repayable. This means that A&B Ltd does not have to give back the £100 invested by Arthur and Ben until the company goes into liquidation. The company can buy the shares back from the investors (Arthur and Ben) but this is not quite the same thing.

So, consider the following scenario: imagine that you invested $10,000 into Microsoft when it started in 1975; Microsoft did not pay a dividend for the first 28 years – i.e. until 2003; so, in 2002, you are reflecting on the fact that after 27 years you have received no (dividend) income and there is no prospect of receiving your $10,000 back – as Microsoft has no intention of going into liquidation in the foreseeable future. How happy would you be with your investment?

If you think that you would **not** be very happy, you are wrong. Why? Well, while you have received no dividend income and the company is not intending to go into liquidation in the foreseeable future, the reason that you should be exceedingly happy with your investment is that the value of the Microsoft shares that you now own will have risen. So the value of your investment would greatly exceed the $10,000 that you put in originally (so much so, that by now you would probably have retired on your own private yacht somewhere in the Caribbean).

? Are the shares of your business publicly traded?

? If so, what is the share price?

? How has that price changed over the last 5–10 years?

? What do you think has caused this change?

Who sets the value of Microsoft shares? The answer is the market. If you want to buy a share in Microsoft, it is a relatively straightforward process; you can do it over the Internet these days but it is more fun if you do it on the phone because you get to shout. So, you phone up your stockbroker and you shout, 'MICROSOFT – BUY! BUY! BUY!'

31

Let us assume that Microsoft is trading on the market at $100 per share. How much of that $100 do you think Microsoft will receive? $100? $90? Less? The answer is nothing. Why? Because when you phone up your stockbroker and shout, 'MICROSOFT – BUY! BUY! BUY!', someone somewhere else in the world is phoning up their stockbroker and shouting, 'MICROSOFT – SELL! SELL! SELL!'. The stockbroker matches the two trades together, deducts their commission, and the shares are exchanged independently of Microsoft.

This is what is known as a **secondary** market transaction. The secondary market is where you and I trade shares between each other. A **primary** market transaction is where a company sells its shares for the first time, for example a flotation or an initial public offering (IPO). The existence of the secondary market allows the primary market to function. So you may choose to buy shares in a company that has just listed on the stock exchange because you know that it is very easy to sell their shares again – the investment is said to be very liquid, that is it is very easy to turn into cash. The same is true for companies like BP who have been in public ownership for many years – they are still traded on the secondary market.

This is very important because, if your friend asks you to make an equity investment in his pub you should consider his intentions. If you are making a lifestyle investment because you always wanted to tell your friends that you own a pub with your own barstool and own pint glass then that is fine. But if you are making a financial investment you should consider, 'what is the exit strategy?' to realise your investment before making that investment. Thus it is important to know how to get **out** of an equity investment before you get **in**.

How much of a company do you need to own?

If you buy a share in Microsoft, you will own a very small proportion of the number of shares in issue, and therefore own a very small part of the company. Each year, as an owner, you will receive the annual report and accounts and will be invited to the annual general meeting (AGM) of the company. However, as a very small (in terms of ownership, not stature) shareholder, you will have very little influence on the company. As you buy more shares, so your influence will increase. If you own over 50 per cent of the shares, ultimately you control the company – you can remove board members if you are unhappy with their performance, and thus, ultimately, you can control the dividend policy of the company.

What are the different types of equity investment?

? How much equity is invested in your business?

? How much is this in proportion to the amount of debt funding the business?

? Is the equity primarily from investment by shareholders?

? Or is the primary source of equity investment from profits being reinvested back into the business?

What are derivatives?

So far in this chapter we have looked at the funding options available to Arthur and Ben and A&B Ltd and have examined the differences between debt and equity.

This final section is a brief look at derivatives and the role that they play in financing a business.

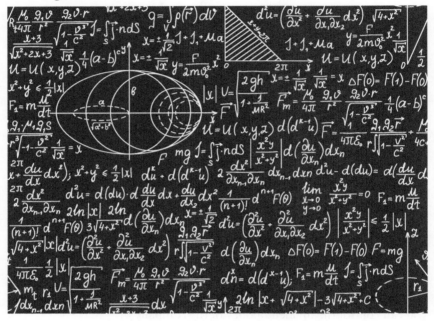

Now, at the first mention of derivatives most people's eyes glaze over and they rapidly start to lose the will to live, but bear with this section – they are not that complicated once you understand them!

Let us define a derivative:

'A derivative is a contract between two parties where neither party owns the item being bought or sold.'

Now, if you are looking at that definition and thinking that you are none the wiser, don't worry. Let us look at a few examples.

Derivatives – what is a future?

Imagine that Arthur is planning a trip from the USA to Europe in a year's time. He has discovered that the cost of the trip will be €5,000 and the travel company has given him the option to pay when he arrives in Europe.

Let us assume that the exchange rate between the US dollar and the Euro is $1=€1 (this will make the maths easier!). Arthur therefore works out that the cost of the trip will be $5,000 and this is within his budget – he is happy!

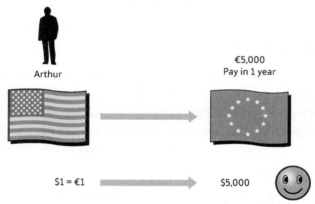

Arthur

€5,000
Pay in 1 year

$1 = €1 $5,000

But then Arthur gets to thinking – what if the exchange rate changes during the year? What if, in a year's time, $1 will buy only €0.50? Then the trip will cost him $10,000 and this is outside of his budget, making him very unhappy.

$1 = €0.5 $10,000

Arthur could buy the Euros now, but this will tie up cash that he could use for other things in the meantime. So, instead, he purchases a **future** from a financial institution, such as a bank.

FUTURE   The obligation to buy (call) or sell (put) at a future point in time

A future is the **obligation** of Arthur to buy €5,000 for $5,000 in a year's time. The obligation to buy is known as a call, whereas the obligation to sell is known as a put.

You will notice that, at the time of sale, neither the bank nor Arthur owns the Euros. The value of the contract is **derived** from the underlying exchange rate, and thus is a derivative contract. If Arthur no longer needs the contract (perhaps he has cancelled his trip), he can sell the contract (the pricing of which is too complicated for this book!).

Meanwhile, the bank has just been on the phone to a Frenchman who is planning to make a trip to the USA and wanted to buy $5,000 for €5,000 in a year's time. The bank is, therefore, able to hedge the two deals off against each other, thus minimising their exposure to risk.

Derivatives – what is an option?

So, Arthur is happy that the trip is not going to cost him any more than $5,000; but then he gets to thinking further – what if the exchange rate goes the other way? What if, rather than $1=€0.50, the exchange changes so that $1 will buy €2? Then the trip would have cost him $2,500. But he has entered into a contract with the bank where he **has** to buy the Euros from the banks at a $1=€1 rate.

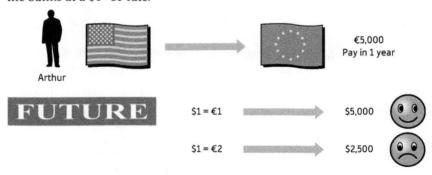

This will leave him worse off and so he would not be happy. In this case, he might choose to purchase an option from the bank.

An option is the right (as opposed to obligation) to buy (call) or sell (put) at a future point in time. In this case if, in a year's time, Arthur is better off buying the Euros from the bank, then he will buy them from the bank, and if he is better off buying them from the local travel agent, then he will do this and the contract with the bank will lapse, as it has become worthless.

You will notice that the option involves a significant transfer of risk from Arthur to the bank and so the bank will charge considerably more for this.

The right to buy (call) or sell
(put) at a future point in time

So we can now see that any company trading internationally in different currencies most likely will use futures and options to manage their exposure to the risk of exchange rate movements. There are many risks in business, and the last thing a company needs is for the exchange rate to mean that the goods that it is purchasing in Country A are now more expensive than the price at which they can be sold in Country B.

So Arthur is now happy that he has managed his exposure to a future exchange rate movement. But then he starts thinking about the airline, which will fly him to Europe. He wants to book his seat today, and the airline must ensure that the price at which it sells all of the seats exceeds the cost of flying the aeroplane to Europe. What do you think is the biggest cost of flying from the USA to Europe for an airline (clue – it is not the bar bill!)?

The answer is fuel. Now, the airline could nip down to the local petrol station and fill up enough jerry cans with fuel to fill up the aeroplane and then store them at the back of the office for a year until Arthur makes the flight. However, this is not very practical (apart from the smell, Health & Safety would have a few words to say) and anyway – it is the wrong type of fuel! So, instead, the airline may purchase the fuel on the futures and options market. This way they can guarantee how much it will cost them to make the flight, and thus enable them to price the seat.

And so we can see that all commodities are traded on the futures and options markets: hard commodities, such as gold, silver, zinc, copper, steel; and soft commodities such as sugar, coffee, cocoa, wheat, barley and cotton.

Derivatives – what is a swap?

The final class of derivative is known as a swap.

Arthur has a house that he purchased using a fixed rate mortgage (a fixed rate means that, if interest rates change, the interest on Arthur's mortgage will not change, but will remain the same). Ben has a house that he purchased using a variable rate mortgage (which means that the interest that he pays on the mortgage will vary in line with interest rates).

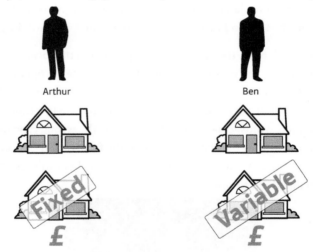

For reasons best known to Arthur, he wants a variable rate mortgage and for reasons best known to Ben, he wants a fixed rate mortgage (remember, whenever there is a trade in the market place, there are two sides to the trade – a buyer and a seller).

They could go back to their respective banks and renegotiate their mortgages, but this takes time and is costly; alternatively, they could choose to swap their interest streams. Arthur agrees to pay the interest on Ben's mortgage in exchange for Ben agreeing to pay the interest on Arthur's mortgage. They keep their own houses and they keep their own mortgages – they have simply **swapped** interest streams.

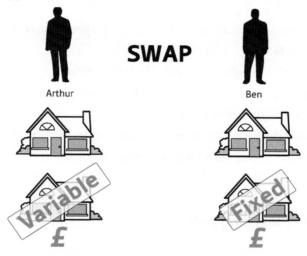

? Does your company use derivatives?

? Why do you think this is?

? What sort of derivative contracts does it enter into?

? How does this mitigate risk?

Chapter summary

In this chapter we have examined the business cycle of the business and how businesses are funded. We have looked at debt and equity in detail and finally we gained a brief overview of derivative products, and how companies use them to manage risk.

In the next chapter we will build on this knowledge in examining the financial statements of a company.

Next steps

▶ If you were starting a new business, would you prefer to use debt or equity to fund it?

▶ What are the benefits and drawbacks of each option?

▶ Now consider if you were asked to invest in a new business – again, which would you prefer and why?

▶ Now consider what sorts of businesses are funded with debt?

▶ And what sorts are more likely to be equity funded?

 Key learning points

▶ Businesses are funded primarily through debt and equity.

▶ Debt is of lower risk to the investor, but higher risk to the borrower.

▶ At each stage of investment, equity investors are looking to exit their investment.

▶ Debt providers are looking to ensure that the loan can be repaid.

▶ Derivatives fall into three categories – futures, options and swaps.

 Test yourself

2.1 The business cycle shows:

  (a) how cash flows within a business ☐

  (b) how goods and services flow within a business ☐

  (c) the role of employees in a business ☐

  (d) how a business responds to the global economic climate ☐

2.2 A business can raise investment/cash from:

  (a) equity and shareholders ☐

  (b) debt and equity ☐

  (c) shareholders and employees ☐

  (d) debt and banks/loans ☐

2.3 Debt is:

(a) riskier than equity ☐

(b) unlikely to be repaid ☐

(c) a loan, usually bearing interest ☐

(d) probably interest free ☐

2.4 Equity is:

(a) a combination of retained profit and dividends ☐

(b) the shareholders' stake in the business ☐

(c) the concept of all shareholders being treated equally ☐

(d) an investment that will attract interest ☐

2.5 The primary market is where:

(a) companies raise money from investors ☐

(b) investors trade shares that they own ☐

(c) companies trade goods and services ☐

(d) companies resell goods and services ☐

2.6 The secondary market is where:

(a) companies raise money from investors ☐

(b) investors trade shares that they own ☐

(c) companies trade goods and services ☐

(d) companies resell goods and services ☐

2.7 Capital is a combination of:

(a) debt and equity ☐

(b) debt and dividends ☐

(c) dividends and equity ☐

(d) debt, equity and dividends ☐

2.8 A derivative is:

(a) something only bankers know about ☐

(b) a trade between two parties where neither owns the underlying asset ☐

(c) a trade between two parties where both own the underlying asset ☐

(d) a swap ☐

2.9 An option is:

(a) the right to buy an asset at a future point in time ☐

(b) the obligation to buy an asset at a future point in time ☐

(c) a swap ☐

(d) a derivative product that is traded only in the USA ☐

2.10 Companies usually use derivatives to:

(a) bet on markets going up ☐

(b) bet on markets going down ☐

(c) bet on markets going up and down ☐

(d) hedge risk ☐

CHAPTER 3
The financial statements

'The longer I go on, the more I am aware of the power of finance.'

Justin Welby

 ## Aim

The aim of this chapter is to understand the primary financial statements of a business and how they interact with each other.

 ## Outcomes

By the end of this chapter you will understand:

▶ the main elements of the balance sheet

▶ the main elements of the income statement (also known as the profit and loss account)

▶ how the balance sheet and income statement interact

▶ the main elements of the cash flow statement and how it reconciles the profit and loss account to the balance sheet.

 ## Additional resources

▶ Links to videos are all available at:
www.wainman.net/wainman.net/resources.html

Introduction to the annual report and accounts

In this chapter we will be examining the accounts of National Grid. You can access them online either by searching for 'National Grid Annual Report and Accounts 2013' or by visiting **http://www2.nationalgrid.com/About-us/ Corporate-governance/Annual-Report-and-Accounts-2012-13/.**

National Grid is responsible for the transportation of gas and electricity around the UK. The power companies (such as Centrica, E.ON, npower, etc.) are responsible for generating the power and National Grid is responsible for getting it to your home. Here is an extract from the accounts where Steve Holliday, the chief executive (who runs the business on a day-to-day basis), explains in his own words what his business does:

'National Grid's job is to connect people to the energy they use, safely. We are at the heart of one of the greatest challenges facing our society – delivering clean energy to support our world long into the future. We work with all our stakeholders to promote the development and implementation of sustainable, innovative and affordable energy solutions. And we are proud that our work, and our people, underpin the prosperity and wellbeing of our customers, communities and investors'.

What is in the balance sheet?

In Chapter 1 we were first introduced to the balance sheet when Arthur and Ben set up A&B Ltd. The balance sheet is represented by the accounting equation, which states that the assets of a business less the liabilities (i.e. the net assets) are equal to the shareholders' funds.

The balance sheet is a snapshot of the business at a particular point in time. The only two things that you will find in a balance sheet are the assets and liabilities.

Assets

Liabilities

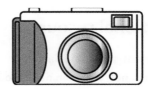

What are assets?

The assets of a business can be divided into current assets and non-current assets (sometimes referred to as fixed assets). These are defined as follows:

▶ **Current assets** are things that the company owns (assets) that it is actively trying to turn into cash (or that it expects to become cash within 12 months of the balance sheet date). The main items that you will find under current assets in the balance sheet are:

(a) stock or inventories (which the company is trying to sell)

(b) debtors (also known as receivables – amounts that are owed to the company by customers who have bought goods or services but have not yet paid for them – these are amounts that the company is trying to collect in and turn into cash) and

(c) cash.

▶ **Non-current assets** are things that the company owns (assets) and that it needs to run the business – such as tables and chairs, computers, plant, machinery and buildings (unless the company rents the building rather than owning it). The company can, of course, sell the non-current assets if it wanted to (put all the tables, chairs and computers, etc. on eBay), but it does not want to, as the staff would have nowhere to sit!

What are liabilities?

The liabilities of the business can be divided in a similar way to the assets – between current liabilities and non-current liabilities (sometimes called long-term liabilities). These are defined as follows:

▶ **Current liabilities** are amounts that the company owes to third parties and has to pay within 12 months of the balance sheet date – mainly these are items such as creditors (also known as payables) – the amounts owed to suppliers who have not yet been paid for providing goods and services.

▶ **Non-current liabilities** (sometimes called long-term liabilities) represent amounts owed to third parties, which are payable more than 12 months from the balance sheet date – usually long-term loans that are due to be repaid at some point in the distant future.

As discussed in Chapter 1, deducting the assets from the liabilities leaves the net assets. This is the same as the shareholders' funds (sometimes called share capital and reserves or 'equity'). Remember, shareholders' funds are also treated as a liability as it is the amount that is owed back to the shareholders.

We can now break the assets and liabilities of the business into the five main sections:

Non current (Fixed) assets
Plus current assets

Less current liabilities
Less non current (Long term) liabilities

Equals Shareholders' funds

? See if you can obtain the financial statements of your business. See if you can identify the above 5 sections on the balance sheet of your company.

What does the balance sheet tell me about the business?

We have now identified the five main elements of a balance sheet. Identifying these five elements will allow you to 'crack' the balance sheet.

Let us first consider the balance sheet of National Grid (responsible for transporting gas and electricity around the UK). Below is its balance sheet for the year ended 2012. Have a look at the numbers, and see if you can work out how much cash the company had on 31 March 2012.

National Grid's Balance Sheet 2012

Consolidated statement of financial position
as at 31 March

	Notes	2013 £m	2012 £m
Non-current assets			
Goodwill	8	5,028	4,776
Other intangible assets	9	589	546
Property, plant and equipment	10	36,592	33,701
Other non-current assets	11	104	95
Pension assets	22	195	155
Financial and other investments	12	278	251
Investments in joint ventures and associates	13	371	341
Derivative financial assets	14	1,972	1,819
Total non-current assets		45,129	41,684
Current assets			
Inventories and current intangible assets	15	291	376
Trade and other receivables	16	2,910	1,971
Financial and other investments	12	5,431	2,391
Derivative financial assets	14	273	317
Cash and cash equivalents	17	671	332
Total current assets		9,576	5,387
Assets of businesses held for sale	18	–	264
Total assets		54,705	47,335
Current liabilities			
Borrowings	19	(3,448)	(2,492)
Derivative financial liabilities	14	(407)	(162)
Trade and other payables	20	(3,051)	(2,685)
Current tax liabilities		(231)	(383)
Provisions	23	(308)	(282)
Total current liabilities		(7,445)	(6,004)
Non-current liabilities			
Borrowings	19	(24,647)	(20,533)
Derivative financial liabilities	14	(1,274)	(1,269)
Other non-current liabilities	21	(1,884)	(1,921)
Deferred tax liabilities	5	(4,076)	(3,738)
Pensions and other post-retirement benefit obligations	22	(3,694)	(3,088)
Provisions	23	(1,452)	(1,449)

Total non-current liabilities		(37,027)	(31,998)
Liabilities of businesses held for sale	18	–	(87)
Total liabilities		**(44,472)**	**(38,089)**
Net assets		**10,233**	**9,246**
Equity			
Called up share capital	24	**433**	422
Share premium account		**1,344**	1,355
Retained earnings		**13,132**	12,297
Other equity reserves	25	**(4,681)**	(4,835)
Shareholders' equity		**10,228**	**9,239**
Non-controlling interests		**5**	7
Total equity		**10,233**	**9,246**

The consolidated financial statements set out on pages 97 to 164 were approved by the Board of Directors on 15 May 2013 and were signed on its behalf by:

Sir Peter Gershon Chairman

Andrew Bonfield Finance Director

You should be able to identify the answer as £671 million – see the last line (cash and cash equivalents) under current assets (remember, National Grid is a very big company!). £671 million is part of the current assets of National Grid, which total £9,576 million. So National Grid has approximately £9.6 billion of things that it owns (assets) that either are cash or something it is actively trying to turn into cash.

National Grid's non-current assets (sometimes called fixed assets) total £45,129 million. So it has approximately £45.1 billion of things that it owns (assets) that it is not trying to turn into cash but is using to run the business.

Total assets are, therefore, £54,705 million – or almost £54.7 billion – as shown on the balance sheet.

Current liabilities – that is the amount that National Grid owes to third parties and is going to have to pay by 31 March 2014 – amount to £7,445 million and the non-current liabilities total £37,027 million. Thus the total liabilities amount to £44,472 million – or about £44.5 billion.

Thus the net assets are the total assets (£54,705 million) less the total liabilities (£44,472 million), which equals £10,233 million.

We can show the five main elements as follows (we have rounded to the nearest billion to make it easier to follow the numbers).

Balance sheet analysis

	National Grid £ bn
Non-current assets	£ 45.1
Current assets	£ 9.6
Current liabilities	£ 7.5
Non-current liabilities	£ 37.0
Net assets/shareholders' funds	£ 10.2

How does a balance sheet show how a company is funded?

Having identified the five elements of the balance sheet, we are now in a position to see what this tells us about the company.

If you refer back to Chapter 2, you will remember that we identified the two primary sources of funds that are available to a business as being debt and equity.

In which of the above sections of the balance sheet do you think that you will find the debt that National Grid uses to fund its operations?

We can work this out through a process of elimination. It will not be in assets (either non-current or current) as the debt is a liability of the company. Nor will it be in the shareholders' funds, as this represents the amount owed to the shareholders of the business (not to third parties).

So the debt must be either in the current liabilities or the non-current liabilities. For the same reason that you do not (should not!) buy a house on a credit card, so you should not use short-term sources of funding for long-term funding needs.

As National Grid has used the debt for long-term investment in its infrastructure, it makes sense to borrow on a long-term basis. The debt, therefore, sits in the non-current liabilities. Check back to National Grid's balance sheet and you will see that the biggest number making up the non-current liabilities is £24.6 billion of borrowings. There are a few other things that National Grid owes and does not have to pay for over a year (for example a deferred tax liability), but the main element is the debt.

The other source of funding available to a business is from the share-holders. This is represented on the balance sheet as the shareholders' funds (sometimes called equity or capital and reserves). For National Grid, this is the £10.2 billion.

The debt plus the equity represents the total capital employed in a business. So, on an approximate basis, we can see that the balance sheet shows us where a business obtained its funding from, and the balance between those two sources of funding, as shown in the following analysis.

Balance sheet analysis

	National Grid £ bn	
Non-current assets	£ 45.1	
Current assets	£ 9.6	
Current liabilities	£ 7.5	
Non-current liabilities	£ 37.0	} Capital £ 47.2
Net assets/shareholders' funds	£ 10.2	

National Grid has £37 billion of debt plus £10.2 billion of equity, which makes the total capital employed in the business £47.2 billion.

How does a balance sheet show what a company did with those funds?

So what did it do with all of that capital that has been invested?

Well, a company like National Grid needs lots of assets to run its business – things like pylons, towers, pipes and substations – all of which are repre-sented in the non-current assets section. National Grid has £45.1 billion of investment capital.

But National Grid also needs some money in its pocket to make sure that it can pay its staff at the end of each month, as well as its suppliers, etc. This is called the working capital of the business and is represented by the current assets net of (or less) the current liabilities (i.e. the net current assets). For National Grid, the current assets of £9.6 billion less the current liabilities of £7.5 billion gives net current assets of £2.1 billion – which is the working capital. Working capital of £2.1 billion plus the investment capital of £45.1 billion gives total capital employed of £47.2 billion.

Balance sheet analysis

	National Grid			
	£ bn			
			Investment	
Non-current assets	£ 45.1		capital	£ 45.1
Current assets	£ 9.6		Working	£ 2.1
Current liabilities	£ 7.5		capital	
Non-current liabilities	£ 37.0			
Net assets/shareholders' funds	£ 10.2			£ 47.2

So the balance sheet tells us how a company is funded – debt plus equity. It also tell us what the company did with that funding – how much was invested (investment capital) and how much is being used to run the business on a day-to-day basis (the working capital).

Balance sheet analysis

	National Grid			
	£ bn			
Non-current assets	£ 45.1		Investment capital £ 45.1	
Current assets	£ 9.6		Working	£ 2.1
Current liabilities	7.5		Capital	
Non-current liabilities	£ 37.0		Debt	capital £ 47.2
Net assets/shareholders' funds	£ 10.2		Equity	

What do the balance sheets of different types of business look like?

We have examined National Grid's balance sheet in a reasonable amount of detail. What do you think the balance sheet of a service company would look like in comparison? What about a manufacturing company? Below are two fictitious companies – Company M and Company S.

? Which do you think is most likely to be a manufacturing business and which is most likely to be a service company?

? What made you decide on your answers?

Balance sheet analysis

	National Grid £ bn	Company S £ bn	Company M £ bn
Non-current assets	£ 45.1	£ 5.0	£ 20.0
Current assets	£ 9.6	£ 10.2	£ 15.6
Current liabilities	£ 7.5	£ 9.3	£ 8.3
Non-current liabilities	£ 37.0	£ 0.4	£ 14.3
Net assets/shareholders' funds	£ 10.2	£ 5.5	£ 13.0

Company M clearly has more investment capital than Company S – plant and machinery – suggesting that M is more likely to be a manufacturing business. Service companies do not need a lot of fixed assets (remember, they probably rent their offices), but do need a lot of working capital. Company M has a lot of fixed assets on which it can secure loans, so is more likely to have some debt funding, but probably not to the extent of an infrastructure business like National Grid.

So the answer is that:

▶ National Grid is an infrastructure business – high investment capital and low working capital, primarily funded though debt

▶ Company M is a manufacturing business – high investment capital and high working capital, funded through a mix of debt and equity

▶ Company S is a services business – low investment capital and high working capital, funded primarily via equity.

? What other companies can you think of?

? What do you think their balance sheets will look like?

What is in the detail of the current assets section?

Once you have managed to identify the five elements, you can use this information to work out to what each line refers.

Have another look at the current assets of National Grid. We have identified that the company has **cash and cash equivalents** of £671 million. Cash equivalents are things that are like cash, but not quite cash: the cash in your pocket is cash; money in your current account is also treated as cash (you can access it quickly); and the money in your deposit account. But what about a 30-day deposit account? Or 90-day deposit account? Money residing in these types of account is like cash, but is not as liquid as cash.

Listed just above cash and cash equivalents you will find **derivative financial assets**. We covered derivatives in Chapter 2 and, while we may not be exactly sure to what the £273 million refers, we know that they must be derivative contracts that are due to mature within 12 months and are currently treated as an asset by the business.

Just above derivative financial assets you will find **financial and other investments** of £5,431 million. Again, we may not be sure exactly to what this refers, but, given where they appear in the balance sheet, we can deduce that they must be investments by National Grid, which are of a liquid nature, that is they can be turned into cash within 12 months. You will notice just to the left of the £5,431 million figure is the number 12. This tells us that, if we require more information on the contents of this line, we can have a look at Note 12 of National Grid's accounts to find out the detail.

Just above financial and other investments is **trade and other receivables**. This figure relates to organisations with whom National Grid has traded and who have not yet paid, as well as other amounts owing to the company; this line is sometimes referred to as trade and other debtors.

The first item in the current assets section is **inventories and current intangible assets**; inventories is another word for stock – goods that have been purchased or made and are being held for resale (National Grid has very little stock, as it provides a service of transporting gas and electricity around the UK).

What is in the detail of the non-current assets section?

There are two types of assets that the company owns: **tangible** and **intangible**. Tangible assets are things that you can touch, such as tables and chairs, plant and machinery, buildings and other equipment. Intangible assets are things that you cannot touch, such as patents, licences and research and development.

Let us look at some of the items in the non-current assets section. Goodwill is the difference between the amount that one company pays to buy another and the fair value of that company's assets and liabilities. It essentially reflects the added value of the business being considered as a going concern.

National Grid is an infrastructure business, so most of its assets are of the tangible variety – property, plant and equipment (this will be the pylons and substations around the country).

The rest of the numbers under non-current assets are relatively small and so we will not go in detail here as to what they all relate. Once again, additional information on the detail of these items is available in the notes, which are indicated to the left of the main numbers. We can conclude that all of the entries relate to items that the business has treated as assets, and that are not expected to become cash within the next 12 months.

What is in the detail of the current liabilities section?

The first item under current liabilities is **borrowings**. These are loans from the bank that have to be repaid within 12 months and so might relate to overdrafts – loans from the bank that are repayable on demand. £3,445 million looks like quite a large overdraft, and so this is more likely to be the current portion of long-term borrowings. If you think about taking out a mortgage for 25 years, most of the amount that you owe will be treated as long-term i.e. it is paid next year, the year after and the year after that (for 25 years!). But you may also have to make capital payments (if it is a repayment mortgage) over the next 12 months. Those payments due to be made during the next 12 months will be accounted for as a current liability and the balance (payments due to be made from month 13 to the end of the mortgage term) as a non-current liability. The next year you will once again show the payments that are made over the next 12 months as a current liability and the remainder (this time the payments for years 2–24, as you have now paid off one year of the mortgage) will be treated as a non-current liability.

After borrowings comes **derivative financial liabilities**; in exactly the same way that derivative financial assets are derivative contracts, which the company has treated as an asset, so this refers to derivative contracts that are due to mature within 12 months of the balance sheet date and that the company is treating as a liability.

Just below derivative financial liabilities we find **trade and other payables**. If trade and other receivables related to debtors of the business, i.e. companies that owe National Grid money, so trade and other payables refers to trade creditors of the business – suppliers from whom National Grid has purchased goods and services but who have not yet been paid, as well as other amounts owed.

Current tax liabilities relates to the tax that National Grid has incurred on this year's profits, but has not yet paid to HMRC.

Finally, **provisions** relates to the amounts the company has put aside in order to pay potential future liabilities. For example, if you visited Arthur at A&B Ltd and, during your visit, tripped on a carpet and broke your leg, you might choose to sue A&B Ltd. A&B Ltd might assess the case and conclude that there was a high likelihood that they were going to have to pay out, say £5,000, and so would provide for that amount. They do not owe you £5,000 (if they did, then it would appear as part of other payables) but, as they believe that there is a high likelihood that they will have to pay, to be prudent they will provide for the amount in the accounts. Note – this is merely an accounting entry – they have not, necessarily, physically set aside the cash.

What is in the detail of the non-current liabilities section?

Non-current liabilities are amounts that National Grid owes to third parties, but does not have to pay within 12 months. The biggest number here is borrowings, which we have already covered in detail under current liabilities.

Other non-current liabilities relates to other amounts that the company owes but it does not have to pay within 12 months of the balance sheet date, and again additional information is available in Note 21.

Deferred tax liabilities relates to tax that is owed but does not have to be paid for over 12 months. For more information about this number speak to the tax department!

Pensions and other post-retirement benefit obligations relates to the pension scheme of National Grid. The appearance of this figure here suggests that National Grid has a **defined benefit** (as opposed to **defined contribution**) pension scheme for some or all of its employees, which will pay out, for example, 3/5 of final annual salary of each member when they retire. In order to ensure that the company can make the payments, a separate pension fund will have been set up. Both the company and the employees will make payments into the separate fund, which is invested with a view to growing sufficiently large to be able to make the pension payments to National Grid staff once they have retired. Each year the actuaries review this separate pension scheme in order to assess whether the funds contained therein are adequate for the payments that will have to be paid out in the future. If the actuaries believe there is a shortfall, then this shortfall will appear as a (non-current) liability on the balance sheet of National Grid. Once again, additional information on this number is available in the notes.

Finally, **provisions** relates to amounts that have been set aside to make potential payments but, again, these potential payments are not expected to mature for another 12 months.

What is in the detail of the equity section?

The final section of National Grid's balance sheet is called **equity**. Sometimes this is referred to by other names, such as: **shareholders' funds** or **capital and reserves**. This represents the amounts that are due back to the shareholders in the event that the business is wound up.

The **called up share capital** and the **share premium account** together relates to the amount that the investors actually have invested into the business. The difference between these two accounts is explained below.

Retained earnings relates to the total amount of profit that National Grid has made ever since it started trading and that has not yet been given back to the shareholders. This is the profit that has been reinvested back into the business on behalf of the shareholders. This is a bit like your bank account. The balance this morning is the sum total of all of the money that you have ever put into your account, less the total that you have ever withdrawn.

Other equity reserves relate to amounts owed to the shareholders, but that cannot be classified as profit or investment – an example of another reserve might be a **revaluation reserve**, which is explained below.

The balance sheet of National Grid is titled 'Consolidated statement of financial position'. This means that the balance sheet is the combined balance sheets of all the different companies through which National Grid conducts its business. It is quite possible that it does not own 100 per cent of all of its subsidiary companies. If another party owns a very small part of the business, for example, 2 per cent of one of the subsidiaries, then this share will be shown under equity as non-controlling or minority interests.

What is the difference between share capital and share premium?

When Arthur and Ben set up A&B Ltd, they issued two shares (one to each of them) at a nominal value of £50 each. This £100 investment would have been accounted for as **share capital**. After two days' trading, Arthur may decide to raise additional equity investment by creating (for example) an additional two shares, which he intends to sell to Poppy.

If Poppy buys these two shares, she will own 50 per cent of the company and therefore will be entitled to 50 per cent of the net assets on the winding up of the company. Given that the net assets of A&B Ltd at the end of day two were £900, it does not appear reasonable to sell the two shares for £100. Therefore, the sale of the additional two shares should be at a premium to the original or nominal value at which the first two shares were issued. Thus, if the additional two shares were sold for (say) £500 each, then, for each share, £50 would be accounted for as share capital and the remaining £450 would be accounted for as **share premium** – i.e. the premium over and above the nominal value of the share.

What is a rights issue?

We have just looked at the difference between the share capital and share premium accounts of the business. Now let us consider Ben's reaction to the process. He originally owned one share, which gave him 50 per cent of the business. However, if A&B Ltd creates two more shares and sells them to

Poppy, then Ben will own only one of the four shares of the business, which will dilute his ownership to 25 per cent of the business. In order to avoid the dilution of his share of the business, Ben may ask Arthur to undertake a rights issue. This gives existing shareholders the right to buy any new shares in proportion to their existing shareholding – in effect allowing existing shareholders to avoid the diluting effects of issuing new shares. In this example, A&B Ltd would undertake a one-for-one rights issue, where every existing shareholder was given the right to buy one new share for every existing share that they own. Thus Arthur and Ben would be given the right to buy an additional share and maintain their holding at 50 per cent of the business; if either of them chose not to take up this offer, then Poppy would be given the opportunity to buy those shares.

What is a revaluation reserve?

Imagine that A&B Ltd bought a building for £1 million and that building was now worth £2 million. A&B Ltd might decide to increase the **property, plant and equipment** on the balance sheet by £1 million. In order for the balance sheet to continue to balance, the equity section of the balance sheet must, therefore, also increase by £1 million. A&B Ltd cannot increase the called up share capital or share premium accounts, as there has been no additional investment in the company. It cannot increase the retained earnings figure, because it has not made a profit on the building (A&B Ltd can recognise a profit on the building only when it actually sells the asset). It may, therefore, choose to set up a revaluation reserve to account for the increase in the value of the building. This would appear in the equity section as **other reserves**. In effect, an increase in the value of the building is merely an increase in the amount that A&B Ltd now owes to the shareholders.

How can I compare balance sheets?

Below are the balance sheets of a variety of different companies. See if you can identify the five elements of each company's balance sheet and complete the following table. What does this information tell you about each company? The answers are given to you at the end of the section, but try to do it yourself before you refer to the answers – clue: if it adds up, then you have probably got it right! Remember, if you look at a balance sheet and it does not look familiar, go back to the basics and try to identify each of the five sections.

Balance sheet analysis

	National Grid	M&S	Tesco	Indesit	BT	NMS
	£m	£m	£m	£m	£m	£m
Non-current assets						
Current assets						
Current liabilities						
Non-current liabilities						
Net assets/share-holders' funds						

Marks & Spencer's balance sheet

Financial statements   Marks and Spencer Group plc   Annual report and financial statements 2014   89
Consolidated statement of financial position

	Notes	As at 29 March 2014 £m	As at 30 March 2013 (restated)[1] £m
Assets			
Non-current assets			
Intangible assets	14	808.4	695.0
Property, plant and equipment	15	5,139.9	5,033.7
Investment property	15.7	15.7	15.8
Investment in joint ventures	12.7	12.7	15.5
Other financial assets	16	3.0	3.0
Retirement benefit asset	11	200.7	249.1
Trade and other receivables	17	313.5	265.4
Derivative financial instruments	21	40.6	65.3
		6,534.5	6,342.8
Current assets			
Inventories		845.5	767.3
Other financial assets	16	17.7	16.9
Trade and other receivables	17	309.5	245.0
Derivative financial instruments	21	13.7	42.5
Current tax assets		–	3.1
Cash and cash equivalents	18	182.1	193.1
		1,368.5	1,267.9
Total assets		7,903.0	7,610.7

59

Liabilities

Current liabilities

Trade and other payables	19	1,692.8	1,503.8
Partnership liability to the Marks & Spencer UK Pension Scheme	12	71.9	71.9
Borrowings and other financial liabilities	20	448.7	558.7
Derivative financial instruments	21	51.5	13.7
Provisions	22	44.8	19.2
Current tax liabilities		39.6	71.0
		2,349.3	2,238.3

Non-current liabilities

Retirement benefit deficit	11	11.7	13.1
Trade and other payables	19	334.0	292.1
Partnership liability to the Marks & Spencer UK Pension Scheme	12	496.8	550.7
Borrowings and other financial liabilities	20	1,655.1	1,727.3
Derivative financial instruments	21	75.4	13.1
Provisions	22	31.4	16.0
Deferred tax liabilities	23	242.6	240.6
		2,847.0	2,852.9
Total liabilities		5,196.3	5,091.2
Net assets		2,706.7	2,519.5

Equity

Issued share capital	24	408.1	403.5
Share premium account		355.5	315.1
Capital redemption reserve		2,202.6	2,202.6
Hedging reserve		(41.8)	9.2
Other reserve		(6,542.2)	(6,542.2)
Retained earnings		6,325.1	6,150.3
Total shareholders' equity		2,707.3	2,538.5
Non-controlling interests in equity		(0.6)	(19.0)
Total equity		2,706.7	2,519.5

1. Restatement relates to the adoption of the revised IAS 19 'Employee Benefits' (see note 1).

The financial statements were approved by the Board and authorised for issue on 22 May 2014. The financial statements also comprise of the notes on pages 92 to 122.

Marc Bolland Chief Executive Officer
Alan Stewart Chief Finance Officer

Tesco's balance sheet

Group balance sheet

	Notes	22 February 2014 £m	23 February 2013 £m
Non-current assets			
Goodwill and other intangible assets	10	3,795	4,362
Property, plant and equipment	11	24,490	24,870
Investment property	12	227	2,001
Investments in joint ventures and associates	13	286	494
Other investments	14	1,015	818
Loans and advances to customers	17	3,210	2,465
Derivative financial instruments	21	1,496	1,965
Deferred tax assets	6	73	58
		34,592	37,033
Current assets			
Inventories	15	3,576	3,744
Trade and other receivables	16	2,190	2,525
Loans and advances to customers	17	3,705	3,094
Derivative financial instruments	21	80	58
Current tax assets		12	10
Short-term investments		1,016	522
Cash and cash equivalents	18	2,506	2,512
		13,085	12,465
Assets of the disposal group and non-current assets classified as held for sale	7	2,487	631
		15,572	13,096
Current liabilities			
Trade and other payables	19	(10,595)	(11,094)
Financial liabilities:			
Borrowings	20	(1,910)	(766)
Derivative financial instruments and other liabilities	21	(99)	(121)
Customer deposits and deposits from banks	23	(6,858)	(6,015)
Current tax liabilities		(494)	(519)
Provisions	24	(250)	(188)
		(20,206)	(18,703)
Liabilities of the disposal group classified as held for sale	7	(1,193)	(282)
Net current liabilities		(5,827)	(5,889)

Non-current liabilities
Financial liabilities:

Borrowings	20	**(9,303)**	(10,068)
Derivative financial instruments and other liabilities	21	**(770)**	(759)
Post-employment benefit obligations	26	**(3,193)**	(2,378)
Deferred tax liabilities	6	**(594)**	(1,006)
Provisions	24	**(183)**	(272)
		(14,043)	(14,483)
Net assets		**14,722**	16,661
Equity			
Share capital	27	**405**	403
Share premium		**5,080**	5,020
All other reserves		**(498)**	685
Retained earnings		**9,728**	10,535
Equity attributable to owners of the parent		**14,715**	16,643
Non-controlling interests		**7**	18
Total equity		**14,722**	16,661

The notes on pages 74 to 121 form part of these financial statements.
Philip Clarke
Directors
The financial statements on pages 69 to 121 were authorised for issue by the Directors on 2 May 2014 and are subject to the approval of the shareholders at the Annual General Meeting on 27 June 2014.

Indesit's balance sheet

Consolidated statement of financial position at 31 December 2013[2]

(million euro)	Note	31.12.2013	31.12.2012 restated	01.01.2012 restated
Assets				
Property, plant and equipment	9.1	615.4	673.1	623.2
Goodwill and other intangible assets with an indefinite useful life	9.2	240.1	242.2	236.5
Other intangible assets with a finite useful life	9.3	98.7	103.8	100.1
Investments in associates	9.4	0.5	0.5	0.5
Other non-current assets	9.5	2.3	0.9	28.0
Deferred tax assets	9.6	129.5	118.8	81.4
Other non-current financial assets	9.13.5	1.9	1.5	1.5
Total non-current assets		**1,088.3**	**1,140.8**	**1,071.2**

Inventories	9.7	302.4	331.8	323.2
Trade receivables	9.8	426.5	465.3	440.5
Current financial assets	9.13.1	17.9	29.4	20.9
Tax receivables	9.9	14.1	16.3	12.9
Other receivables and current assets	9.10	63.2	75.4	67.8
Cash and cash equivalents	9.13.2	330.8	142.8	234.4
Assets held for sale	9.21	2.1	20.4	11.8
Total current assets		**1,157.0**	**1,081.4**	**1,111.4**
Total assets		**2,245.4**	**2,222.2**	**2,182.6**
Equity				
Share capital	9.11	92.8	92.8	92.8
Reserves	9.11	(191.0)	(103.9)	(129.1)
Retained earnings	9.11	560.2	506.3	470.6
Profit attributable to owners of the Parent	9.11	3.2	61.7	58.7
Equity attributable to owners of the Parent		**465.3**	**556.9**	**493.0**
Non-controlling interests	9.12	0.0	0.0	0.0
Total equity		**465.3**	**557.0**	**493.0**
Liabilities				
Medium and long-term loans and borrowings	9.13.4	368.6	232.3	246.3
Employee benefits	9.14	81.0	84.3	114.0
Provisions for risks and charges	9.15	56.7	50.1	48.6
Deferred tax liabilities	9.16	30.5	35.5	35.1
Other non-current liabilities	9.17	22.6	29.9	34.9
Total non-current liabilities		**559.5**	**432.1**	**478.9**
Banks and other short-term loans and borrowings	9.13.3	307.4	197.8	228.7
Provisions for risks and charges	9.15	52.3	64.4	58.6
Trade payables	9.18	738.9	844.8	788.7
Tax payables	9.19	25.3	23.6	27.6
Other payables	9.20	96.8	102.7	107.2
Total current liabilities		**1,220.6**	**1,233.1**	**1,210.7**
Total liabilities		**1,780.1**	**1,665.2**	**1,689.6**
Total equity and liabilities		**2,245.4**	**2,222.2**	**2,182.6**

BT's balance sheet

Group balance sheet

At 31 March	Notes	2014 £m	2013 £m
Non-current assets			
Intangible assets	12	3,087	3,258
Property, plant and equipment	13	13,840	14,153
Derivative financial instruments	26	539	1,080
Investments	22	34	64
Associates and joint ventures		18	28
Trade and other receivables	16	214	184
Deferred tax assets	9	1,460	1,438
		19,192	**20,205**
Current assets			
Programme rights	15	108	–
Inventories		82	103
Trade and other receivables	16	2,907	2,930
Current tax receivable		26	16
Derivative financial instruments	26	114	170
Investments	22	1,774	531
Cash and cash equivalents	23	695	924
		5,706	**4,674**
Current liabilities			
Loans and other borrowings	24	1,873	1,736
Derivative financial instruments	26	139	74
Trade and other payables	17	5,261	5,574
Current tax liabilities		315	100
Provisions	18	99	120
		7,687	**7,604**
Total assets less current liabilities		**17,211**	**17,275**
Non-current liabilities			
Loans and other borrowings	24	7,941	8,277
Derivative financial instruments	26	679	802
Retirement benefit obligations	19	7,022	5,856
Other payables	17	898	883
Deferred tax liabilities	9	829	1,209
Provisions	18	434	510
		17,803	**17,537**
Equity			
Ordinary shares		408	408
Share premium		62	62
Own shares	20	(829)	(832)
Other reserves	27	1,447	1,790
Retained loss		(1,680)	(1,690)
Total (deficit) equity		**(592)**	**(262)**
		17,211	**17,275**

NMS's balance sheet

Consolidated balance sheet					
At 5 April 2013	Note		2013		2012
		£000's	£000's	£000's	£000's
Fixed assets					
Tangible assets	13		**2,858**		2,478
Investments	14		5		–
Intangible assets	12		3,028		–
			5,891		2,478
Current assets					
Work in progress		10,546		10,343	
Debtors	15	87,609		73,501	
Cash at bank		21,670		12,142	
		119,825		95,986	
Creditors: amounts falling	16	(87,643)		(70,567)	
due within one year					
Net current assets			32,182		25,419
Total assets less current			38,073		27,897
liabilities					
Creditors: amounts falling	17		(15,024)		(8,066)
due after more than one year					
Net assets			23,049		19,831
Capital and reserves					
Called up share capital	18		62		62
Share premium account	19		3,754		3,754
Capital contribution reserve	19		6,961		6,961
Profit and loss account	19		12,272		9,054
Equity shareholders' funds	19		23,049		19,831

How can I compare balance sheets? – The answer

Here are the results of the various balance sheets. See if you managed to identify all of the figures correctly. Review the brief conclusions and see if you managed to draw the same inferences from your analysis.

Balance sheet analysis

	National Grid £m	M&S £m	Tesco £m	Indesit £m	BT £m	NMS £m
Non-current assets	£ 45,129	£ 6,534.5	£ 34,592	£ 1,088.4	£ 19,192	£ 5.9
Current assets	£ 9,576	£ 1,368.5	£ 15,572	£ 1,157.0	£ 5,706	£ 119.0
Current liabilities	£ 7,445	£ 2,349.3	£ 21,399	£ 1,220.6	£ 7,687	£ 87.6
Non-current liabilities	£ 37,027	£ 2,847.0	£ 14,043	£ 559.5	£ 17,803	£ 15.0
Net assets/share-holders' funds	£ 10,233	£ 2,706.7	£ 14,722	£ 465.3	–£ 592	£ 23.0

National Grid

National Grid is, as discussed, a large infrastructure business (£45 billion of non-current assets) with very little working capital. Mainly funded via debt.

M&S

M&S is a retail business but owns many of its shops (large non-current asset figure) and appears to need very little working capital. Funded via debt and equity.

Tesco

Tesco is similar to M&S – a retail business and, again, owns most of the property from which it trades – again with very little working capital. Funded via debt and equity.

Indesit

Indesit is a manufacturing business (making washing machines and dishwashers) where the plant and machinery for manufacturing (non-current assets) are the same size as the working capital. Funded via debt and equity.

BT

BT is a large infrastructure telecoms business (think of all those phone networks) with little working capital. The debt is so big that the liabilities of the business are bigger than the assets – giving a negative equity figure.

Is this a problem? BT's negative balance sheet is a bit like being in negative equity – where the mortgage that you have taken out to buy your house exceeds the value of the house. This is not a particularly nice position to be in, but it is not disastrous – as long as you can keep up the interest repayments on your house (remember, in Chapter 2, we looked at the need for a company to be able to service its debt – i.e. keep up the interest repayments – which will allow it to refinance). This is a similar situation for BT. The negative balance sheet does not look particularly healthy, but as long as BT can service the debt then it is not the end of BT.

Have another look at BT's balance sheet. What is the largest number making up its non-current liabilities? The answer is loans and other borrowings of £7.9 billion (and we would expect this to be the case). But what is the second-largest figure? It is the retirement benefit obligations of £7 billion. We have already covered what this figure relates to when we undertook the detailed analysis of National Grid's balance sheet. What this is telling us is that BT has a negative balance sheet because its pension fund is very underfunded.

NMS

NMS is a small company that you have probably never heard of. It offers building managed services (i.e. it will look after your building, run reception, sort out cleaning, fix the air conditioning when it breaks and other services). As a service company, NMS does not need much in the way of non-current assets (plant and machinery, etc.) but it does need a lot of working capital. On the face of it, the company appears to be funded through a mixture of debt and equity; however, examination of the accounts will show that the non-current liabilities actually relate to a long-term incentive plan for the senior management. Thus the company is, in fact, entirely equity funded.

What is in the income statement or profit & loss account?

Whereas the balance sheet is a snapshot in time showing the assets and liabilities of a business, the income statement (also known as the profit & loss account – P&L a/c) shows the **income** (also known as turnover, revenue or sales) and **expenses** (also known as costs or outgoings) of a business over a period of time.

While you will have seen different balance sheets presenting information in different order to each other, the P&L a/c is always structured in the same order. If you can identify this order, then, again, you have cracked the P&L.

How is the P&L account structured?

Sales		
Less		Cost of sales
Equals	=	Gross profit
Less		Operating costs
Equals	=	Operating profit
Less		Interest
Less		Tax
Equals	=	Net profit

What are the different definitions contained within the P&L?

Sales will sometimes be referred to as turnover, income or revenue. Under the accrual accounting concept, this figure refers to what has been sold, irrespective of whether or not it has been paid for.

Cost of sales relates to the cost of the things that are sold. Remember when Arthur and Ben purchased the apples (see Chapter 1), the apples would have been treated as stock (an asset). At the point of purchase, there was no impact on the profit & loss account of A&B Ltd; Arthur and Ben were merely turning one form of asset – cash – into another form of asset – apples or stock. Only when A&B Ltd sold the apples, did they appear in the P&L as a cost of sale (sometimes referred to as **cost of goods sold**). The cost of sales usually relates to the variable costs of running the business (on the basis that the more apples that A&B has to sell, the more apples they have to buy).

Operating costs relates to the fixed costs of running the business. These are things such as rent, rate, light, heat and other overheads. As A&B Ltd sells more apples, we would expect the operating costs to remain constant and so usually these are referred to as fixed costs.

? See if you can obtain the financial statements of your business. Undertake the following analysis for the profit & loss account.

How can I compare P&L accounts?

Now have a look at the different P&L accounts of the six companies for whom we analysed the balance sheet. See if you can complete the matrix. Some items will have to be grouped together, but you should be able to build up a high-level picture of each business. What sort of conclusions do you draw?

Profit & loss accounts

	National Grid £m	M&S £m	Tesco £m	Indesit £m	BT £m	NMS £m
Sales						
Cost of sales						
Gross profit						
Operating costs						
Operating profit						
Interest						
Tax						
Net profit						

National Grid's P&L account

	Notes	2013 £m	2013 £m	2012 £m	2012 £m	2011 £m	2011 £m
Revenue	1(a)		14,359		13,832		14,343
Operating costs	2		(10,605)		(10,293)		(10,598)
Operating profit							
Before exceptional items, remeasurements and stranded cost recoveries	1(b)	3,644		3,495		3,600	
Exceptional items, remeasurements and stranded cost recoveries	3	110		44		145	
Total operating profit	1(b)		3,754		3,539		3,745
Finance income							
Before exceptional items	4	1,252		1,301		1,281	
Exceptional items	3,4	–		–		43	
Total finance income	4		1,252		1,301		1,324

Finance costs				
Before exceptional items and remeasurements	4	**(2,172)**	(2,218)	(2,415)
	3,4	**68**	(70)	(37)
Total finance costs	4	**(2,104)**	(2,288)	(2,452)
Share of post-tax results of joint ventures and associates	13	**18**	7	7
Profit before tax				
Before exceptional items, remeasurements and stranded cost recoveries	1(b)	**2,742**	2,585	2,473
Exceptional items, remeasurements and stranded cost recoveries	3	**178**	(26)	151
Total profit before tax	1(b)	**2,920**	2,559	2,624
Taxation				
Before exceptional items, remeasurements and stranded cost recoveries	5	**(686)**	(755)	(722)
Exceptional items, remeasurements and stranded cost recoveries	3,5	**62**	234	261
Total taxation	5	**(624)**	(521)	(461)
Profit after tax				
Before exceptional items, remeasurements and stranded cost recoveries		2,056	1,830	1,751
Exceptional items, remeasurements and stranded cost recoveries	3	**240**	208	412
Profit for the year		**2,296**	2,038	2,163
Attributable to:				
Equity shareholders of the parent		**2,295**	2,036	2,159
Non-controlling interests		**1**	2	4
		2,296	2,038	2,163
Earnings per share*				
Basic	6	**62.6p**	55.6p	61.2p
Diluted	6	**62.3p**	55.4p	60.9p

*Comparative amounts have been restated to reflect the impact of additional shares issued as scrip dividends

The notes on pages 105 to 164 form part of the consolidated financial statements.

Marks & Spencer's P&L account

Consolidated income statement

	Notes	52 weeks ended 29 March 2014	52 weeks ended 30 March 2013 (restated)[1]
		£m	£m
Revenue	2, 3	10,309.7	10,026.8
Operating profit	2, 3	694.5	753.0
Finance income	6	25.0	12.4
Finance costs	6	(139.1)	(218.2)
Profit before tax	4	580.4	547.2
Income tax expense	7	(74.4)	(102.4)
Profit for the year		506.0	444.8

Tesco's P&L account

Year ended 22 February 2014	Notes	52 weeks 2014	52 weeks 2013 (restated*)
		£m	£m
Continuing operations			
Revenue	2	63,557	63,406
Cost of sales		(59,547)	(59,252)
Gross profit		4,010	4,154
Administrative expenses		(1,657)	(1,482)
Profits/losses arising on property-related items		278	(290)
Operating profit		2,631	2,382
Share of post-tax profits of joint ventures and associates	13	60	72
Finance income	5	132	120
Finance costs	5	(564)	(517)
Profit before tax	3	2,259	2,057
Taxation	6	(347)	(529)
Profit for the year from continuing operations		1,912	1,528
Discontinued operations			
Loss for the year from discontinued operations	7	(942)	(1,504)
Profit for the year		970	24

Indesit's P&L account

(million euro)	Note	Year 2013	Year 2012 restated
Revenue	8.1	2,671.1	2,893.7
Cost of sales	8.2	(2,054.8)	(2,180.2)
Selling and distribution expenses	8.3	(437.3)	(468.9)
General and administrative expenses	8.4	(110.9)	(108.8)
Operating profit	8.5	**68.1**	**135.8**
Net interest		(27.8)	(26.8)
Exchange rate	8.6	(18.8)	(2.5)
Fees and other net financial expenses	8.6	(4.7)	(5.3)
Share of profit (losses) of associates and other	8.6	(0.0)	0.3
Profit before tax		**16.9**	**101.5**
Income taxes	8.7	(13.7)	(39.8)
Profit for the year		**3.2**	**61.7**

BT's P&L account

Year ended 31 March 2012	Notes	Before specific items Restated[b] £m	Specific items[a] Restated[b] £m	Total Restated[b] £m
Revenue	4	**19,397**	**(410)**	**18,987**
Operating costs	5	(16,335)	237	(16,098)
Operating profit (loss)	4	**3,062**	**(173)**	**2,889**
Finance expense	25	(692)	(98)	(790)
Finance income		11	–	11
Net finance expense		**(681)**	**(98)**	**(779)**
Share of post tax profit of associates and joint ventures		10	–	10
Profit (loss) before taxation		**2,391**	**(271)**	**2,120**
Taxation	9	(576)	212	(364)
Profit (loss) for the year		**1,815**	**(59)**	**1,756**

NMS's P&L account

Consolidated profit and loss account
for the 53 weeks ended 5 April 1013

	Note	2013 £000's Trading	2013 £000's Other	2013 £000's Total	2012 £000's Total
Turnover		384,838	–	384,838	312,089
Cost of sales		(328,888)	–	(328,888)	(266,994)
Mobilisation costs		(1,080)	–	(1,080)	–
Total cost of sales		(329,968)	–	(329,968)	(266,994)
Gross **profit**		54,870	–	54,870	45,095
Administrative expenses		(33,573)	–	(33,573)	(27,028)
Goodwill amortisation	12	–	(336)	(336)	–
FRS20 charges	8	–	(6,958)	(6,958)	(8,066)
Total administrative expenses		(33,573)	(7,294)	(40,867)	(35,094)
Operating profit		21,297	(7,294)	14,003	10,001
Exceptional restructuring costs	9			(1,375)	–
Share of associate's results	14			1,082	–
Profit on sale of associate	14			37	–
Interest receivable and similar income	5			405	390
Interest payable and similar charges	6			(84)	(48)
Profit on ordinary activities before taxation	4			14,068	10,343
Current and deferred tax	11			(4,424)	(2,127)
Group relief charge	11			(1,628)	(3,633)
Tax on profit on ordinary activities	11			(6,052)	(5,760)
Profit for the period	19			8,016	4,583

How can I compare P&L accounts? – The answer

Here are the results of the various P&L accounts.

Profit & loss accounts

	National Grid £m	M&S £m	Tesco £m	Indesit £m	BT £m	NMS £m
Sales	£ 14,359	£ 10,309.7	£ 63,557	£ 2,671.1	£ 19,397	£ 384.8
Cost of sales			£ 59,547	£ 2,054.8		£ 330.0
Gross profit			£ 4,010	£ 616.3		£ 54.9
Operating costs	£ 10,605		£ 1,379	£ 548.2	£ 16,335	£ 40.9
Operating profit	£ 3,754	£ 694.5	£ 2,631	£ 68.1	£ 3,032	£ 14.0
Interest	£ 834	£ 114.1	£ 372	£ 51.2	£ 671	£ -
Tax	£ 624	£ 74.4	£ 347	£ 13.7	£ 576	£ 6.0
Net profit	£ 2,296	£ 506.0	£ 1,912	£ 3.2	£ 1,815	£ 8.0

National Grid

National Grid transports gas and electricity around the UK. The costs of running the business when the UK is watching *Coronation Street* on TV are about the same as when the programme finishes and the nation turns the kettle on to brew a cuppa. Thus, the cost of sales is relevant – it is a fixed-cost business, so opts not to show gross profit (which would be the same as the sales). There is a reasonable amount of interest, due to the debt used to fund the business.

M&S

M&S is a retail business and has chosen not to split its costs between fixed (operating costs) and variable (cost of sales).

Tesco

Tesco spends a lot on the food and clothes that it sells; while Tesco turns over £64 billion, it spends about £60 billion buying the stuff to sell. In comparison, it costs only £1.4 billion to run the business (back-office staff, head office costs, etc.)

Indesit

Indesit spends a lot of money making the products (dishwashers and washing machines, etc.) that it sells.

BT

BT is very similar to National Grid in so far as it is a fixed-cost business. It is clearly profitable, and so the fact that there is negative equity on the balance sheet does not signify that BT must cease trading.

NMS

NMS's cost of sales relates to the cost of the employees who are providing the services to its clients. Like Tesco's cost of sales (food), this is quite a high figure when compared to the sales. There is no interest payable, because there is no debt on the balance sheet.

? What other organisations can you think of?

? How profitable do you think they are?

? What do you think are the biggest (and smallest) numbers in their P&L accounts?

How does the income statement or profit & loss account interact with the balance sheet?

In Chapter 1, we saw how A&B Ltd accounted for its trading. At the end of day one the company had made total profits of £400. During day two, it made an additional profit of £400, so, by the end of day two, the total profits generated, but not yet paid back to shareholders, was £800. This amount appeared on the balance sheet as **retained earnings** in the **shareholders' funds** section – also known as **equity** or **capital and reserves**.

We should be able to perform this reconciliation for each of our companies. We will do this for NMS.

NMS made a profit of £8,016,000 as per the P&L a/c.

Consolidated profit and loss account
for the 53 weeks ended 5 April 1013

	Note	2013 £000's Trading	2013 £000's Other	2013 £000's Total	2012 £000's Total
Turnover		384,838	–	384,838	312,089
Cost of sales		(328,888)	–	(328,888)	(266,994)
Mobilisation costs		(1,080)	–	(1,080)	–
Total cost of sales		(329,968)	–	(329,968)	(266,994)
Gross profit		54,870	–	54,870	45,095
Administrative expenses		(33,573)	–	(33,573)	(27,028)
Goodwill amortisation	12	–	(336)	(336)	–
FRS20 charges	8	–	(6,958)	(6,958)	(8,066)
Total administrative expenses		(33,573)	(7,294)	(40,867)	(35,094)
Operating profit		21,297	(7,294)	14,003	10,001
Exceptional restructuring costs	9			(1,375)	–
Share of associate's results	14			1,082	–
Profit on sale of associate	14			37	–
Interest receivable and similar income	5			405	390
Interest payable and similar charges	6			(84)	(48)
Profit on ordinary activities before taxation	4			14,068	10,343
Current and deferred tax	11			(4,424)	(2,127)
Group relief charge	11			(1,628)	(3,633)
Tax on profit on ordinary activities	11			(6,052)	(5,760)
Profit for the period	19			8,016	4,583

The total amount of profit that NMS has made, ever since it started trading, and has not yet given back to the shareholders, can be found in the balance sheet under **capital and reserves**.

Consolidated balance sheet
At 5 April 2013

	Note	2013 £000's	2013 £000's	2012 £000's	2012 £000's
Fixed assets					
Tangible assets	13		2,858		2,478
Investments	14		5		–
Intangible assets	12		3,028		–
			5,891		2,478
Current assets					
Work in progress		10,546		10,343	
Debtors	15	87,609		73,501	
Cash at bank		21,670		12,142	
		119,825		95,986	
Creditors: amounts falling due within one year	16	(87,643)		(70,567)	
Net current assets			32,182		25,419
Total assets less current liabilities			38,073		27,897
Creditors: amounts falling due after more than one year	17		(15,024)		(8,066)
Net assets			23,049		19,831
Capital and reserves					
Called up share capital	18		62		62
Share premium account	19		3,754		3,754
Capital contribution reserve	19		6,961		6,961
Profit and loss account	19		12,272		9,054
Equity shareholders' funds	19		23,049		19,831

NMS started the year with £9,054k and finished the year with £12,272k.

Remember, A&B Ltd started day two with £400, made an additional £400 profit, and finished day two with £800.

So, NMS started the year with £9,054k, made an additional £8,016k profit and finished with £12,272k. These figures do not appear to add up – so something else must have happened during the year. Perhaps NMS paid a dividend? We can find the answer in Note 19 (you can see the number 19 just to the right of where it says Profit and loss account in the balance sheet, indicating that if you need more information on this area then that is where to find it).

Note 19 from the accounts of NMS shows the following:

19 Reserves					
	Share Capital	Share Premium	Capital Contribution Reserve	Profit and Loss Account	Total
Group	£000's	£000's	£000's	£000's	£000's
Opening balance	62	3,754	6,961	9,054	19,831
Dividends paid	–	–	–	(4,777)	(4,777)
Profit for the period	–	–	–	8,016	8,016
Other movements in reserves	–	–	–	–	–
Exchange rate gain	–	–	–	(21)	(21)
At end of period	62	3,754	6,961	12,272	23,049

Note 19 shows us that NMS paid a dividend during the year of £4,777k. So, in conclusion, the company started with approximately £9 million of retained profits, made an additional £8 million in profit during the year (total £17 million), paid out nearly £5 million in dividends, leaving £12 million of retained earnings or retained profits reinvested back in to the business.

What is in the cash flow statement?

The final section of this chapter deals with the cash flow statement.

The cash flow statement aims to reconcile the profit from the P&L a/c with the movement in cash on the balance sheet. It aims to highlight where else on the balance sheet cash has either been tied up or released.

This is best demonstrated by looking at a practical example, such as National Grid:

National Grid made an operating profit of £3,754 million for 2013:

	Notes	2013 £m	2013 £m	2012 £m	2012 £m	2011 £m	2011 £m
Revenue	1(a)		**14,359**		13,832		14,343
Operating costs	2		**(10,605)**		(10,293)		(10,598)
Operating profit							
Before exceptional items, remeasurements and stranded cost recoveries	(b)	**3,644**		3,495		3,600	
Exceptional items, remeasurements and stranded cost recoveries	3	<u>**110**</u>		<u>44</u>		<u>145</u>	
Total operating profit	1(b)		3,754		3,539		3,745

If we now turn to the balance sheet, we can see that National Grid started the year with £332 million in **cash and cash equivalents** (right-hand column – remember that the cash balance at the end of last year is the same as the cash balance at the beginning of this year) and finished the year with £671 million:

	Notes	2013 £m	2012 £m
Non-current assets			
Goodwill	8	**5,028**	4,776
Other intangible assets	9	**589**	546
Property, plant and equipment	10	**36,592**	33,701
Other non-current assets	11	**104**	95
Pension assets	22	**195**	155
Financial and other investments	12	**278**	251
Investments in joint ventures and associates	13	**371**	341
Derivative financial assets	14	**1,972**	1,819
Total non-current assets		**45,129**	41,684
Current assets			
Inventories and current intangible assets	15	**291**	376
Trade and other receivables	16	**2,910**	1,971
Financial and other investments	12	**5,431**	2,391
Derivative financial assets	14	**273**	317
Cash and cash equivalents	17	671	332
Total current assets		**9,576**	5,387
Assets of businesses held for sale	18	–	264
Total assets		**54,705**	47,335

So, the company made a profit of £3,754 million, but saw an increase in its cash of only £339 million (i.e. from £332 million at the beginning of the year to £671 million at the end of the year). The aim of the cash flow statement is to assist us in understanding this difference.

In Chapter 1, when we looked at how A&B Ltd trades, we saw that profit and cash is not the same thing. This is due to the accrual concept (where we recognise sales when we earn them, not when we receive payment and costs when we incur them, not when we make payment). Thus the £3,754 million of profit is based on this accrual accounting method.

So, the first aim of the cash flow statement is to see what sort of profit the company would have generated, if it had been counting on a cash basis (where we recognise sales when we receive payment and costs when we make a payment). One way to achieve this would be to rerun every single P&L transaction on a cash basis, but this would take a very long time. An alternative method is to start with the operating profit and then make a number of adjustments to turn the **operating** profit into a **cash** profit.

For example, consider **depreciation**. If A&B Ltd bought a table 7 years ago for £100 and intended to use that table for 10 years, the company would depreciate the £100 over 10 years – that is £10 a year. What impact does that £10 depreciation have on A&B Ltd's profit in this year? The answer is that it reduces their profit by £10 because depreciation is a charge against profits. But what impact does this expense have on cash? The answer is nothing. Why? Because depreciation is an **accounting** adjustment but not a **cash** adjustment (don't forget, the company paid for the table seven years ago – that is when it affected their cash).

So, if we are trying to work out our **cash** profit and we are starting with our **accounting** profit, we need to **add back** depreciation; this becomes a **reconciling** item. Below we can see the first part of the cash flow statement from National Grid. The first section of the cash flow statement aims to turn the accounting profit into a cash profit by adding and subtracting various reconciling items such as depreciation.

This section of the cash flow statement is called **cash flows from operating activities** – the aim is to turn an accounting profit into a cash profit. Sometimes this section of the cash flow does not appear in the main cash flow statement, but will be hidden in the notes to the accounts.

	Notes	2013 £m	2012 £m	2011 £m
Cash flows from operating activities				
Total operating profit	1(b)	3,754	3,539	3,745
Adjustments for:				
Exceptional items, remeasurements and stranded cost recoveries	3	(110)	(44)	(145)
Depreciation, amortisation and impairment		1,361	1,282	1,245
Share-based payment charge		20	24	25
Changes in working capital		(410)	146	185
Changes in provisions		(53)	(116)	(93)
Changes in pensions and other post-retirement benefit obligations		(413)	(386)	(304)
Cash flows relating to exceptional items		(112)	(205)	(147)
Cash flows relating to stranded cost recoveries		–	247	343
Cash generated from operations		4,037	4,487	4,854
Tax (paid)/received		(287)	(259)	4
Net cash inflow from operating activities		3,750	4,228	4,858

You can see from looking at the various reconciling items that depreciation is one of the biggest adjustments. Incidentally, amortisation is merely depreciation by another name – we **depreciate** tangible assets (things that we can touch) and **amortise** intangible assets (things that we cannot touch).

After all the adjustments, we see that National Grid made a **cash** operating profit (as opposed to an **accounting** operating profit) of £3,750 million, so the two figures are broadly the same, although this is not always the case. For example, in 2006 Vodafone reported a net loss for the year of £22 billion, but still managed to generate £12 billion in cash from its trading operations.

But what did National Grid do with that cash? The next section of the cash flow statement, called **cash flows from investing activities**, answers that question:

	Notes	2013 £m	2012 £m	2011 £m
Cash flows from investing activities				
Acquisition of investments		**(14)**	(13)	(135)
Proceeds from sale of investments in subsidiaries		**183**	365	11
Purchases of intangible assets		**(175)**	(203)	(176)
Purchases of property, plant and equipment		**(3,214)**	(3,147)	(2,958)
Disposals of property, plant and equipment		**32**	24	26
Dividends received from joint ventures		**21**	26	9
Interest received		**29**	24	26
Net movements in short-term financial investments		**(2,992)**	553	(1,577)
Net cash flow used in investing activities		**(6,130)**	(2,371)	(4,774)

The biggest expenditure was the investment in property, plant and equipment of £3,214 million, as shown above. There was also an additional investment of £2,992 million in financial investments.

Overall, National Grid has invested £6,130 million. So, the company made a (cash) profit of £3,750 million but has spent (invested) £6,130 million. The difference it must have made up with additional funding.

This is where the third section of the cash flow statement comes in – **cash flows from financing activities**. This section examines whether the company has generated cash from financing activities (for example, taking out loans or issuing new shares) or used cash to pay down loans or buy back shares. It also shows the cost to the company of obtaining that financing – interest that is paid on the debt and dividends that are paid to the shareholders or equity investors.

	Notes	2013 £m	2012 £m	2011 £m
Cash flows from financing activities				
Proceeds of rights issue		–	–	3,214
Proceeds from issue of treasury shares		19	13	18
Purchase of own shares		(6)	(4)	(3)
Proceeds received from loans		5,062	1,809	767
Repayment of loans		(1,210)	(1,914)	(2,878)
Net movements in short-term borrowings and derivatives		452	(49)	348
Interest paid		(792)	(749)	(965)
Exceptional finance costs on the redemption of debt		–	–	(73)
Dividends paid to shareholders		(810)	(1,006)	(858)
Net cash flow from/(used in) financing activities		2,715	(1,900)	(430)

The main items from the financing section show that National Grid issued new debt of £5,062 million, and used £1,210 million of that to repay existing loans – i.e. some of the debt was rolled over or refinanced (you will remember in Chapter 2 that we gave the example of National Grid refinancing its debt). In total, National Grid raised £2,715 million from financing activities.

So, to summarise so far, National Grid made a £3,750 million (cash) profit, invested £6,130 million and has raised £2,715 million from financing activities. The net effect of these three amounts is a decrease in cash of £333 million.

The final section of the cash flow statement reconciles this figure back to the balance sheet. Our first examination of the balance sheet concluded that the total cash had risen by £339 million, which is close to the £333 million above. The difference is that the cash flow is looking at the movement in cash and cash equivalents, which will include both the cash balances and any overdrafts. You can see from the section below that some overdrafts have also been included (if you look on the balance sheet, the overdrafts will be included in the borrowings section under current liabilities).

	Notes	2013 £m	2012 £m	2011 £m
Net increase/(decrease) in cash and cash equivalents	26(a)	335	(43)	(346)
Exchange movements		14	–	(3)
Net cash and cash equivalents at start of year		299	342	691
Net cash and cash equivalents at end of year (i)	17	648	299	342

(i) Net of bank overdrafts of £23m (2012: £33m; 2011: £42m).

So, the summary of the cash flow statement for National Grid looks like this:

	Notes	2013 £m	2012 £m	2011 £m
Cash flows from operating activities				
Total operating profit	1(b)	**3,754**	3,539	3,745
Adjustments for:				
Exceptional items, remeasurements and stranded cost recoveries	3	**(110)**	(44)	(145)
Depreciation, amortisation and impairment		**1,361**	1,282	1,245
Share-based payment charge		**20**	24	25
Changes in working capital		**(410)**	146	185
Changes in provisions		**(53)**	(116)	(93)
Changes in pensions and other post-retirement benefit obligations		**(413)**	(386)	(304)
Cash flows relating to exceptional items		**(112)**	(205)	(147)
Cash flows relating to stranded cost recoveries		**–**	247	343
Cash generated from operations		**4,037**	4,487	4,854
Tax (paid)/received		**(287)**	(259)	4
Net cash inflow from operating activities		**3,750**	4,228	4,858
Cash flows from investing activities				
Acquisition of investments		**(14)**	(13)	(135)
Proceeds from sale of investments in subsidiaries		**183**	365	11
Purchases of intangible assets		**(175)**	(203)	(176)
Purchases of property, plant and equipment		**(3,214)**	(3,147)	(2,958)
Disposals of property, plant and equipment		**32**	24	26
Dividends received from joint ventures		**21**	26	9
Interest received		**29**	24	26
Net movements in short-term financial investments		**(2,992)**	553	(1,577)

Net cash flow used in investing activities		**(6,130)**	(2,371)	(4,774)
Cash flows from financing activities				
Proceeds of rights issue		–	–	3,214
Proceeds from issue of treasury shares		**19**	13	18
Purchase of own shares		**(6)**	(4)	(3)
Proceeds received from loans		**5,062**	1,809	767
Repayment of loans		**(1,210)**	(1,914)	(2,878)
Net movements in short-term borrowings and derivatives		**452**	(49)	348
Interest paid		**(792)**	(749)	(965)
Exceptional finance costs on the redemption of debt		–	–	(73)
Dividends paid to shareholders		**(810)**	(1,006)	(858)
Net cash flow from/(used in) financing activities		**2,715**	(1,900)	(430)
Net increase/(decrease) in cash and cash equivalents	26(a)	**335**	(43)	(346)
Exchange movements		**14**	–	(3)
Net cash and cash equivalents at start of year		**299**	342	691
Net cash and cash equivalents at end of year (i)	17	**648**	299	342

(i) Net of bank overdrafts of £23m (2012: £33m; 2011: £42m).

The main constituent elements of the cash flow statement are as follows:

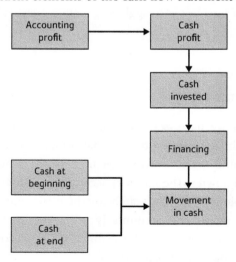

See if you can complete this table for National Grid.

Cash flow statement

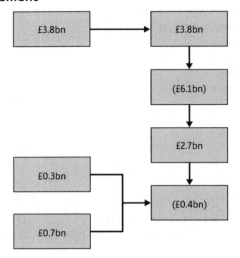

? See if you can obtain the financial statements of your business. Has a cash flow statement been prepared? If so, see if you can undertake the analysis for the cash flow statement.

? What sort of businesses are good at generating lots of cash, do you think?

? What sort of businesses struggle to generate cash? Why do you think this is?

Chapter summary

In this chapter we have examined the key financial statements of a company to gain an overview of how that company is structured financially. You should see if you can get hold of the annual report and accounts (also known as the statutory accounts) for your company. Many will be available online (just search for them by typing in '[company name] annual report and accounts [year]'). Alternatively, you could search for them on Companies House for all UK listed companies. Go to **http://www.companieshouse.gov.uk** and:

▶ click on 'Find company information'

▶ type in the name of the company (or number if you know it)

▶ select the company from the list

▶ click on the number of the company that you wish to select

▶ click on 'Order information on this company'

▶ click on the latest 'AA' (which stands for annual accounts).

It will cost you £1!

Next steps

▶ See if you can obtain the financial statements for your business – they should be available on your website, from the finance team or from Companies House.

▶ Now break down the balance sheet, profit & loss account and cash flow statement into their constituent parts. What does this tell you about the business?

▶ Revisit your answers to the Next steps from Chapters 1 and 2. How correct were your informed guesses?

▶ Try to make a habit of obtaining the financial statements of your suppliers/clients/competitors. Use them as a reference as we analyse the accounts in the next chapter.

Key learning points

▶ The balance sheet contains the assets and liabilities of a business – it is a snapshot in time.

▶ The assets and liabilities are divided into five main classifications: non-current (or fixed) assets; current assets; current liabilities; non-current (or long-term) liabilities; and shareholders' funds.

▶ The profit and loss account (or income statement) is the trading account – showing the income and costs between two points in time.

▶ Any profit not paid (in the form of a dividend) will appear on the balance sheet as an amount still owing to the shareholders.

HOW TO TALK FINANCE

The cash flow statement reconciles the profit in the profit and loss account with the movement in cash in the balance sheet.

The cash flow statement shows how much cash was used in investing activities and how much was generated from funding activities.

 Test yourself

3.1 The financial objective of a business might include:

(a) maximising the wealth of the shareholders ☐

(b) paying creditors early ☐

(c) maximising staff bonuses ☐

(d) tax evasion ☐

3.2 Who of the following might be interested in a company's annual report?

(a) suppliers to competitors ☐

(b) suppliers ☐

(c) the general public ☐

(d) ex-employees ☐

3.3 In which month must I show the cost of a service for the following?

(a) purchase order raised in February ☐

(b) invoice received in March ☐

(c) service delivered in April ☐

(d) invoice paid in May ☐

3.4 The financial statements are:

(a) always correct ☐

(b) a clear picture of the future of a company ☐

(c) a clear picture of the past of a company ☐

(d) never to be relied upon due to accounting manipulation techniques ☐

3.5 The balance sheet contains:

(a) assets and liabilities ☐

(b) assets and expenses ☐

(c) income and liabilities ☐

(d) income and expenses ☐

3.6 Assets are categorised as:

(a) fixed and non-current ☐

(b) fixed, non-current and current ☐

(c) non-current and current ☐

(d) long-term and current ☐

3.7 Cash will appear in:

(a) non-current assets ☐

(b) current assets ☐

(c) current liabilities ☐

(d) non-current liabilities ☐

3.8 Plant and machinery will appear in:

(a) non-current assets ☐

(b) current assets ☐

(c) current liabilities ☐

(d) non-current liabilities ☐

3.9 Current assets are:

(a) assets that the business needs to keep to do business ☐

(b) assets that the business is trying to sell ☐

(c) assets that the business is trying to turn into cash ☐

(d) not really assets at all ☐

3.10 Non-current (or fixed) assets are:

(a) assets that the business needs to keep to do business ☐

(b) assets that the business is trying to sell ☐

(c) assets that the business is trying to turn into cash ☐

(d) not really assets at all ☐

3.11 Liabilities are categorised as:

(a) current and fixed ☐

(b) non-current and fixed ☐

(c) current, non-current and shareholders' funds ☐

(d) current, short-term, non-current and long-term ☐

3.12 An overdraft is most likely to appear in:

(a) non-current assets ☐

(b) current assets ☐

(c) current liabilities ☐

(d) non-current liabilities ☐

3.13 An interest-only mortgage is most likely to appear in:

   (a) non-current assets ☐

   (b) current assets ☐

   (c) current liabilities ☐

   (d) non-current liabilities ☐

3.14 Current liabilities are:

   (a) liabilities that need to be repaid soon ☐

   (b) liabilities that do not need to be repaid soon ☐

   (c) amounts owed to shareholders ☐

   (d) dividends payable ☐

3.15 Non-current (or long-term) liabilities are:

   (a) liabilities that need to be repaid soon ☐

   (b) liabilities that do not need to be repaid soon ☐

   (c) amounts owed to shareholders ☐

   (d) dividends payable ☐

3.16 Equity is:

   (a) liabilities that need to be repaid soon ☐

   (b) liabilities that do not need to be repaid soon ☐

   (c) amounts owed to shareholders ☐

   (d) dividends payable ☐

3.17 Share capital is:

   (a) the initial investment in the business by shareholders ☐

   (b) the nominal value of all investments in the business by shareholders ☐

   (c) debt and equity ☐

   (d) reinvested profits ☐

3.18 Capital is:

   (a) debt and current assets ☐

   (b) total assets and current liabilities ☐

   (c) total liabilities and current assets ☐

   (d) equity and current liabilities ☐

3.19 Capital is used for:

   (a) investment capital and equity ☐

   (b) debt and equity ☐

   (c) debt and working capital ☐

   (d) investment capital and working capital ☐

3.20 Capital comes from:

  (a) investment capital and equity ☐

  (b) debt and equity ☐

  (c) debt and working capital ☐

  (d) investment capital and working capital ☐

3.21 The income statement contains:

  (a) assets and liabilities ☐

  (b) assets and expenses ☐

  (c) income and liabilities ☐

  (d) income and expenses ☐

3.22 Turnover is **not** also known as:

  (a) sales ☐

  (b) deferred income ☐

  (c) income ☐

  (d) revenue ☐

3.23 Cost of sales usually contains:

  (a) fixed costs ☐

  (b) sunk costs ☐

  (c) variable costs ☐

  (d) marginal costs ☐

3.24 Gross profit is sales less:

  (a) turnover ☐

  (b) administration costs ☐

  (c) cost of sales ☐

  (d) cost of sales and administration costs ☐

3.25 Administration costs usually contain:

  (a) fixed costs ☐

  (b) sunk costs ☐

  (c) variable costs ☐

  (d) marginal costs ☐

3.26 Operating profit is sales less:

  (a) turnover ☐

  (b) administration costs ☐

  (c) cost of sales ☐

  (d) cost of sales and administration costs ☐

3.27 Interest costs are:

(a) the costs of servicing the equity investment ☐

(b) the costs of servicing the debt investment ☐

(c) the costs of servicing both debt and equity investments ☐

(d) only included on the balance sheet ☐

3.28 Profit before tax is sales less:

(a) cost of sales ☐

(b) cost of sales and administration costs ☐

(c) cost of sales, administration costs and dividends ☐

(d) cost of sales, administration costs and interest ☐

3.29 Dividends are paid out of:

(a) gross profit ☐

(b) net profit ☐

(c) operating profit ☐

(d) retained profit ☐

3.30 Retained earnings appears:

(a) in the balance sheet ☐

(b) in the cash flow statement ☐

(c) in the income statement ☐

(d) in the balance sheet and the income statement ☐

3.31 The difference between brought forward and carried forward retained earnings is:

(a) operating profit less interest ☐

(b) operating profit less dividends ☐

(c) net profit less interest ☐

(d) net profit less dividends ☐

3.32 A retained loss is:

(a) an asset ☐

(b) a liability ☐

(c) an income ☐

(d) an expense ☐

3.33 The reason for a difference in accrual and cash profit will **not** be due to:

    (a) a sales invoice that has been paid ☐

    (b) amortisation ☐

    (c) a supplier's invoice that has not yet been settled ☐

    (d) rent that has been paid in advance ☐

3.34 The cash flow statement will include:

    (a) a reconciliation between accrual profit and cash profit ☐

    (b) a cash flow forecast ☐

    (c) a reconciliation between actual and budgeted cash ☐

    (d) a reconciliation between cash and overdraft balances ☐

3.35 Depreciation will appear in the cash flow reconciliation because:

    (a) it is always a big figure ☐

    (b) it affects cash profit but not accrual profit ☐

    (c) it affects accrual profit but not cash profit ☐

    (d) it affects both accrual and cash profit ☐

3.36 The cash flow statement will also include sections covering:

    (a) cash from sales and investments ☐

    (b) how cash was invested and cash from sales ☐

    (c) cash from sales and cash from financing activities ☐

    (d) how cash was invested and cash from financing activities ☐

4 CHAPTER 4
Financial analysis

'It is incumbent upon each of us to improve spending and savings practices to ensure our own individual financial security and preserve the collective economic well-being of our great society.'

Ron Lewis

 ## Aim

In Chapter 3, we examined the three primary financial statements (balance sheet, profit & loss account – or income statement – and cash flow statement) and how they interact. Now that we have established **what** is in each of the statements, this chapter will help us to **read** the financial statements.

 ## Outcomes

By the end of this chapter you will understand:

▶ the core key financial indicators (KFIs) that are used to run a company
▶ whether these KFIs are relevant to your business.

How do you measure return on investment (ROI)?

In Chapter 3 we examined the accounts of National Grid, who made a profit of £2,296 million (nearly £2.3 billion) in the year to 31 March 2013. Was this good or bad?

Any question of this type to the finance team usually elicits the reply, 'It depends…' (usually followed by, 'What would you like it to be?' or 'Are you buying or selling?'). So, on what does it depend?

Imagine that India owns a house in London, which she rents out for £1 million per year. Is that good or bad? Your initial reaction might be good – £1 million per year in rental income would be quite nice (just think of the holidays!). But the correct answer would be, 'It depends.' On what does it depend? It depends on the value of the house. If the house is worth £1 million, then this would be a very good investment (investing £1 million and receiving income of £1 million per year is a 100 per cent return and is very good!); but, if the house is worth £1 billion (i.e. £1,000 million) then the return is 0.01 per cent and is very bad. In effect, if the house is worth £1 billion, you should be able to rent it out for more than £1 million per year.

Now let us apply this logic to National Grid. Is a £2.3 billion profit good or bad? It depends. On what does it depend? Well, just like India's house in the above example, it depends on the investment in National Grid. So, how can we work out the investment in the company? Well, you may remember in Chapter 2 that we examined the two primary sources of investment that are available to a business – debt and equity. In Chapter 3, we discovered that this information is available on the balance sheet, as shown below.

Balance sheet analysis

	National Grid £bn			
Non-current assets	£ 45.1	Investment capital	£ 45.1	
Current assets	£ 9.6	Working	£ 2.1	
Current liabilities	£ 7.5	Capital		
Non-current liabilities	£ 37.0	Debt		Capital £ 47.2
Net assets/shareholders' funds	£ 10.2	Equity		

You will remember that the above analysis is an approximation to the actual figures (for example, some of the non-current liabilities do not relate to long-term borrowings, and some long-term borrowings actually appear in current liabilities), but, for the sake of a quick overview of the business, this gives us a reasonable picture of the company.

So, National Grid has capital of £47.2 billion (made up of £37 billion debt and £10.2 billion equity), which it has invested in the business (£45.1 billion of investment capital and £2.1 billion of working capital).

? What do you think is an acceptable rate of return?

? How would your answer change with what you can achieve by putting your money on deposit in the bank?

? How would your answer change if the investment was high risk?

What is return on capital employed (ROCE)?

So, the return on investment, also known as return on capital employed (ROCE) is:

Return on capital employed

	National Grid £bn
Profit	£ 2.3
Capital	£ 47.2
	5%

So for National Grid, the return on investment, or return on capital employed, is 5 per cent. What do you think it is for NMS? Don't forget, we have already established that the non-current or long-term liabilities relate to a long-term incentive plan (LTIP– in effect a bonus scheme for the senior management of the business), so the company is 100 per cent equity funded:

Return on capital employed

	National Grid £bn	NMS £m
Profit	£ 2.3	£ 8.0
Capital	£ 47.2	£ 23.0
	5%	35%

On the face of it, it appears that NMS is much more efficient than National Grid. For every £1 invested in National Grid, the company generates 5p of profit, but for every £1 invested in NMS, the company generates 35p of profit.

We have to be careful here; as discussed in Chapter 3, National Grid and NMS are very different companies. National Grid is an infrastructure company, depending heavily on investment in fixed assets; NMS is a service company – so does not need a lot of capital. Therefore return on investment is not really an important key financial indicator (KFI) for NMS.

?   What is the ROCE for your business?

?   Think of other businesses. For what types of business would a ROCE calculation be less relevant?

What is EBITDA?

Let us look at the return on investment, or ROCE, of National Grid in a little more detail. The profit figure we used of £2.3 billion is after deducting tax. But what determines the tax that a company pays? The tax is dependent on the profit that a company makes and the rate (usually set by the Government). Now, while companies will take steps to mitigate the amount of tax that they pay, the general rule is that, if you make a profit then you will have to pay tax, and the more profit that you make, the more tax you will pay.

So, how much influence does the management team have over the amount of tax that they pay? Well, they could reduce their tax bill by reducing the profits that they make, but this does not make commercial sense; so perhaps we should judge the result of the business on the profit (or earnings) before tax.

EBITDA

Profit	£2.3 bn			National Grid £bn
Earnings				£2.9bn = EBT
Before				
I				
Tax	profit	x	rate	£0.6
D				
A				

Now we might consider the interest that the company pays, and again ask what determines the amount of interest that appears in the P&L. In the same way that tax is a function of profit and rate, so interest is a function of debt and rate.

The rate is set by the banks or the financial institutions, which lend to National Grid, so the company has little influence over this. The amount of debt that National Grid has is a function of historical long-term funding decisions – again the company has very little influence over the amount of debt on its balance sheet (in the same way that you probably could not pay off your mortgage tomorrow, unless you sold your house).

So, just as we considered the profit before tax for National Grid, we might also consider profit (or earnings) before both tax and interest. This figure is known as earnings before interest and tax (EBIT). What is another name for EBIT?

If you remember back to Chapter 3 and the analysis of the income statement, you will remember that the profit before interest and tax is, in fact, the operating profit:

Profit & loss accounts

	National Grid £m	
Sales	£	14,359
Cost of sales		
Gross profit		
Operating costs	£	10,605
Operating profit	£	3,754
Interest	£	834
Tax	£	624
Net profit	£	2,296

So we can now look at National Grid on an EBIT basis:

EBITDA

Profit	£2.3 bn			National Grid £bn	
Earnings				£	3.8bn = EBIT
Before					
Interest	Debt	x	Rate	£	0.8
Tax	Profit	x	Rate	£	0.6
D					
A					

Now let us revisit the original return on investment calculation. What if we use EBIT as the return? The return increases to 8 per cent. Don't forget, the company still has to pay tax and still has to service its debt, but the 8 per cent is closer to the underlying performance of the actual business.

Return on capital employed

	National Grid £bn
EBIT	£ 3.8
Capital	£ 47.2
	8%

What other costs are in the P&L that the management team have no (or very little) control over? The answer is depreciation and amortisation. We touched on these in Chapter 2 – depreciation effectively is the spreading (or matching) the cost of an asset over its useful economic life. We used the example of a table, purchased 7 years ago, that we are going to use for 10 years. The depreciation charge in the accounts this year is £10 (the table cost £100 when it was purchased originally). The management team can reduce this cost only by selling the table – and then they would have nowhere to put their computers, etc. So the depreciation charge that appears in the P&L is a function of fixed assets (like the table) that have been purchased in prior years and the rates of depreciation that are applied to those assets. Not only can the management team not affect the historical purchasing decisions, they also have very little influence over the rates.

The policy that National Grid adopts towards depreciation is explained in their accounts:

'10. Property, plant and equipment

The following note shows the physical assets controlled by us. The cost of these assets primarily represents the amount initially paid for them. A depreciation expense is charged to the income statement to reflect annual wear and tear and the reduced value of the asset over time. Depreciation is calculated by estimating the number of years we expect the asset to be used (useful economic life) and charging the cost of the asset to the income statement equally over this period.

Our strategy in action

We operate an energy networks business and therefore have a significant physical asset base. We continue to invest in our networks to maintain reliability, create new customer connections and ensure our networks have the flexibility and resilience necessary to meet future challenges. Our business plan envisages these additional investments will be funded through a mixture of cash generated from operations and the issue of new debt.'

Depreciation periods	Years
Freehold and leasehold buildings	up to 65
Plant and machinery	
Electricity transmission plant	15 to 60
Electricity distribution plant	15 to 60
Electricity generation plant	20 to 40
Interconnector plant	15 to 60
Gas plant – mains, services and regulating equipment	30 to 100
Gas plant – storage	15 to 21
Gas plant – meters	10 to 33
Motor vehicles and office equipment	up to 10

The management team cannot just arbitrarily change these policies. They cannot decide that last year the table was being depreciated over 10 years, this year it will be depreciated over 2 years and next year 50 years. This is because they must be consistent in applying these accounting policies in order to enable comparability between the accounts of this year and previous years.

Amortisation is merely depreciation by another name. We depreciate tangible assets (assets we can touch) and amortise intangible assets (assets that we cannot touch, such as licences and patents).

So, our conclusion is that the management team of National Grid have no influence over the depreciation or amortisation charge in their P&L, so perhaps we should consider the profit (or earnings) before these items too – and hence we arrive at earnings before interest, taxation, depreciation and amortisation (EBITDA).

Just as we identified interest and taxation in the P&L of National Grid, so we should be able to find the deprecation and amortisation:

	Notes	2013 £m	2013 £m	2012 £m	2012 £m	2011 £m	2011 £m
Revenue	1(a)		**14,359**		13,832		14,343
Operating costs	2		**(10,605)**		(10,293)		(10,598)
Operating profit							
Before exceptional items, remeasurements and stranded cost recoveries	1(b)	**3,644**			3,495		3,600
Exceptional items, remeasurements and stranded cost recoveries	3	**110**			44		145
Total operating profit	1(b)		**3,754**		3,539		3,745
Finance income							
Before exceptional items	4	**1,252**			1,301		1,281
Exceptional items	3,4	**–**			–		43
Total finance income	4		**1,252**		1,301		1,324
Finance costs							
Before exceptional items and remeasurements	4	**(2,172)**			(2,218)		(2,415)
Exceptional items and remeasurements	3,4	**68**			(70)		(37)
Total finance costs	4		**(2,104)**		(2,288)		(2,452)
Share of post-tax results of joint ventures and associates	13		**18**		7		7
Profit before tax							
Before exceptional items, remeasurements and stranded cost recoveries	1(b)	**2,742**			2,585		2,473
Exceptional items, remeasurements and stranded cost recoveries	3	**178**			(26)		151
Total profit before tax	1(b)		**2,920**		2,559		2,624
Taxation							
Before exceptional items, remeasurements and stranded cost recoveries	5	**(686)**			(755)		(722)
Exceptional items, remeasurements and stranded cost recoveries	3,5	**62**			234		261
Total taxation	5		**(624)**		(521)		(461)
Profit after tax							
Before exceptional items, remeasurements and stranded cost recoveries		**2,056**			1,830		1,751
Exceptional items, remeasurements and stranded cost recoveries	3	**240**			208		412
Profit for the year			**2,296**		2,038		2,163

If you are looking at National Grid's P&L and struggling to find the depreciation and amortisation, it is because it is not explicitly stated. It will be included somewhere in the operating costs of £10.6 billion.

But, if you remember back in Chapter 3, we found the depreciation and amortisation somewhere else – in the cash flow statement. They were added back to the operating profit to determine the cash profit of the business:

	Notes	2013 £m	2012 £m	2011 £m
Cash flows from operating activities				
Total operating profit	1(b)	**3,754**	3,539	3,745
Adjustments for:				
Exceptional items, remeasurements and stranded cost recoveries	3	**(110)**	(44)	(145)
Depreciation, amortisation and impairment		**1,361**	1,282	1,245
Share-based payment charge		**20**	24	25
Changes in working capital		**(410)**	146	185
Changes in provisions		**(53)**	(116)	(93)
Changes in pensions and other post-retirement benefit obligations		**(413)**	(386)	(304)
Cash flows relating to exceptional items		**(112)**	(205)	(147)
Cash flows relating to stranded cost recoveries		**–**	247	343
Cash generated from operations		**4,037**	4,487	4,854
Tax (paid)/received		**(287)**	(259)	4
Net cash inflow from operating activities		**3,750**	4,228	4,858

We can see that the depreciation and amortisation charge that has been added back is £1,361 million – so we can now establish what the EBITDA for National Grid is. Incidentally, you will notice that the figure also includes impairments. This merely relates to one-off write-downs in the value of an asset.

Imagine that our table was currently worth £30 in the balance sheet (we purchased it 7 years ago, so we have reduced the value by 7 years × £10 per year) and then someone sat on it and broke it. It now has a value of £nil, so to continue to show it in the balance sheet with a value of £30 would be misleading, so we would have to impair, or write down, the asset to £nil.

EBITDA

Profit	£2.3 bn			National Grid £bn	
Earnings				£	5.1 = EBITDA
Before					
Interest	debt	×	rate	£	0.8
Tax	profit	×	rate	£	0.6
Deprecation	prior year	×	rate	£	1.4
Amortisation	capex				

So the EBITDA of National Grid is £5.1 billion. We can now consider the return that National Grid is generating on an EBITDA basis:

Return on capital employed

	National Grid £bn
EBITDA	£ 5.1
Capital	£ 47.2
	11%

This suggests that National Grid is generating an underlying return on its assets of 11 per cent, which is not too bad. Remember, it is effectively a monopoly (there are lots of energy companies in the UK generating power, but only one transports the power to your home). They could abuse this monopoly by charging as much as they like, so a regulator will ensure that they do not charge an excessive amount and make sufficient ongoing investment in the company's infrastructure.

Here is another comment from the annual report and accounts of National Grid, reinforcing the fact that the company is undertaking ongoing investment in infrastructure:

'Impressions and reflections on 2012/13

This has been a significant year for National Grid, which has seen substantial change in both the UK and US.

One of the most important changes we have seen is Ofgem's introduction of RIIO, a new eight year regulatory framework in the UK. In February 2013, we agreed all the UK RIIO price control arrangements proposed by Ofgem. The Board believes the combination of revenue allowances and incentive mechanisms provides a good opportunity to earn appropriate returns for investors, while delivering essential infrastructure investment for the benefit of consumers and the UK economy.'

Do you think that EBITDA is a measure of KFI that will be in use at NMS? Well, let us think about their business:

They will pay tax, because they are a profitable business.

They pay very little interest, because they have no debt.

There is no significant depreciation or amortisation in their accounts, because they have very little in the way of fixed assets (remember – they are a service provider, not an infrastructure business, so need very little in the way of property, plant and machinery).

So EBITDA is not relevant to NMS. This shows us that we need to understand the KFI and the business to determine whether or not the KFI is relevant to our business.

? Does your business measure EBITDA?

? EBITDA will be important for some companies and not for others. Why do you think this is?

How do you measure profitability?

Examining profitability allows us to analyse the ability of a company to control costs while generating revenue. There are a number of different calculations for profitability, each of which uses the figures in the income statement.

What is the gross profit margin and why is it important?

The gross profit is calculated as the revenue (also known as sales, turnover or income) of a business, less the cost of sales (variable costs, sometimes called the cost of goods sold). When expressed as a percentage of the revenue figure, this gives the margin. It is useful to express this as a percentage in order to compare this period with previous periods and so examine whether there are any underlying trends that we should be aware of (a falling margin may reflect increasing competition – causing prices to fall – or increasing raw material costs that are not being passed on).

Usually we would expect the gross margin to remain constant over time on the basis that, if revenue doubles, then the business will have to buy twice as much to sell and so cost of sales will double (and hence gross profit will double – keeping the percentage constant). So, if A&B Ltd buy one apple for £1 and sell that apple for £5, they will make a gross profit of £4. £4 expressed as a percentage of £5 is 80 per cent, so the company is operating at a gross margin of 80 per cent. If the company buys 100 apples, they will cost £100, and can be sold for £500 – giving a profit of £400, and maintaining the gross margin at 80 per cent.

The gross margin is calculated as follows:

$$\frac{Gross\ profit}{Revenue}$$

Let us look at the gross margin of our six companies.

Profit & loss accounts

	National Grid	M&S	Tesco	Indesit	BT	NMS
	£m	£m	£m	£m	£m	£m
Sales	£ 14,359	£ 10,309.7	£ 63,557	£ 2,671.1	£ 19,397	£ 384.8
Cost of sales			£ 59,547	£ 2,054.8		£ 330.0
Gross profit			£ 4,010	£ 616.3		£ 54.8
Operating costs	£ 10,605		£ 1,379	£ 548.2	£ 16,335	£ 40.9
Operating profit	£ 3,754	£ 694.5	£ 2,631	£ 68.1	£ 3,032	£ 14.0
Interest	£ 834	£ 114.1	£ 372	£ 51.2	£ 671	£ -
Tax	£ 624	£ 74.4	£ 347	£ 13.7	£ 576	£ 6.0
Gross profit	£ 2,296	£ 506.0	£ 1,912	£ 3.2	£ 1,815	£ 8.0
Gross margin						
Gross Profit			£4,010	£616		£55
Sales			£63,557	£2,617		£385
× 100%			6%	23%		14%

We are not provided with the gross profit for three of the companies, so we cannot calculate the gross margin.

For Tesco, the gross margin is 6 per cent. This means that, for every £1 that the company sells, the cost of the thing that they sell is 94p – leaving them with 6p. Tesco is a very low-margin business – it competes on cost, trying to pay as little as it can for the food and then selling it on at as low a price as possible. If Tesco started to charge a higher price (and therefore obtain a higher margin) the customers might go elsewhere.

Indesit, on the other hand, makes a higher margin. Consumers are less discerning when buying dishwashers – the perception that a higher price gains higher quality allows Indesit to charge a higher price and therefore make a higher margin.

NMS operates in a competitive market and therefore makes a smaller gross margin than Indesit but higher than Tesco. However, comparatively speaking, it has higher fixed costs of running the business and therefore makes a higher gross margin than Tesco.

Now, consider the following information for the accounts of a fictional company called Importers-R-Us (IRU):

I have worked out the gross margin for you below:

Profit & loss accounts

	Note	2009 £	2008 £
Turnover	1	14,696,742	9,037,882
Cost of sales		11,096,720	6,073,743
Gross profit		3,600,022	2,964,139

We have worked out the Gross Margin got you below –

Gross Margin

Gross Profit	£3,600,022	£2,964,139
Sales	£14,696,742	£9,037,883
x 100%	24%	33%

You will notice that the sales (turnover) for IRU have increased from £9 million to £14.7 million. Based on the above analysis, we would expect the gross margin to remain constant at 33 per cent; but the gross margin has actually fallen to 24 per cent. What do you think could have caused this?

There are two main explanations:

1   The price at which IRU is selling its products has fallen.
2   The cost to IRU of buying the products that it is selling has risen.

Which of these two explanations do you think is most relevant?

It might be tempting to go with (2) – after all the cost of sales has almost doubled. But look at the sales. They have increased – by over 60 per cent! That is a massive increase to achieve in just one year! How do you think that they achieved this? Perhaps through effective marketing, but it looks like they dropped the price (1). So it appears that IRU has dropped the price of its products, sacrificing margin, in order to increase market share.

?   What is the gross margin for your business?
?   How has it changed over the last few years?
?   What do you think might be the reasons for any change?

What is the operating profit margin and why is it important?

The operating profit is the gross profit less any administration (or fixed) costs. The operating margin will be lower than the gross margin due to the inclusion of these additional costs. As we have seen above, as a company grows its revenues, it would expect to see its variable costs grow at the same rate. However, it would not expect to see its fixed costs growing at the same rate (for example, if A&B Ltd doubled sales, it would not necessarily have to pay twice as much rent, or double the finance team, although they may need to increase). Thus the operating margin reflects the **economies of scale** that a business can achieve by growing.

The operating margin is calculated as follows:

$$\frac{Operating\ profit}{Revenue}$$

We can calculate the operating margin for our six companies as follows:

Profit & loss accounts

	National Grid	M&S	Tesco	Indesit	BT	NMS
	£m	£m	£m	£m	£m	£m
Sales	£ 14,359	£ 10,309.7	£ 63,557	£ 2,671.1	£ 19,397	£ 384.8
Cost of sales			£ 59,547	£ 2,054.8		£ 330.0
Gross profit			£ 4,010	£ 616.3		£ 54.8
Operating costs	£ 10,605		£ 1,379	£ 548.2	£ 16,335	£ 40.9
Operating profit	£ 3,754	£ 694.5	£ 2,631	£ 68.1	£ 3,032	£ 14.0
Interest	£ 834	£ 114.1	£ 372	£ 51.2	£ 671	£ -
Tax	£ 624	£ 74.4	£ 347	£ 13.7	£ 576	£ 6.0
Gross profit	£ 2,296	£ 506.0	£ 1,912	£ 3.2	£ 1,815	£ 8.0
Operating margin						
Operating Profit	£3,754	£695	£2,631	£68	£3,062	£14
Sales	£14,359	£10,310	£63,557	£2,671	£19,397	£385
× 100%	26%	7%	4%	3%	16%	4%

You will remember that Tesco had a very low gross margin when compared to Indesit (6 per cent versus 23 per cent), but from the above analysis you will notice that they are at the same operating margins – this means that Indesit has a (relatively) much higher fixed cost base than Tesco.

We have compared various businesses from different sectors here. This comparison is, however, fairly meaningless. Tesco, with an operating margin of 4 per cent, should not look at National Grid and think, 'If they can achieve a margin of 26 per cent, then so can we.' Tesco would be better off comparing itself to Sainsbury and Morrisons.

An operating margin of 4 per cent for Tesco means that, for every £1 of goods that it sells, it has to spend 94p buying that item and an additional 2p on running the business, leaving the company with just 4p for every £1 of sale.

? What is the operating margin for your business?

? How has it changed over the last few years?

? What do you think might be the reasons for any change?

What is the net profit margin and why is it important?

The net profit is also known as the **bottom line** – the profit that the company is left with after all other costs (including tax and interest) have been deducted. In a similar way to the operating margin, we would expect a company to benefit from economies of scale and so be able to increase its net margin as it grows in size (diseconomies of scale, on the other hand, are where a company suffers as it grows – seeing its fixed costs grow at a quicker rate than its revenues; this may happen as a result of increased regulatory burdens or IT complexity as it becomes bigger).

The net margin is calculated as follows:

$$\frac{Net\ profit}{Revenue}$$

The net margins for our six companies are calculated as follows:

Profit & loss accounts

	National Grid	M&S	Tesco	Indesit	BT	NMS
	£m	£m	£m	£m	£m	£m
Sales	£ 14,359	£ 10,309.7	£ 63,557	£ 2,671.1	£ 19,397	£ 384.8
Cost of sales			£ 59,547	£ 2,054.8		£ 330.0
Gross profit			£ 4,010	£ 616.3		£ 54.8
Operating costs	£ 10,605		£ 1,379	£ 548.2	£ 16,335	£ 40.9
Operating profit	£ 3,754	£ 694.5	£ 2,631	£ 68.1	£ 3,032	£ 14.0
Interest	£ 834	£ 114.1	£ 372	£ 51.2	£ 671	£ -
Tax	£ 624	£ 74.4	£ 347	£ 13.7	£ 576	£ 6.0
Net profit	£ 2,296	£ 506.0	£ 1,912	£ 3.2	£ 1,815	£ 8.0
Net margin						
Net Profit	£3,296	£506	£1,912	£3	£1,815	£8
Sales	£14,359	£10,310	£63,557	£2,671	£19,397	£385
× 100%	16%	5%	3%	0%	9%	2%

Indesit is left with almost nothing at all once it has paid all the costs of running the business. NMS and Tesco are very low-margin businesses – suggesting that they operate in highly competitive environments (Tesco), or ones with low barriers to entry (NMS) where it is easy for competitors to enter the market if they are seen to be making too much profit. National Grid is, on the other hand, making a healthy profit margin.

We might also want to run this analysis on an EBITDA basis. Not only does this remove the costs that the management team cannot control, it also allows us to compare businesses in the same sector more accurately. (If Company A has more debt than Company B, then Company A will make a lower net margin, for example.)

Profit & loss accounts

	National Grid	M&S	Tesco	Indesit	BT	NMS
	£m	£m	£m	£m	£m	£m
Sales	£ 14,359	£ 10,309.7	£ 63,557	£ 2,671.1	£ 19,397	£ 384.8
Cost of sales			£ 59,547	£ 2,054.8		£ 330.0
Gross profit			£ 4,010	£ 616.3		£ 330.0
Operating costs	£ 10,605		£ 1,379	£ 548.2	£ 16,335	£ 40.9
Operating profit	£ 3,754	£ 694.5	£ 2,631	£ 68.1	£ 3,032	£ 14.0
Interest	£ 834	£ 114.1	£ 372	£ 51.2	£ 671	£ -
Tax	£ 624	£ 74.4	£ 34.7	£ 13.7	£ 576	£ 6
Net profit	£ 2,296	£ 506.0	£ 1,912	£ 3.2	£ 1,815	£ 8.0
Note D&A (from the cashflow statement)	£ 1,361	£ 504.7	£ 1,567	£ 110.3	£ 2,695	£ 1.4
= EBIDTA	£ 5,115	£ 1,199.2	£ 4,198	£ 178.4	£ 5,757	£ 15.4
EBIDTA Margin						
EBIDTA	£ 5,115	£ 1,199	£ 4,198	£ 178	£ 5,757	£ 15
Sales	£ 14,359	£ 10,310	£ 63,557	£ 2,671	£ 19,397	£ 385
EBIDTA Profit	£5,115	£1,199	£4,198	£178	£5,757	£15
Sales	£14,359	£10,310	£63,557	£2,671	£19,397	£385
× 100%	36%	12%	7%	7%	30%	4%

You will notice that, on an EBITDA basis, BT is generating significant profit margins. This is very much a feature of the telecoms industry.

? What is the net margin for your business?

? How has it changed over the last few years?

? What do you think might be the reasons for any change?

What is operational gearing?

Having analysed the profitability of a business, we can now examine its operational gearing. Operational gearing tells us how price sensitive a company is and how risky its business model is.

Consider the following example for Company A:

Operational gearing

Company A		
	Budget	
	£m	
Sales	£	100
Cost of sales	£	90
Gross profit	£	10
Operating costs	£	5
Operating profit	£	5

Company A has sales of £100 million with a gross profit of £10 million (10 per cent gross margin) and an operating profit of £5 million (5 per cent operating margin). The sales director wants to increase sales, and so advocates a discount in the sales price of 5 per cent in order to achieve this. With no change in volume, the income statement will look like this:

Operational gearing

Company A				
	Budget		**5% discount**	
	£m		**£m**	
Sales	£	100	£	95
Cost of sales	£	90	£	90
Gross profit	£	10	£	5
Operating costs	£	5	£	5
Operating profit	£	5	£	–

The 5 per cent discount will reduce the sales revenue but will not have any effect on the cost of sales; the administration expenses (fixed costs) obviously remain constant. This has wiped out the profit that the company was originally making which is clearly unacceptable.

What is the minimum increase in volume of sales that the sales director must achieve to at least get back to where the business was originally? On the face of it, this might look like quite a straightforward question – the answer being 5 per cent. But, if we increase sales by 5 per cent due to the volume increase, then we must also increase the cost of sales by 5 per cent, and so the operating profit by 5 per cent. Increasing £5 million by 5 per cent achieves only £5.25 million, which will result in an operating profit of £0.25 million – way below the original £5 million that was being achieved.

Because of the way that the variable costs operate, it is going to take considerably more than a 5 per cent increase in sales volume to get back to where the company was originally. The answer is, in fact, the sales volume has to double!

Operational gearing

	Company A		
	Budget	5% discount	Target
	£m	£m	£m
Sales	£ 100	£ 95	£ 190
Cost of sales	£ 90	£ 90	£ 180
Gross profit	£ 10	£ 5	£ 10
Operating costs	£ 5	£ 5	£ 5
Operating profit	£ 5	£ –	£ 5

With a doubling in sales volume, the sales revenue doubles to £190 million and the cost of sales doubles to £180 million and hence gross profit is restored to £10 million. A company with high variable costs and low fixed costs is said to have a low level of operational gearing – they will be very sensitive to price changes.

Now consider Company B – with a different cost structure:

Operational gearing

	Company A			Company B
	Budget	5% discount	Target	Budget
	£m	£m	£m	£m
Sales	£ 100	£ 95	£ 190	£ 100
Cost of sales	£ 90	£ 90	£ 180	£ 5
Gross profit	£ 10	£ 5	£ 10	£ 95
Operating costs	£ 5	£ 5	£ 5	£ 90
Operating profit	£ 5	£ –	£ 5	£ 5

Company B has the same level of sales (£100 million) and the same operating profit (£5 million) as the previous company, but its cost structure is different – it has very high fixed costs but very low variable costs.

Operational gearing

	Company A			Company B	
	Budget	5% discount	Target	Budget	5% discount
	£m	£m	£m	£m	£m
Sales	£ 100	£ 95	£ 190	£ 100	£ 95
Cost of sales	£ 90	£ 90	£ 180	£ 5	£ 5
Gross profit	£ 10	£ 5	£ 10	£ 95	£ 90
Operating costs	£ 5	£ 5	£ 5	£ 90	£ 90
Operating profit	£ 5	£ –	£ 5	£ 5	£ –

Once again, the sales director is advocating a 5 per cent reduction in sales price to achieve an increase in sales; once again, this reduction will result in the operating profit being eliminated.

However, this time the business does not need to double sales in order to achieve the original operating profit.

In fact, sales need to rise only by a small fraction to maintain the level of operating profit.

Operational gearing

	Company A			Company B		
	Budget	5% discount	Target	Budget	5% discount	Target
	£m	£m	£m	£m	£m	£m
Sales	£ 100	£ 95	£ 190	£ 100	£ 95	£ 100.28
Cost of sales	£ 90	£ 90	£ 180	£ 5	£ 5	£ 5.28
Gross profit	£ 10	£ 5	£ 10	£ 95	£ 90	£ 95
Operating costs	£ 5	£ 5	£ 5	£ 90	£ 90	£ 90
Operating profit	£ 5	£ –	£ 5	£ 5	£ –	£ 5

In this case, Company B is said to have high operational gearing. It is much less price sensitive, but has very high fixed costs compared with its variable costs.

Now let us return to Company A:

Operational gearing

	Company A	
	Budget	
	£m	
Sales	£ 100	
Cost of sales	£ 90	
Gross profit	£ 10	
Operating costs	£ 5	
Operating profit	£ 5	

If Company A sold nothing, what profit would it make? Don't forget, when a company buys something to sell, this transaction appears in the balance sheet under current assets – as stock (or inventories) – and so has no impact on the P&L. Only when the item is sold, is it transferred into the cost of sales and therefore into the P&L account. So, if Company A sells nothing, then its sales will be nil and its cost of sales will be nil:

Operational gearing

	Company A	
	Budget	**Sell nothing**
	£m	**£m**
Sales	£ 100	£ –
Cost of sales	£ 90	£ –
Gross profit	£ 10	£ –
Operating costs	£ 5	£ 5
Operating profit	£ 5	£ 5

Fixed costs remain constant, and so the company will book a loss of £5 million.

However, if, on the other hand, Company A was to double sales (no discount this time) it would make a profit of £15 million:

Operational gearing

	Company A		
	Budget £m	**Sell nothing** £m	**Double sales** £m
Sales	£ 100	£ –	£ 200
Cost of sales	£ 90	£ –	£ 180
Gross profit	£ 10	£ –	£ 25
Operating costs	£ 5	£ 5	£ 5
Operating profit	£ 5	£ 5	£ 15

Now let us run the same analysis for Company B.

Operational gearing

	Company A			Company B
	Budget £m	**Sell nothing** £m	**Double sales** £m	**Budget** £m
Sales	£ 100	£ –	£ 200	£ 100
Cost of sales	£ 90	£ –	£ 180	£ 5
Gross profit	£ 10	£ –	£ 25	£ 95
Operating costs	£ 5	£ 5	£ 5	£ 90
Operating profit	£ 5	£ 5	£ 15	£ 5

If Company B sold nothing, it would book a loss of £90 million:

Operational gearing

	Company A			Company B	
	Budget £m	**Sell nothing** £m	**Double sales** £m	**Budget** £m	**Sell nothing** £m
Sales	£ 100	£ –	£ 200	£ 100	£ –
Cost of sales	£ 90	£ –	£ 180	£ 5	£ –
Gross profit	£ 10	£ –	£ 25	£ 95	£ –
Operating costs	£ 5	£ 5	£ 5	£ 90	£ 90
Operating profit	£ 5	£ 5	£ 15	£ 5	£ 90

But if Company B doubled sales, then it would make a profit of £100 million:

Operational gearing

	Company A			Company B		
	Budget	Sell nothing	Double sales	Budget	Sell nothing	Double sales
	£m	£m	£m	£m	£m	£m
Sales	£ 100	£ –	£ 200	£ 100	£ –	£ 200
Cost of sales	£ 90	£ –	£ 180	£ 5	£ –	£ 10
Gross profit	£ 10	£ –	£ 25	£ 95	£ –	£ 190
Operating costs	£ 5	£ 5	£ 5	£ 90	£ 90	£ 90
Operating profit	£ 5	£ 5	£ 15	£ 5	£ 90	£ 100

So, which company potentially will make you the most money? Company B. Which company potentially will lose you the most money? Company B. Which company is higher risk? Company B. Which company is higher potential return? Company B. Which company is higher operationally geared? Company B.

The operational gearing of a company is the relationship between its fixed and variable costs. Companies that have very high fixed costs relative to their variable costs are said to be very highly operationally geared – they can make a lot of money, but can also lose a lot of money.

Now consider our six companies – we can think about operational gearing in terms of a scale (it is not a question of are you or aren't you?, but where you sit on the scale relative to other companies).

Imagine operational gearing is a little like the volume dial above. 'Min' refers to companies like Company A – minimal operational gearing (all variable costs and little or no fixed costs) – and 'Max' refers to companies like Company B (predominantly fixed-cost businesses with little or no variable costs).

Where on this scale would you put the six companies that we have been looking at? Think about what your answer would be, before progressing.

Profit & loss accounts

	National Grid	M&S	Tesco	Indesit	BT	NMS
	£m	£m	£m	£m	£m	£m
Sales	£ 14,359	£ 10,309.7	£ 63,557	£ 2,671.1	£ 19,397	£ 384.8
Cost of sales			£ 59,547	£ 2,054.8		£ 330.0
Gross profit			£ 4,010	£ 616.3		£ 54.9
Operating costs	£ 10,605		£ 1,379	£ 548.2	£ 16,335	£ 40.9
Operating profit	£ 3,754	£ 694.5	£ 2,631	£ 68.1	£ 3,062	£ 14.0
Operating gearing						
Variable costs	£	£	£ 59,574	£ 2,055		£ 330
Fixed costs	£ 10,605	£	£ 1,379	£ 548	£ 16,355	£ 41
			43.18	3.75		8.07

A company that is highly operationally geared will have a ratio of less than one, whereas those with low operational gearing will have a ratio of more than one. Tesco has by far the highest number, and so can be put furthest to the left – it is very like Company A (this makes sense – the cost of the food that it sells is the biggest cost of the business). National Grid, on the other hand, has no variable costs – and so is very like Company B – on the right-hand side. Again, this makes sense following the conclusions in Chapter 2 when we first examined as to why National Grid has no cost of sales figure.

BT is similar to National Grid – it sells services using its network – so will also be like Company B. Indesit is very much in the middle (slightly on the Company A side) and NMS is somewhere between Tesco and Indesit.

So, what about M&S? We were not given any information on the fixed or variable costs, so we will have to have a guess. M&S is a retailer, so will have fairly substantial variable costs (think of all the food and clothes they have to buy), so probably they will be closer to Tesco; however, they are probably not operating on quite the same margins as Tesco; so an educated guess at the six companies might be:

Low operational gearing					*High operational gearing*
Company A					*Company B*
Tesco	M&S	NMS	Indesit	BT	National Grid

? Is your company more like Company A or Company B?

? What sorts of businesses can you think of that are likely to be more like Company A?

? What sorts of businesses can you think of that are likely to be more like Company B?

? How can a Company A become more like a Company B and vice versa?

What is financial gearing – the use of debt?

Imagine that Oscar had won £100,000 on the lottery (you may think that the lottery is more of a tax on hope, or you may be more of the you have got to be in it to win it persuasion) and is considering investing in property.

He has identified two houses that he is thinking of buying. The first is valued at £100,000 and the second at £1 million:

Cost	£100,000	£1,000,000

If Oscar wants to buy the first house, he can use the £100,000 that he has just won. If he wants to buy the second house, then he will need to borrow an additional £900,000 to make the full £1 million.

Cost	£	100,000	£	1,000,000
Debt	£	-	£	900,000
Equity	£	100,000	£	100,000
	£	100,000	£	1,000,000

Now Oscar starts thinking about what will happen if house prices double in value. The first house will be worth £200,000 – a 100 per cent return on his investment – which would leave Oscar happy.

But the second house would be worth £2 million. Oscar owes the bank £900,000, so his investment is now worth £1.1 million – and he would be **very** happy!

Cost	£	100,000		£	1,000,000	
Debt	£	-		£	900,000	
Equity	£	100,000		£	100,000	
	£	100,000		£	1,000,000	
House price doubles						
Debt	£	-		£	900,000	
Equity	£	200,000	happy	£	1,100,000	very happy
	£	200,000		£	2,000,000	

? Does your business use a lot of debt?

? Why is this?

? Has debt been increasing or decreasing over the past few years?

What is leverage?

So, in buying the second house using debt, Oscar has increased the return on his own (equity) investment. The reason for Oscar's increase in return is due to leverage. Leverage is defined as:

$$\frac{Capital}{Equity}$$

The capital is the total investment (the cost of the house), which in this case is £1 million. The equity is Oscar's personal investment (the remainder coming from the bank), which is £100,000. So, Oscar is said to be 10 times leveraged (£1,000,000 divided by £100,000). As the underlying asset doubles in value, so Oscar sees his return grow 10 times.

But then Oscar starts thinking about the downside. What if house prices were to halve in value?

Cost	£ 100,000		£ 1,000,000	
Debt	£ -		£ 900,000	
Equity	£ 100,000		£ 100,000	
	£ 100,000		£ 1,000,000	
House price doubles				
Debt	£ -		£ 900,000	
Equity	£ 200,000	happy	£ 1,100,000	very happy
	£ 200,000		£ 2,000,000	
House price halves				
Debt	£ -		£ 900,000	
Equity	£ 50,000	unhappy	£ (400,000)	very unhappy
	£ 50,000		£ 500,000	

In this case the first house would be worth £50,000. Oscar has now lost £50,000 of his winnings – and he would be unhappy.

The second house would be worth only £500,000. But Oscar still owes the bank £900,000. Not only has he lost all of the money that he won, but also he now owes the bank £400,000 that he does not have – and he would be **very** unhappy!

So the question remains – should Oscar use debt to buy the second house or should he stick with just buying the first house? Again, the answer is 'it depends' – in this case, it depends on his future expectations of house prices and his appetite for risk; if Oscar thinks house prices are going to rise, then he should borrow as much as he can afford and buy the biggest house on the street!

Financial gearing (the use of debt) is a little like operational gearing (the use of fixed costs) and can be compared to the gearing on Oscar's bicycle. In which gear should Oscar be when riding his bike? The answer obviously is based on the terrain. If he is going downhill, then he wants to be in a high gear – if the economy is performing well and your business is growing, then debt is good. But if Oscar starts the long, slow and lonely ascent to Alpe d'Huez, then he is going to want to be in as low a gear as possible – if the economy is not performing well and your business is not performing well, then debt is not good.

Think about that for a minute. If the economy turns from performing well to performing badly (as happened in Japan in 1990 or the USA in 2008), then companies are incentivised to pay down their debt rather than reinvest. Their reaction to a deflationary environment actually causes more deflation (paying down debt takes money out of the economy). Central banks here in the UK, as well as in the US, Japan and Europe, have therefore responded by printing money (called quantitative easing) to create inflationary forces to stave off deflation.

How can you determine the financial gearing for companies?

The ratio for determining the gearing for companies is therefore:

$$\frac{Debt}{Capital}$$

Balance sheet

	National Grid	M&S	Tesco	Indesit	BT	NMS
	£m	£m	£m	£m	£m	£m
Non-current assets	£ 14,129	£ 6,534.5	£ 34,592	£ 1,088.4	£ 19,192	£ 5.9
Current assets	£ 9,576	£ 1,368.5	£ 15,572	£ 1,157.0	£ 5,706	£ 119.8
Current liabilities	£ 7,445	£ 2,349.3	£ 21,399	£ 1,220.6	£ 7,687	£ 87.6
Non-current liabilities	£ 32,027	£ 2,847.0	£ 14,043	£ 559.5	£ 17,083	£ 15.0
Net assets/share-holders' funds	£ 10,233	£ 2,706.7	£ 14,722	£ 465.3	-£ 592	£ 23.0
Financial gearing						
Debt	£37,027	£2,847	£14,043	£560		£–
Capital	£47,260	£5,554	£28,765	£1,025		£23
	78%	51%	49%	55%		0%
Leverage						
Capital	£47,260	£5,554	£28,765	£1,025		£23
Equity	£10,233	£2,707	£14,722	£465		£23
	4.62	2.05	1.95	2.20		1.00

You will notice that National Grid has a very high financial gearing. Why do you think this is? First of all, it has a lot of fixed assets on which to secure the debt (you may remember from Chapter 2 that securing debt is lower risk for the lender and therefore less expensive for the borrower); National Grid is also a fairly safe bet (there are no competitors) so banks are more prepared to lend it money. As a result, the equity investors are nearly five times leveraged (in a similar way that Oscar managed to leverage his equity investment in the second house). If National Grid continues to expand, then the equity investors will do very well.

M&S, Tesco and Indesit are all around the 50 per cent mark; and BT has been ignored, as the pension deficit, discussed in Chapter 2, distorted the numbers.

NMS has no debt at all (remember the non-current liability actually refers to a long-term incentive plan for the senior management) and so has no leverage.

Why is interest cover – the ability to service the debt – important?

It would appear from the section on gearing that, as long as things are going well, we should take on as much debt as we can – it is higher risk, but the rewards are greater.

The crucial thing to consider is whether or not a company can service its debt – i.e. can it meet the interest payments as they fall due?

The key ratio to consider here is the interest cover ratio.

What is the interest cover ratio?

The interest cover shows the extent to which a company can meet (or service) its interest payments. Here we see why the order of the income statement, as explained previously, is so important – interest is paid out of **operating profit** (i.e. after the cost of sales and other administration or fixed costs of running the business).

The interest cover is therefore calculated as:

$$\frac{Operating\ profit}{Interest\ payable}$$

Profit & loss accounts

	National Grid £m	M&S £m	Tesco £m	Indesit £m	BT £m	NMS £m
Sales	£ 14,359	£ 10,309.7	£ 63,557	£ 2,671.1	£ 19,397	£ 384.8
Cost of sales			£ 59,547	£ 2,054.8		£ 330.0
Gross profit			£ 4,010	£ 616.3		£ 54.9
Operating costs	£ 10,605		£ 1,379	£ 548.2	£ 16,335	£ 40.9
Operating profit	£ 3,754	£ 694.5	£ 2,631	£ 68.1	£ 3,062	£ 14.0
Interest	£ 834	£ 114.1	£ 372	£ 51.2	£ 671	£ -
Tax	£ 624	£ 74.4	£ 347	£ 13.7	£ 576	£ 6.0
Net profit	£ 2,296	£ 506.0	£ 1,912	£ 3.2	£ 1,815	£ 8.0
Interest cover						
EBIT	£ 3,754	£ 695	£ 2,631	£ 68	£ 3,062	£ 14
Interest	£ 834	£ 114	£ 372	£ 51	£ 671	£
EBIT	£3,754	£695	£2,631	£68	£3,062	£14
Interest	£834	£114	£372	£51	£671	£ -
	4.50	6.09	7.07	7.33	4.56	

When looking at the interest cover, National Grid (even though it has a lot of debt) is easily able to pay the interest on that debt (i.e. if interest rates doubled, then the interest payable could double, but there is still sufficient operating profit to pay this interest). Indesit, on the other hand, is sailing much closer to the wind. Its interest cover is only 1.33 times, so the company is much more sensitive to a change in interest rates.

For NMS this measure is, of course, irrelevant – the company has no debt and so does not pay interest.

? Is your company able to service its debts?

? How much room is there?

What are the additional benefits of debt? The tax shield

Debt has one additional attraction – that of a tax shield.

Consider the following:

▶ Interest is paid out of operating profit; so

▶ the more debt that a company has, the more interest it will pay; so

▶ the more interest it pays, the more is deducted from operating profit; so

▶ the lower will be the profit before tax (i.e. operating profit less interest = PBT); so

▶ the lower will be the tax payable.

This is known as the tax shield and provides an extra (tax) incentive for companies to take on additional debt.

What is working capital and why is it important?

So far we have examined the return on investment for a business. We have examined operational gearing – in the income statement – and financial gearing – in the balance sheet.

In this final section, we turn our attention to another part of the balance sheet – the current assets and the current liabilities, which together are referred to as working capital.

You may remember from the section on the balance sheet that capital comes from two sources:

▶ debt and

▶ equity.

This capital can be put to work in one of two ways:

▶ investment capital and

▶ working capital.

Balance sheet analysis

	National Grid £bn				
Non-current assets	£ 45.1	Investment capital	£ 45.1		
Current assets	£ 9.6	Working	£ 2.1		
Current liabilities	£ 7.5	Capital			
Non-current liabilities	£ 37.0	Debt		Capital	£ 47.2
Net assets/Shareholders' funds	£ 10.2	Equity			

Investment capital is the investment in fixed (or non-current) assets that a business needs to trade – such as property, plant and machinery, etc.

Working capital is what the business uses to meet its obligations as they fall due. In effect, investment capital is like the engine of a car (the bigger the engine, the faster the car) and working capital is like the oil in the engine. It doesn't matter how big your engine is, if you don't have any oil then it will cease to work. In the same way for a business, if it cannot meet its obligations as they fall due then the business will cease to be a going concern (i.e. will not be able to continue to trade) and will therefore fail.

There are a number of different ways of assessing whether or not a business has sufficient working capital, which we will look at in the following sections.

What is the liquidity ratio?

The liquidity ratio is a snapshot of the state of affairs of a company's working capital. The formula for calculating the liquidity ratio is:

$$\frac{Current\ assets}{Current\ liabilities}$$

This ratio measures the ability of a business to **meet its obligations as they fall due**. For a manufacturing business, typically this ratio should be above 2.0; for a service company 1.0 is acceptable.

Let us see what liquidity ratios we can calculate for the six companies:

Balance sheet

	National Grid	M&S	Tesco	Indesit	BT	NMS
	£m	£m	£m	£m	£m	£m
Non-current assets	£ 45,129	£ 6,534.5	£ 34,592	£ 1,088.4	£ 19,192	£ 5.9
Current assets	£ 9,576	£ 1,368.5	£ 15,572	£ 1,157.0	£ 5,706	£ 119.8
Current liabilities	£ 7,445	£ 2,349.3	£ 21,399	£ 1,220.6	£ 7,687	£ 87.6
Non-current liabilities	£ 32,027	£ 2,847.0	£ 14,043	£ 559.5	£ 17,083	£ 15.0
Net assets/ shareholders' funds	£ 10,233	£ 2,706.7	£ 14,722	£ 465.3	-£ 592	£ 23.0
Liquidity ratio						
Current assets	£9,576	£1,369	£15,572	£1,157	£5,706	£120
Current liabilities	£7,445	£2,349	£21,399	£1,221	£7,687	£88
	1.29	0.58	0.73	0.95	0.74	1.37

The liquidity ratio for National Grid is 1.29. This means that for every £1 that National Grid owes and has to pay soon (current liability), it has £1.29 either as cash or going to become cash very soon (current asset). We can conclude, therefore, that this is a good ratio and that National Grid is a going concern as it appears to have sufficient working capital to allow it to meet its obligations as they fall due.

NMS is on a similar ratio and is therefore also reasonably healthy. But, what about the companies with a ratio of less than 1.0? Indesit is only just below 1.0, but BT, M&S and Tesco are all operating on liquidity ratios that are significantly lower than 1.0. Does this cause us concern? Or is there a reason that they can operate like this? We will come back to that question later.

? What is the liquidity ratio of your business?

? Is this cause for concern?

? Why?

? How can it be improved?

What is the acid test?

Before we do, let us consider the acid test. The acid test is exactly like the liquidity ratio, but ignores stock:

$$\frac{Current\ assets\ less\ stock}{Current\ liabilities}$$

Why is this an important ratio? Well, consider the nature of the current assets. Imagine that the creditors (suppliers who have not yet been paid) are now banging on the door of A&B Ltd. A&B needs to pay them quickly.

▶ How easy is it to turn cash into cash? Silly question – cash already is cash! – and so A&B can easily pay the suppliers.

▶ How easy is it to turn debtors into cash? Relatively easy; they have already entered into the contract, which is legally binding. If A&B needs cash quickly it could either call them up nicely and offer a discount or, if they are in arrears, consider legal proceedings to recover the amounts due.

▶ How easy is it to turn stock into cash? Pretty difficult – if it was that easy then it would not be sitting on their shelves as stock (think about a high street shop – they don't have sales for your benefit, but rather because they couldn't sell the stock at the original high price and so have to reduce the price in order to shift it. So, the next time you see a sign in a shop window reading 'sale extended due to popular demand', you now know that they lie like a cheap watch – the only reason to extend a sale is due to **lack** of popular demand).

Let us examine the acid test for the six companies:

Balance sheet

	National Grid	M&S	Tesco	Indesit	BT	NMS
	£m	£m	£m	£m	£m	£m
Non-current assets	£ 45,129	£ 6,534.5	£ 34,592	£ 1,088.4	£ 19,192	£ 5.9
Current assets	£ 9,576	£ 1,368.5	£ 15,572	£ 1,157.0	£ 5,706	£ 119.8
Current liabilities	£ 7,445	£ 2,349.3	£ 21,399	£ 1,220.6	£ 7,687	£ 87.6
Non-current liabilities	£ 32,027	£ 2,847.0	£ 14,043	£ 559.5	£ 17,083	£ 15.0
Net assets/ shareholders' funds	£ 10,233	£ 2,706.7	£ 14,722	£ 465.3	-£ 592	£ 23.0
Liquidity ratio						
Current assets	£9,576	£1,369	£15,572	£1,157	£5,706	£120
Current liabilities	£7,445	£2,349	£21,399	£1,221	£7,687	£88
	12.9	0.58	0.73	0.95	0.74	1.37
Note – Stock	£ 291	£ 845.5	£ 3,576	£ 302.4	£ 82	–
Acid test						
CA less stock	£9,285	£523	£11,996	£855	£5,624	£120
Current liabilities	£7,445	£2,349	£21,399	£1,221	£7,687	£88
	1.25	0.22	0.56	0.70	0.73	1.37

The acid test is not relevant to businesses such as National Grid, BT and NMS – as they do not hold stock (or not very much). It is much more relevant to the likes of M&S, Tesco and Indesit. Traditionally, we would expect the acid test for a company with a lot of stock to be no less than 1.0; so, again, we need to examine these businesses in more detail to understand why they are operating with so little working capital.

? Is the acid test relevant to your business?

? If so, what is it?

? Is this cause for concern?

? Why?

? How can it be improved?

What is the liquidity ratio – target value?

As a general rule, a company should try to keep a liquidity ratio of at least 1.0, and for a manufacturing business it should be 2.0 (with 1.0 for the acid test ratio).

So, if we should be wary of a business with a liquidity ratio of 0.5, happy with 1.0, what would be our reaction to a business having, for example, 8.0?

The best way to answer this question is to examine the four main elements of the liquidity ratio:

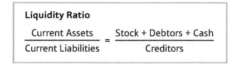

In order to achieve a liquidity ratio of 8.0, either one (or more) of the top three elements must be **high** or creditors on the bottom must be **low**:

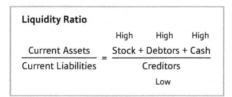

Let us examine each of these in turn:

▶ **Low** creditors – in order to achieve low creditors, they must be paid as soon as possible. Is this desirable? Well, we don't want to pay them so late that they will no longer do business with us, but there is no point in paying them sooner than we should. We should wait until the last possible minute before paying creditors, and so this figure should **not** be low!

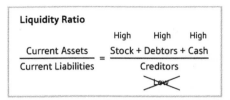

▶ **High** stock – what are we trying to do with stock? Sell it! The more stock we have, the more likely that it will be damaged, pilfered, stolen, become obsolete, etc. Our aim, therefore, is to hold just enough stock, but not too much (think of a just in time approach to stock), and so this figure should **not** be high!

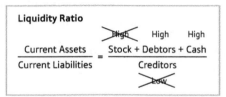

▶ **High** debtors – do we want high debtors? No! We want to collect the money due to us as soon as possible; if we can convince those who owe us money to pay us early, then so much the better, so this figure should **not** be high!

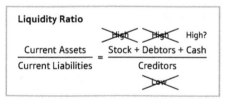

▶ **High** cash – our initial reaction may be that this is desirable, but think about the (unlikely) scenario where you won the jackpot on the lottery – would you put all of the money in your current account? The answer is probably not – you may keep some money aside to celebrate your win, but you would invest a large amount in savings or other asset classes to maximise your return. In the same way, if a company is achieving a return on its assets of (say) 12 per cent, it is unlikely to be earning this on its cash in the bank – the company is therefore not working or sweating its assets hard enough. In this case, the business should either invest the cash in the future of the business (and achieve the desired return) or, if no such investment opportunities exist, return the cash to the shareholders in the form of a dividend and allow them to maximise their return elsewhere in the market.

There are, of course, a number of different reasons why a company may choose to hold higher than normal amounts of cash – for example, to defend against a takeover, to undertake a takeover or to fund an uncertain future – but usually a business needs enough cash, not too much (in the same way that a car needs enough oil but not too much).

Take a look at Apple's balance sheet in 2012:

CONSOLIDATED BALANCE SHEETS		
(In millions, except number of shares which are reflected in thousands)		
	September 29, 2012	September 24, 2011
	$m	$m
ASSETS:		
Current assets:		
Cash and cash equivalents	10,746	9,815
Short-term marketable securities	18,383	16,137
Accounts receivable, less allowances of $98	10,930	5,369
and $53, respectively		
Inventories	791	776
Deferred tax assets	2,583	2,014
Vendor non-trade receivables	7,762	6,348
Other current assets	6,458	4,529
Total current assets	57,653	44,988
Long-term marketable securities	92,122	55,618
Property, plant and equipment, net	15,452	7,777
Goodwill	1,135	896
Acquired intangible assets, net	4,224	3,536
Other assets	5,478	3,556
Total assets	$176,064	$116,371
LIABILITIES AND SHAREHOLDERS' EQUITY:		
Current liabilities:		
Accounts payable	$21,175	$14,632
Accrued expenses	11,414	9,247
Deferred revenue	5,953	4,091
Total current liabilities	38,542	27,970
Deferred revenue – non-current	2,648	1,686
Other non-current liabilities	16,664	10,100
Total liabilities	57,854	39,756
Commitments and contingencies		
Shareholders' equity:		
Common stock, no par value; 1,800,000	16,422	13,331
shares authorized; 939,208 and 929,277 shares		
issued and outstanding, respectively		
Retained earnings	101,289	62,841
Accumulated other comprehensive income	499	443
Total shareholders' equity	118,210	76,615
Total liabilities and shareholders' equity	$176,064	$116,371

How much cash does it have? Our initial answer is $11 billion ($10,746 million, to be precise). But look at the next line down – 'Short-term marketable securities'. This is extra cash that the company has, which it has invested in short-term (very liquid) investments. It will be earning a very small return on these investments.

If you are now thinking that Apple has a total of £29 billion in cash, have a look at the non-current assets section. The first line is 'Long-term marketable securities' – these are investments, but do not mature for a long time (although they can be sold reasonably easily). Apple is, therefore, sitting on over $120 billion in cash! What is it doing with this cash? Nothing! It should either reinvest into the business (and invent the next big thing after the iPhone and iPad) or give it back to the shareholders. Pressure from shareholders has forced Apple to agree to give back $45 billion over the next three years in a combination of share buybacks and dividends.

? How much cash is there on the balance sheet of your business?

? Do you think that this is too much, too little or about right?

What is the working capital cycle?

The working capital cycle looks at how quickly a business can sell its stock from the time of purchase and how quickly it can collect the money from its customers; this is then compared with the amount of time it takes to pay its creditors and thus defines its **working capital requirement**.

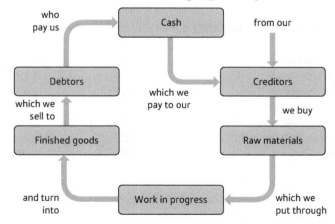

Let us examine the working capital requirement (WCR) for Tesco.

What is stock turnover?

Stock turnover measures the number of days, on average, it takes for a business to sell an item of stock from the day that it purchases that item of stock:

$$\text{Stock Turnover}$$
$$\frac{\text{Average Stock}}{\text{Cost of Sales}} \times 365$$

As all we have to work with are the statutory accounts of the company, we can calculate average stock by taking the stock at the end of the last year (closing stock for the end of last year is the opening stock for the beginning of this year) and the closing stock at the end of this year, adding them together and dividing by two.

	Notes	22 February 2014 £m	23 February 2013 £m
Non-current assets			
Goodwill and other intangible assets	10	3,795	4,362
Property, plant and equipment	11	24,490	24,870
Investment property	12	227	2,001
Investments in joint ventures and associates	13	286	494
Other investments	14	1,015	818
Loans and advances to customers	17	3,210	2,465
Derivative financial instruments	21	1,496	1,965
Deferred tax assets	6	73	58
		34,592	37,033
Current assets			
Inventories	15	3,576	3,744
Trade and other receivables	16	2,190	2,525
Loans and advances to customers	17	3,705	3,094
Derivative financial instruments	21	80	58
Current tax assets		12	10
Short-term investments		1,016	522
Cash and cash equivalents	18	2,506	2,512
		13,085	12,465
Assets of the disposal group and non-current assets classified as held for sale	7	2,487	631
		15,572	13,096

The calculation for Tesco is therefore:

Stock turnover

$$\frac{\text{Average stock}}{\text{Cost of sales}} \times 365$$

Open stock	£3,774		
Close stock	£3,576		
Average stock	£3,675	$\dfrac{£3,675}{£59,547}$ $\times 365$	
	=	22.53 days	

On average, from the day that Tesco buys something, it takes them 23 days to sell it. This probably makes sense. Tesco has very efficient logistics, which means that it can sell what it buys very quickly. Milk and bread probably sell more quickly than 23 days, while tins of baked beans and DVD players may be a little slower.

? What is the stock turnover (in days) for your business?

? How can this be improved?

What is debtor turnover?

Debtor turnover, or debtor days, calculates the time taken to collect monies due from clients. The formula for calculating this is:

Debtor Turnover

$$\frac{\text{Average trade debtors}}{\text{Sales}} \times 365$$

As all we have to work with are the statutory accounts of the company, we can calculate average debtors by taking the debtors at the end of the last year (the closing debtors figure for the end of last year is the opening debtors figure for the beginning of this year) and the closing debtors at the end of this year, adding them together and dividing by two.

The calculation for Tesco is therefore:

Debtor turnover

$$\frac{\text{Average trade debtors}}{\text{Sales}} \times 365$$

Open debtors	£2,525
Close debtors	£2,190
Average debtors	£2,358

$$\frac{£2,358}{£63,557} \times 365$$

$$= 13.54 \text{ days}$$

Again, we can check as to whether this makes sense. If you try to leave Tesco without paying, the security guard will probably accost you. Tesco does not really offer credit to the likes of you and I. Even if you pay by credit card, the credit card company will pay Tesco within a day or so of the transaction. However, there may be some customers (probably corporates) that Tesco supplies and who will pay Tesco after 30 days; so 14 days does not appear unreasonable.

So, Tesco buys the goods on day 0, sells the goods on day 24 and collects the money in (on average) 14 days later – on day 38.

? What is the debtor days for your business?

? How can this be improved?

What is creditor turnover?

Creditor turnover, or creditor days, calculates the time taken to pay monies due to suppliers. The formula for calculating this is:

Creditor turnover

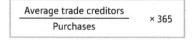

$$\frac{\text{Average trade creditors}}{\text{Purchases}} \times 365$$

Another problem is that the purchases figure is not shown anywhere in the accounts. All we have currently is cost of sales, which is not the same thing.

How to calculate purchases

Imagine that Rufus is travelling from A to B in his car. When he set off, Rufus noticed that he had a quarter of a tank of petrol. On the journey, he twice had to fill up, purchasing a full tank of gas on each occasion. When Rufus arrived at B, he noticed that he still had half a tank of petrol in his car.

During Rufus' journey he had had to purchase two tanks of petrol; but it would be incorrect to say that it takes two tanks of petrol to get from A to B. Why? Because we can see that it actually takes only 1¾ tanks of petrol.

To work this out we do the following calculation:

Petrol at the start plus petrol purchased less petrol at the end equals petrol used

In our example:

$$¼ + 2 - ½ = ¾$$

For a business, a similar calculation is conducted to arrive at the cost of sales of a business:

Opening stock plus purchases less closing stock equals cost of sales

	Petrol at the start	Opening stock
Plus	Petrol purchased	Purchases (this is the figure to be calculated)
Less	Petrol at the end	Closing stock
Equals	Petrol used	Cost of sales

For Tesco, we can, therefore, populate the above equation with the known numbers (i.e. all of the figures apart from purchases):

How to calculate purchases

Open stock	£ 3,774
+ Purchases	
– Closing stock	£ 3,576
= Cost of sales	£ 59,547

We can, therefore, (reasonably easily) work out the purchases figure:

How to calculate purchases

Open stock	£ 3,774
+ Purchases	£ 59,349
– Closing stock	£ 3,576
= Cost of sales	£ 59,547

We need to revisit the balance sheet to pull out the creditor figures from the current liabilities section:

	Notes	22 February 2014 £m	23 February 2013 £m
Non-current assets			
Goodwill and other intangible assets	10	3,795	4,362
Property, plant and equipment	11	24,490	24,870
Investment property	12	227	2,001
Investments in joint ventures and associates	13	286	494
Other investments	14	1,015	818
Loans and advances to customers	17	3,210	2,465
Derivative financial instruments	21	1,496	1,965
Deferred tax assets	6	73	58
		34,592	37,033
Current assets			
Inventories	15	3,576	3,744
Trade and other receivables	16	2,190	2,525
Loans and advances to customers	17	3,705	3,094
Derivative financial instruments	21	80	58
Current tax assets		12	10
Short-term investments		1,016	522
Cash and cash equivalents	18	2,506	2,512
		13,085	12,465
Assets of the disposal group and non-current assets classified as held for sale	7	2,487	631
		15,572	13,096
Current liabilities			
Trade and other payables	19	(10,595)	(11,094)
Financial liabilities:			
Borrowings	20	(1,910)	(766)
Derivative financial instruments and other liabilities	21	(99)	(121)
Customer deposits and deposits from banks	23	(6,858)	(6,015)
Current tax liabilities		(494)	(519)
Provisions	24	(250)	(188)
		(20,206)	(18,703)
Liabilities of the disposal group classified as held for sale	7	(1,193)	(282)
Net current liabilities		(5,827)	(5,889)

We can now plug all of the figures into our creditor turnover calculation:

Creditor turnover

$$\frac{\text{Average trade creditors}}{\text{Purchases}} \times 365$$

Open creditors	£11,094		
Close creditors	£10,595		
Average creditors	£10,845	$\dfrac{£10,845}{£59,349}$	× 365
	=	66.69 days	

Tesco is a very large company and will use its size to negotiate very good terms with its suppliers. Not only will Tesco negotiate the price down (and it needs to – remember the low margin that it operates at) but it will also negotiate very good payment terms.

? What is the creditor days for your business?

? How might you improve this?

What is the working capital requirement?

We have now calculated the main elements of Tesco's working capital requirement:

> Tesco buys stock on day 0
>
> Tesco sells stock on day 24
>
> Tesco pays its suppliers on day 66 (66 creditor days after purchase)
>
> Tesco receives payment on day 38 (14 days after sale of the stock)

This means that Tesco is collecting the money on day 38 from its customers – 28 days before it has to pay its suppliers. This is a very strong cash flow model and means that Tesco can operate on a very low working capital requirement – i.e. the fact that its liquidity ratio is below 1.0 is not a concern, due to the way it collects money due long before having to pay money out.

Chapter summary

In this chapter, we have examined some of the key ratios that might be used to analyse the financial performance of a business. This is not an exhaustive list, and there are other books that go into greater depth on these ratios, as well as introducing other ratios. However, using these core ratios should give you a grasp of the financial performance of a business:

▶ Return on capital employed

▶ Profitability

▶ Operational gearing

▶ Financial gearing

▶ Working capital.

In the next chapter, you will have the opportunity to apply these ratios to a case study.

 Next steps

▶ Apply the above analysis to the financial statements that you obtained in Chapter 3 (of your suppliers/clients/competitors, etc.).

▶ What does it tell you about the business that you are looking at?

▶ Can you match your financial analysis above with your practical and operational understanding of the business that you are looking at?

▶ Are all of the ratios relevant?

▶ If not, why not?

▶ Does the business talk about any other key financial indicators (KFIs)?

▶ Do you think these are industry specific or should have been included in this book?

Key learning points

This chapter examines the use of the following ratios to assess the financial performance of a business:

▶ Return on capital employed (ROCE)

▶ Profitability – gross, operating and net margins

▶ Operational gearing and price sensitivity

▶ Financial gearing and interest cover

▶ Working capital – the liquidity ratio, the acid test and the working capital requirement.

 Test yourself

4.1 Return on investment gives an indication of:
- **(a)** profitability compared to the cash flow ☐
- **(b)** cash generated compared to the capital invested ☐
- **(c)** profitability compared to the capital investment ☐
- **(d)** cash generated compared to profitability ☐

4.2 Capital is a combination of:
- **(a)** debt and working capital ☐
- **(b)** equity and investment capital ☐
- **(c)** debt, equity and working capital ☐
- **(d)** debt and equity ☐

4.3 The return on capital employed compares:
- **(a)** net profit with debt ☐
- **(b)** net profit with equity ☐
- **(c)** net profit with investment and working capital ☐
- **(d)** net profit with debt, equity, investment and working capital ☐

4.4   EBITDA stands for:

    (a)   earnings between interest, taxation, depreciation and amortisation ☐

    (b)   excess before income, taxation, depreciation and amortisation ☐

    (c)   earnings before interest, taxation, depreciation and amortisation ☐

    (d)   earnings before income, taxation, depreciation and amortisation ☐

4.5   Gross margin is:

    (a)   sales expressed as a percentage of cost of sales ☐

    (b)   gross profit expressed as a percentage of sales ☐

    (c)   sales expressed as a percentage of gross profit ☐

    (d)   gross profit expressed as a percentage of cost of sales ☐

4.6   As a company increases turnover, the gross margin is expected to:

    (a)   increase ☐

    (b)   decrease ☐

    (c)   stay the same ☐

    (d)   impossible to say ☐

4.7   Operating margin is:

    (a)   administration costs expressed as a percentage of sales ☐

    (b)   operating profit expressed as a percentage of administration costs ☐

    (c)   sales expressed as a percentage of operating profit ☐

    (d)   operating profit expressed as a percentage of sales ☐

4.8   As a company increases turnover, the operating margin is expected to:

    (a)   increase ☐

    (b)   decrease ☐

    (c)   stay the same ☐

    (d)   impossible to say ☐

4.9   Net profit is:

    (a)   sales less all costs ☐

    (b)   sales less all costs and interest ☐

    (c)   sales less all costs and interest and tax ☐

    (d)   sales less all costs and interest and tax and dividends ☐

4.10   Net margin is:

(a)   EBITDA expressed as a percentage of net profit ☐

(b)   net profit expressed as a percentage of sales ☐

(c)   dividends expressed as a percentage of net profit ☐

(d)   sales expressed as a percentage of net profit ☐

4.11   As a company increases turnover, the net margin is expected to:

(a)   increase ☐

(b)   decrease ☐

(c)   stay the same ☐

(d)   impossible to say ☐

4.12   Operational gearing is reflected in the relationship between:

(a)   sales and fixed costs ☐

(b)   fixed costs and variable costs ☐

(c)   variable costs and operating profit ☐

(d)   operating profit and sales ☐

4.13   A company with high operational gearing will have:

(a)   high variable costs and high fixed costs ☐

(b)   high variable costs and low fixed costs ☐

(c)   low variable costs and high fixed costs ☐

(d)   low variable costs and low fixed costs ☐

4.14   A company with low operational gearing will have:

(a)   high variable costs and high fixed costs ☐

(b)   high variable costs and low fixed costs ☐

(c)   low variable costs and high fixed costs ☐

(d)   low variable costs and low fixed costs ☐

4.15   We should only take on additional debt if:

(a)   interest rates are high ☐

(b)   things are going badly ☐

(c)   things are going well ☐

(d)   things are going well and we can afford the interest payments ☐

4.16   Financial gearing is:

(a)   debt expressed as a percentage of equity ☐

(b)   debt expressed as a percentage of capital ☐

(c)   capital expressed as a percentage of debt ☐

(d)   capital expressed as a percentage of debt and equity ☐

4.17   Financial gearing shows:

    (a)   whether a company is insolvent ☐

    (b)   the proportion of funding coming from employees ☐

    (c)   the proportion of funding coming from the banks and loans ☐

    (d)   whether a company can meet its interest payments ☐

4.18   The interest cover ratio shows:

    (a)   how much interest a company pays compared to dividends ☐

    (b)   how much interest a company pays compared to net profit ☐

    (c)   how much interest a company pays compared to operating profit ☐

    (d)   how much interest a company pays compared to gross profit ☐

4.19   The tax shield means that:

    (a)   debt is more tax efficient than equity as a source of funding ☐

    (b)   equity is more tax efficient than debt as a source of funding ☐

    (c)   debt and equity are both as tax efficient as each other ☐

    (d)   companies are not obliged to pay interest if they do not want to ☐

4.20   Leverage shows:

    (a)   how equity multiplies the return on equity ☐

    (b)   how debt multiplies the return on equity ☐

    (c)   how equity multiplies the return on debt ☐

    (d)   how debt multiplies the return on debt ☐

4.21   Working capital is:

    (a)   fixed assets and current assets ☐

    (b)   current assets and current liabilities ☐

    (c)   current liabilities and non-current liabilities ☐

    (d)   non-current liabilities and non-current assets ☐

4.22   Working capital is used to:

    (a)   fund the long-term investment of the business ☐

    (b)   fund the repayment of debt ☐

    (c)   fund the day-to-day trading operations of the business ☐

    (d)   fund the payment of dividends ☐

4.23   Stock turnover measures the number of days:

    (a)   from buying an item of stock to selling it ☐

    (b)   from buying an item of stock to paying for it ☐

    (c)   from buying an item of stock to returning it ☐

    (d)   from buying an item of stock to receiving the invoice for it ☐

4.24   Debtor turnover measures the number of days:

    (a)   from selling an item of stock to invoicing for it ☐

    (b)   from selling an item of stock to having it returned ☐

    (c)   from selling an item of stock to receiving payment for it ☐

    (d)   from selling an item of stock to paying for it ☐

4.25   Creditor turnover measures the number of days:

    (a)   from buying an item of stock to selling it ☐

    (b)   from buying an item of stock to paying for it ☐

    (c)   from buying an item of stock to returning it ☐

    (d)   from buying an item of stock to receiving the invoice for it ☐

4.26   Cost of sales reconciles:

    (a)   goods purchased with goods on order ☐

    (b)   goods purchased with goods held in stock offsite ☐

    (c)   goods purchased with goods returned ☐

    (d)   goods purchased with goods sold ☐

4.27   A company's working capital requirement is the difference between:

    (a)   when it sells a good and when it receives payment for that good ☐

    (b)   when it buys a good and when it sells a good ☐

    (c)   when it pays for a good and when it receives payment for that good ☐

    (d)   when it buys a good and when it pays for that good ☐

4.28   The liquidity ratio compares:

    (a)   current assets with current liabilities ☐

    (b)   current assets with non-current liabilities ☐

    (c)   non-current assets with current liabilities ☐

    (d)   non-current assets with non-current liabilities ☐

4.29   The liquidity ratio:

   (a)   must always be more than 1.0 ☐

   (b)   must never be more than 1.0 ☐

   (c)   shows whether a business is insolvent or not ☐

   (d)   indicates potential areas of concern for further investigation ☐

4.30   A liquidity ratio of 8.0 is:

   (a)   very desirable – the company is very liquid ☐

   (b)   very undesirable – the company is insolvent ☐

   (c)   indicates potential inefficient allocation of capital ☐

   (d)   indicates highly efficient allocation of capital ☐

4.31   The acid test is the same as the liquidity ratio but without stock because:

   (a)   stock is the most difficult to turn into cash quickly ☐

   (b)   stock costs extra to store ☐

   (c)   stock can be sold quickly in a sale ☐

   (d)   stock may become obsolete ☐

4.32   A lot of cash held on the balance sheet may indicate:

   (a)   an insolvent company ☐

   (b)   inefficient allocation of capital ☐

   (c)   a company struggling to make payments to suppliers ☐

   (d)   a company has just made a significant dividend payment ☐

5

Case study

'Debt can cause more social problems than some drugs, yet drugs are illegal and debt is tax-deductable.'

www.fool.com

 Aim

In Chapter 4, we examined how to read and understand a set of financial statements and considered some of the key financial indicators that we might use to analyse these accounts. The aim of this chapter is to consolidate what we have covered so far and to apply the techniques to a new company.

 Outcomes

By the end of this chapter you will be able to:

▶ read a set of financial accounts

▶ identify warning signals

▶ devise corrective action.

The case study – Importers-R-Us

It is 2010. You have just arrived at the office one morning when your bosses call you into their office. They explain that they are meeting a new (fictional) supplier (Importers-R-Us – hereafter called IRU) in a few hours' time and they need your assistance. The supplier is an import/distribution company (i.e. they don't actually make anything) and, potentially, is going to supply a key product to your company – so your boss wants to be confident that IRU is financially, as well as operationally, stable. He has managed to obtain the latest set of their accounts* and would like you to analyse these accounts prior to the meeting.

*Not all of the pages have been included, but you have all of the relevant information to undertake your analysis.

Your mission (should you choose to accept it) is to analyse the accounts of the supplier, conclude as to whether you would be happy to use them as a supplier and also identify any areas of concern (and suggestions that you might like to make to IRU).

In order to assist you, below is a checklist of questions that you should answer. When answering the questions and performing the calculations, try to interpret your answers and think about what this is telling you about the business. Try to resist the temptation to refer to the answer until you have completed the exercise! Good luck!

Checklist for Importers-R-Us case study

1 Is it profitable? Can you follow the profit from the P&L through to the movement in retained profits in the balance sheet?

2 What is the operational gearing (ratio of fixed to variable costs) – is it low risk (Company A) or high risk (Company B)?

3 How is it funded? Debt and/or equity?

4 If equity, is it through investment or retained profits?

5 If debt, what is the interest cover (can it service its debt?)

6 Does it have enough working capital (liquidity ratio)?

7 What about the acid test?

8 What is its working capital requirement?

9 Is it generating cash?

10 Can you follow the operating (accounting) profit (P&L) through to the cash profit (cash flow statement) and then through to the movement in cash on the balance sheet?

11 Is there anything else that looks funny?

12 What about commitments and contingent liabilities?

Importers-R-Us case study – the contents

Auditor's report

We planned and performed our audit so as to obtain all the information and explanations which we considered necessary in order to provide us with sufficient evidence to give reasonable assurance that the financial statements are free from material misstatement, whether caused by fraud or other irregularity or error. In forming our opinion we also evaluated the overall adequacy of the presentation of information in the financial statements.

Opinion

In our opinion

– the financial statements give a true and fair view, in accordance with United Kingdom Generally Accepted Accounting Practice, of the state of the company's affairs as at 31 March 2009 and of its profit for the year then ended;
– the financial statements have been properly prepared in accordance with the Companies Act 1985; and
– the information given in the Report of the Directors is consistent with the financial statements.

Grant Thornton UK LLP

GRANT THORNTON UK LLP
REGISTERED AUDITORS
CHARTERED ACCOUNTANTS
MANCHESTER

9 October 2009

Profit & loss account

	Note	2009 £	2008 £
Turnover	1	14,696,742	9,037,882
Cost of sales		11,096,720	6,073,743
Gross profit		3,600,022	2,964,139
Other operation changes	2	2,610,032	2,075,380
Other operating income	3	(150)	(150)
Operating profit	4	990,140	888,909
Interest receivable	7	109	36
Interest payable and similar charges	8	(52,730)	(45,344)
Profit on ordinary activities before taxation		937,519	843,601
Tax on profit on ordinary activities	9	267,647	252,227
Profit for the financial year	25	669,872	591,374

All of the activities of the company are classed as continuing.
The company has no recognised gains or losses other than the results for the year as set out above.

Balance sheet

	Note	2009 £	2008 £
Fixed assets			
Tangible assets	11	286,896	216,367
Investments	12	2	2
		286,898	216,369
Current assets			
Stocks	13	5,440,505	4,101,896
Debtors	14	2,330,581	1,383,277
Cash at bank		44	11,892
		7,771,130	5,497,065
Creditors: amounts falling due within one year	15	5,210,966	3,384,365
Net current assets		2,560,164	2,112,700
Total assets less current liabilities		2,847,062	2,329,069
Provisions for liabilities			
Deferred taxation	17	20,915	–
		2,826,147	2,329,069
Capital and reserves			
Called-up equity share capital	22	26,199	26,199
Share premium account	23	7,651	7,651
Other reserves	24	3,559	3,559
Profit and loss account	25	2,788,738	2,291,660
Shareholders' funds	26	2,826,147	2,329,069

These financial statements were approved by the directors and authorised for issue on 9 October 2009 and are signed on their behalf by:

Cash flow statement

	Note	2009 £	2008 £
Net cash (outflow)/inflow from operating activities	27	(270,135)	419,139
Returns on investments and servicing of finance	27	(52,621)	(45,308)
Taxation	27	(262,297)	(56,930)
Capital expenditure and financial investment	27	(152,855)	(49,542)
Equity dividends paid		(172,794)	(128,676)
Cash (outflow)/inflow before financing		(910,702)	138,683
Financing	27	(17,147)	(14,834)
(Decrease)/increase in cash	27	(927,849)	123,849

Notes to the accounts

1 Turnover

The turnover and profit before tax are attributable to the one principal activity of the company.
An analysis of turnover is given below:

	2009	2008
	£	£
United Kingdom	14,696,742	9,037,882

2 Other operating charges

	2009	2008
	£	£
Distribution costs	215,745	170,879
Administrative expenses	2,394,287	1,904,501
	2,610,032	2,075,380

3 Other operating income

	2009	2008
	£	£
Rent receivable	150	150

4 Operating profit

Operating profit is stated after charging/ (crediting):

	2009	2008
	£	£
Depreciation of owned fixed assets	82,028	41,466
Depreciation of assets held under hire purchase agreements	–	9,250
Loss/ (profit) on disposal of fixed assets	298	(98)
Auditor's remuneration:		
Audit fees	9,960	9,806
Taxation	1,500	1,500

5 Directors and employees

The average number of staff employed by the company during the financial year amounted to:

	2009	2008
	No	No
Number of administrative staff	8	8
Number of management staff	8	7
Number of sales staff	8	5
Number of warehouse staff	7	6
	31	26

The aggregate payroll costs of the above were:

	2009	2008
	£	£
Wages and salaries	989,970	821,255
Social security costs	116,985	144,003
Other pension costs	51,555	53,355
	1,158,510	1,018,613

7 Interest receivable

	2009	2008
	£	£
Bank interest receivable	109	36

8 Interest payable and similar charges

	2009	2008
	£	£
Interest payable on bank borrowing	52,730	47,510
Finance charges payable under hire purchase agreements	–	(2,166)
	52, 730	45,344

9 Taxation on ordinary activities

(a) Analysis of charge in the year

	2009	2008
	£	£
Current tax:		
In respect of the year:		
UK Corporation tax based on the results for the year at 28% (2008- 30%)	244, 732	262,794
Over/ under provision in prior year	–	(567)
Total current tax	244,732	262,227
Deferred tax:		
Origination and reversal of timing differences	22,915	(10,000)
Tax on profit on ordinary activities	267,647	252,227

10 Dividends

Dividends on shares classed as equity

	2009	2008
	£	£
Proposed at the year-end (recognised as a liability):		
Equity dividends on ordinary shares	172,794	172,794

11 Tangible fixed assets

	Leasehold improvements £	Plant & machinery £	Fixtures & fittings £	Motor vehicles £	Computer equipment £	Total £
Cost						
At 1 Apr 2008	172,659	67,604	118,600	106,528	100,770	566,161
Additions	3,028	10,060	10,342	80,988	73,738	178,156
Disposals	–	–	–	(88,439)	–	(88,439)
At 31 Mar 2009	175,687	77,664	128,942	99,077	174,508	655,878
Depreciation						
At 1 Apr 2008	76,833	32,359	88,624	71,033	80,945	349,794
Charge for the year	19,152	5,231	5,977	28,287	23,381	82,028
On disposals	–	–	–	(62,840)	–	(62,840)
At 31 Mar 2009	95,985	37,590	94,601	36,480	104,326	368,982
Net book value						
At 31 Mar 2009	79,702	40,074	34,341	62,597	70,182	286,896
At 31 Mar 2008	95,826	35,245	29,976	35,495	19,825	216,367

Included within the net book value of £286,896 is £Nil (2008–£27,749) relating to assets held under hire purchase agreements. The depreciation charged to the financial statements in the year in respect of such assets amounted to £Nil (2008–£9,250).

13 Stocks

	2009	2008
	£	£
Finished goods	**5,440,505**	4,101,896

14 Debtors

	2009	2008
	£	£
Trade debtors	**2,144,367**	1,273,608
Other debtors	**10,935**	–
Prepayments and accrued income	**175,297**	107,669
Deferred taxation (note 17)	**–**	2,000
	2,330,581	1,383,277

15 Creditors: amounts falling due within one year

	2009	2008
	£	£
Overdrafts	**1,437,505**	521,504
Trade creditors	**2,631,773**	1,932,710
Corporation tax	**244,732**	262,297
Other taxation and social security	**397,717**	170,855
Amounts due under hire purchase agreements	**–**	17,147
Proposed dividends	**172,794**	172,794
Other creditors	**36,163**	–
Director's loan accounts	**39,254**	59,515
Accruals and deferred income	**251,028**	247,543
	5,210,966	3,384,365

The following liabilities disclosed under creditors falling due within one year are secured by the company:

	2009	2008
	£	£
Overdrafts	**1,437,505**	521,504
Amounts due under fmance leases and hire purchase agreements	**–**	17,147
	1,437,505	538,651

Obligations under finance leases and hire purchase contracts are secured on the assets to which they relate.

The bank overdraft is secured by a debenture over the assets of the company.

16 Commitments under hire purchase agreements

Future commitments under hire purchase agreements net of future finance lease charges are as follows:

	2009	2008
	£	£
Amounts payable within 1 year	**=**	17,147
	=	17,147

17 Deferred taxation

The deferred tax included in the Balance sheet is as follows:

	2009	2008
	£	£
Included in debtors (note 14)	–	(2,000)
Included in provisions	20,915	–
	20,915	(2,000)

The movement in the deferred taxation account during the year was:

	2009	2008
	£	£
Balance brought forward	(2,000)	8,000
Profit and loss account movement arising during the year	22,915	(10,000)
Balance carried forward	20,915	(2,000)

The balance of the deferred taxation account consists of the tax effect of timing differences in respect of:

	2009	2008
	£	£
Excess of taxation allowances over depreciation on fixed assets	20,915	(2,000)

18 Financial instruments

The company holds financial instruments in order to manage its exposure to currency risks arising from its operations and from its sources of finance.

The company incurs foreign exchange risk on sales and purchases that are denominated in currencies other than sterling. The currencies principally giving rise to risk are US Dollars. The company uses forward exchange contracts to hedge its foreign currency risk. All of the forward exchange contracts have maturities of less than 12 months after the balance sheet date.

	2009	2008
	£000	£000
At 31 March the company had the following forward contracts:		
Buy US $ and sell £	=	378,419
Fair Value of the forward contract as an asset/ (liability)	=	806

19 Leasing commitments

At 31 March 2009 the company had annual commitments under non-cancellable operating leases as set out below.

	2009		2008	
	Land & Buildings	Other Items	Land & Buildings	Other Items
Operating leases which expire:	£	£	£	£
Within 1 year	–	7,995	–	4,563
Within 2 to 5 years	63,078	29,498	–	19,257
After more than 5 years	–	–	63,078	–
	63,078	37,493	63,078	23,820

20 Contingent liabilities

The company has provided guarantees amounting to £30,000 (2008: £15,000) in connection with the liability for deferred duty under a Customs and Excise bond.

22 Share capital

Authorised share capital:

	2009	2008
	£	£
50,000 Ordinary shares of £1 each	**50,000**	50,000

Allotted, called up and fully paid:

	2009		2008	
	No	**£**	No	£
Ordinary shares of £1 each	**26,199**	**26,199**	26,199	26,199

23 Share premium account

There was no movement on the share premium account during the financial year.

24 Other reserves

	2009	2008
	£	£
Other reserve balance brought forward	**3,559**	3,559

25 Profit and loss account

	2009	2008
Balance brought forward	**2,291,660**	1,873,078
Profit for the financial year	**669,872**	591,374
Equity dividends	**(172,794)**	(172,792)
Balance carried forward	**2,788,738**	2,291,660

26 Reconciliation of movements in shareholders' funds

	2009	2008
	£	£
Profit for the financial year	**669,872**	591,375
Equity dividends	**(172,794)**	(172,792)
Net addition to shareholders' funds	**497,078**	418,582
Opening shareholders' funds	**2,329,069**	1,910,487
Closing shareholders' funds	**2,826,147**	2,329,069

27 Notes to the statement of cash flows

Reconciliation of operating profit to net cash (outflow)/inflow from operating activities

	2009	2008
	£	£
Operating profit	990,140	888,909
Depreciation	82,028	50,716
Loss/(Profit) on disposal of fixed assets	298	(98)
Increase in stocks	(1,338,609)	(1,506,259)
Increase in debtors	(949,304)	(290,569)
Increase in creditors	945,312	1,276,440
Net cash (outflow)/inflow from operating activities	(270,135)	419,139

Returns on investments and servicing of finance

	2009	2008
	£	£
Interest received	109	36
Interest paid	(52,730)	(47,510)
Interest element of hire purchase	–	2,166
Net cash outflow from returns on investments and servicing of finance	(52,621)	(45,308)

Taxation

	2009	2008
	£	£
Taxation	(262,297)	(56,930)

Capital expenditure and financial investment

	2009	2008
	£	£
Payments to acquire tangible fixed assets	(178,156)	(52,096)
Receipts from sale of fixed assets	25,301	2,554
Net cash outflow for capital expenditure and financial investment	(152,855)	(49,542)

Financing

	2009	2008
	£	£
Capital element of hire purchase	(17,147)	(14,834)
Net cash outflow from financing	(17,147)	(14,834)

Importers-R-Us case study – the answer

In order to answer the case study, we will go through each question step by step:

1 Is it profitable? Can you follow the profit from the P&L through to the movement in retained profits in the balance sheet?

 Do you want to enter into business with a profitable company? The answer must be yes – especially if they are going to be a long-term supplier on whom you are going to depend. We do not want them to be making enormous profits (suggesting that we are paying too much) but we want them to be profitable.

Profit and loss account	Note	2009	2008
		£	£
Turnover	1	14,696,742	9,037,882
Cost of sales		11,096,720	6,073,743
Gross profit		3,600,022	2,964,139
Other operating charges	2	2,610,032	2,075,380
Other operating income	3	(150)	(150)
Operating profit	4	990,140	888,909
Interest receivable	7	109	36
Interest payable and similar charges	8	(52,730)	(45,344)
Profit on ordinary activities before taxation		937,519	843,601
Tax on profit on ordinary activities	9	267,647	252,227
Profit for the financial year	25	669,872	591,374

The answer is that yes, it is profitable. IRU made a profit of £670,000 during the year, which is good, and we can award the company a tick ☑.

If you look at the balance sheet, you will see the retained profit (called 'Profit and loss account') under the 'Capital and reserves' heading (another word for shareholders' funds or equity). The company started the year with £2,291,660 and finished the year with £2,788,738.

So, IRU started the year with £2.3 million in retained profit or retained earnings (that is, the total amount of profit that the company has made, ever since it started trading, and has not yet given back to shareholders), it made an additional £0.7 million in profit but ended the year with £2.8 million in retained earnings. Clearly, these numbers do not add up.

Balance sheet	Note	2009	2008
		£	£
Fixed assets			
Tangible assets	11	286,896	216,367
Investments	12	2	2
		286,898	216,369
Current assets			
Stocks	13	5,440,505	4,101,896
Debtors	14	2,330,581	1,383,277
Cash at bank		44	11,892
		7,771,130	5,497,065

Creditors: amounts falling due within one year	15	5,210,966	3,384,365
Net current assets		2,560,164	2,112,700
Total assets less current liabilities		2,847,062	2,329,069
Provisions for liabilities			
Deferred taxation	17	20,915	–
		2,826,147	2,329,069
Capital and reserves			
Called-up equity share capital	22	26,199	26,199
Share premium account	23	7,651	7,651
Other reserves	24	3,559	3,559
Profit and loss account	25	2,788,738	2,291,660
Shareholders' funds	26	2,826,147	2,329,069

You will notice that, just to the left of the £2,788,738 is the number 25. This is the number of the note and, if we want to find out more about these numbers, we should refer to Note 25.

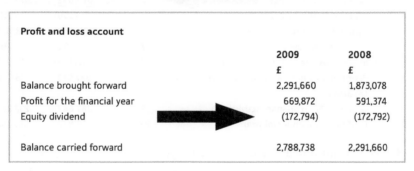

Profit and loss account		
	2009	2008
	£	£
Balance brought forward	2,291,660	1,873,078
Profit for the financial year	669,872	591,374
Equity dividend	(172,794)	(172,792)
Balance carried forward	2,788,738	2,291,660

Note 25 shows us that the company not only made a profit of £670k, but also paid £173k of this profit out to the shareholders, reinvesting the remainder of £497k back into the business. So IRU is a profitable business, which is paying some dividends (to keep the shareholders happy) but is reinvesting most of the profit back into the business, which, again, is good, and earns the company a second tick ☑ ☑

2   What is the operational gearing (ratio of fixed to variable costs) – is it low risk (Company A) or high risk (Company B)?

If you refer to the P&L account, you can see the fixed and variable costs of the business. The cost of sales are generally the variable costs

– remember, the more goods that IRU wants to sell, the more goods it has to buy. The 'Other operating charges' relates to the fixed costs of the business – rent, rates, light, heat, HR, finance, etc. IRU has high variable costs (Cost of sales) relative to its fixed costs (Other operating charges) and is, therefore, low in its operational gearing (i.e. more like Company A). We like to do business with a low-risk supplier, as they are less likely to go bust, so this is good; however, we need to realise that they are very price sensitive, so may not be open to a huge amount of price negotiation! We can, therefore, allocate a third tick to the company ☑ ☑ ☑

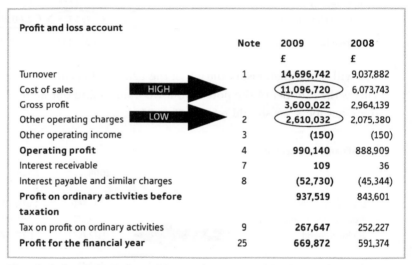

Profit and loss account	Note	2009 £	2008 £
Turnover	1	14,696,742	9,037,882
Cost of sales HIGH →		11,096,720	6,073,743
Gross profit		3,600,022	2,964,139
Other operating charges LOW →	2	2,610,032	2,075,380
Other operating income	3	(150)	(150)
Operating profit	4	990,140	888,909
Interest receivable	7	109	36
Interest payable and similar charges	8	(52,730)	(45,344)
Profit on ordinary activities before taxation		937,519	843,601
Tax on profit on ordinary activities	9	267,647	252,227
Profit for the financial year	25	669,872	591,374

3 How is it funded? Debt and/or equity?

In order to determine how the company is funded, we should first crack the balance sheet by identifying the five main elements. Have another look at the balance sheet and see if you can identify the five main sections:

Balance sheet	Note	2009	2008
		£	£
Fixed assets			
Tangible assets	11	**286,896**	216,367
Investments	12	**2**	2
		286,898	216,369
Current assets			
Stocks	13	**5,440,505**	4,101,896
Debtors	14	**2,330,581**	1,383,277
Cash at bank		**44**	11,892
		7,771,130	5,497,065
Creditors: amounts falling due within one year	15	**5,210,966**	3,384,365
Net current assets		**2,560,164**	2,112,700
Total assets less current liabilities		**2,847,062**	2,329,069
Provisions for liabilities			
Deferred taxation	17	**20,915**	–
		2,826,147	2,329,069
Capital and reserves			
Called-up equity share capital	22	**26,199**	26,199
Share premium account	23	**7,651**	7,651
Other reserves	24	**3,559**	3,559
Profit and loss account	25	**2,788,738**	2,291,660
Shareholders' funds	26	**2,826,147**	2,329,069

IRU has fixed (or non-current) assets of £286,898; this will include the tables and chairs, etc. that are used to run the business. The current assets are £7,771,130 and the current liabilities (referred to here as 'Creditors: amounts falling due within one year') are £5,210,966. Remember, sometimes similar things are referred to by different names; however, you should be able to work out what each item is through a process of logical deduction – 'Creditors' (people to whom we owe money – so 'Liabilities'); 'due within one year' (payable soon – so 'Current').

Just below this number is 'Net current assets' of £2,560,164. These are the current assets (£7,771,130) net of, or less, the current liabilities (£5,210,164). Net current assets is, therefore, another term for working capital.

The next line down states 'Total assets less current liabilities'. This is the net current assets (£2,560,124) plus the fixed assets of £286,898. 'Total assets less current liabilities' is, therefore, another term for 'total capital'!

The provisions for liabilities actually refers to tax that has to be paid, but not for a while. If we had to pay it within a year, it would be included in the current liabilities line. Thus, this must be the non-current (or long-term) liabilities.

Finally, the capital and reserves refers to the shareholders' funds or equity in the business.

We can now, therefore, crack the balance sheet:

Balance sheet analysis

	IEL £bn		£m	£m
Non-current assets	£ 0.287	Investment capital	£ 0.287	
Current assets	£ 7.771	Working	£ 2.560	
Current liabilities	£ 5.211	Capital		
Non-current liabilities	£ 0.021	Debt	Capital	£ 2.847
Net assets/shareholders' funds	£ 2.826	Equity		

The **debt** is £0.021 million and the **equity** is £2.826 million. As we have seen above, the debt is not really debt, but is a deferred tax liability. Therefore, the answer to the question is that IRU is a company funded entirely by equity, with no debt.

Balance sheet	Note	2009 £	2008 £
Fixed assets			
Tangible assets	11	**286,896**	216,367
Investments	12	**2**	2
		286,898	216,369
Current assets			
Stocks	13	**5,440,505**	4,101,896
Debtors	14	**2,330,581**	1,383,277
Cash at bank		**44**	11,892
		7,771,130	5,497,065
Creditors: amounts falling due within one year	15	**5,210,966**	3,384,365
Net current assets		**2,560,164**	2,112,700
Total assets less current liabilities		**2,847,062**	2,329,069
Provisions for liabilities			
Deferred taxation　DEBT ➤	17	**20,915**	
		2,826,147	2,329,069
Capital and reserves			
Called-up equity share capital	22	**26,199**	26,199
Share premium account	23	**7,651**	7,651
Other reserves	24	**3,559**	3,559
Profit and loss account	25	**2,788,738**	2,291,660
Shareholders' funds　EQUITY ➤	26	**2,826,147**	2,329,069

Is this good or bad? Well, as a customer this must be good for us. Why? Because IRU does **not** have to pay a dividend and does **not** have to repay the equity capital invested, so it is a lower risk (remember, if it was funded by debt, then it would **have** to ensure that it could service that debt by paying interest **and** repay the capital), and so this is good for us as a potential customer and earns a fourth tick ☑ ☑ ☑ ☑.

4 If equity, is it through investment or retained profits?

So, we have established that IRU is funded through equity, but is this equity through direct investment by the shareholders or through profits being reinvested back into the business? To find the answer, we need to look at the bottom of the balance sheet under 'Capital and reserves':

Capital and reserves			
Called-up equity share capital **INVESTMENT**	22	26,199	26,199
Share premium account	23	7,651	7,651
Other reserves	24	3,559	3,559
Profit and loss account **RETAINED PROFIT**	25	2,788,738	2,291,660
Shareholders' funds	26	**2,826,147**	**2,329,069**

The shareholders have invested approximately £34k in the business (share capital of £26,199 and share premium of £7,651), while £2,788,738 of profits has been reinvested back into the business. IRU is, therefore, clearly funded through the reinvestment of profits.

Is this good or bad? Well, this must be good. IRU is a profitable business; some of that profit is returned to shareholders as a dividend, but a substantial amount is being reinvested back into the business. We can add another tick to the list ☑ ☑ ☑ ☑ ☑.

5 If debt, what is the interest cover (can it service its debt?)

Under question 4, we established that IRU is funded by equity, with no debt at all appearing on the balance sheet, so this appears to be an irrelevant question. In any case, let us look at the P&L account again:

Profit and loss account			
	Note	**2009**	**2008**
		£	£
Turnover	1	**14,696,742**	9,037,882
Cost of sales		**11,096,720**	6,073,743
Gross profit		**3,600,022**	2,964,139
Other operating charges	2	**2,610,032**	2,075,380
Other operating income	3	**(150)**	(150)
Operating profit **EBIT**	4	**990,140**	888,909
Interest receivable	7	**109**	36
Interest payable and similar charges **INTEREST**	8	**(52,730)**	(45,344)
Profit on ordinary activities before taxation		**937,519**	843,601
Tax on profit on ordinary activities	9	**267,647**	252,227
Profit for the financial year	25	**669,872**	591,374

The company is making an operating profit (also known as earnings before interest and taxation, or EBIT) of nearly £1 million (£990,140, to be precise) and is paying interest of approximately £50,000 (£52,730). This means that the interest cover is 20 x (i.e. the EBIT is 20 × the interest payable) so the company is easily able to service the debt – and earns another tick ☑ ☑ ☑ ☑ ☑ ☑.

But don't you think that this is a little odd? Why is IRU paying interest at all when we have just concluded that it is 100 per cent equity funded, with no debt at all? If you noticed this when going through the case study, then this is good – it means that you are starting to **read** the accounts and not just perform the calculations.

We will revisit the reason that IRU is paying interest when it appears to have no debt later.

6 Does it have enough working capital (liquidity ratio)?

Let us return to the balance sheet and examine the net current assets, or working capital of the business:

Balance sheet	Note	2009 £	2008 £
Fixed assets			
Tangible assets	11	286,896	216,367
Investments	12	2	2
		286,898	216,369
Current assets			
Stocks	13	5,440,505	4,101,896
Debtors	14	2,330,581	1,383,277
Cash at bank		44	11,892
		7,771,130	5,497,065
Creditors: amounts falling due within one year	15	5,210,966	3,384,365
Net current assets		2,560,164	2,112,700
Total assets less current liabilities		2,847,062	2,329,069
Provisions for liabilities			
Deferred taxation	17	20,915	
		2,826,147	2,329,069
Capital and reserves			
Called-up equity share capital	22	26,199	26,199
Share premium account	23	7,651	7,651
Other reserves	24	3,559	3,559
Profit and loss account	25	2,788,738	2,291,660
Shareholders' funds	26	2,826,147	2,329,069

The company has £7.8 million of current assets (£7,771,130) and £5.2 million of current liabilities (£5,210,966). £7.8 million divided by £5.2 million gives a ratio of approximately 1.5; so, for every £1 that IRU owes and has to pay within one year, the company has £1.50 of assets that either are cash or will become cash quite soon. Again, this is good and takes us to seven ticks ☑ ☑ ☑ ☑ ☑ ☑ ☑.

So, let us summarise where we have got to so far. IRU is a profitable company. Some of that profit is being paid out as a dividend, but most is being reinvested back into the business, which is its principal source of funding. It has low operational gearing and low financial gearing. It has no problems meeting its interest payments (although it is a little odd that it is actually paying interest) and it appears to have adequate working capital. If you were starting to think that this is a company with which you could feel comfortable doing business, then you would be right.

7 What about the acid test?

The acid test is exactly the same as the current or liquidity ratio, but ignoring stock:

Balance sheet	Note	2009 £	2008 £
Fixed assets			
Tangible assets	11	286,896	216,367
Investments	12	2	2
		286,898	216,369
Current assets			
Stocks	13	5,440,505	4,101,896
Debtors	14	2,330,581	1,383,277
Cash at bank		44	11,892
		7,771,130	5,497,065
Creditors: amounts falling due within one year	15	5,210,966	3,384,365
Net current assets		2,560,164	2,112,700
Total assets less current liabilities		2,847,062	2,329,069
Provisions for liabilities			
Deferred taxation	17	20,915	
		2,826,147	2,329,069

Capital and reserves			
Called-up equity share capital	22	**26,199**	26,199
Share premium account	23	**7,651**	7,651
Other reserves	24	**3,559**	3,559
Profit and loss account	25	**2,788,738**	2,291,660
Shareholders' funds	26	**2,826,147**	2,329,069

Deducting stock of £5.441 million from current assets of £7.771 million leaves £2.330 million; this, divided by current liabilities of 5.211 million, gives a ratio of 0.45; this means that, for every £1 that the company owes and has to pay soon, it has only 45p of assets that are going to become cash, ignoring stock. This is of concern to us as, if the company cannot sell its stock (for whatever reason - perhaps it has become obsolete), then it will struggle to meet its obligations as they fall due and will no longer be a **going concern**.

Companies that are trading and expected to continue to trade for the foreseeable future are described as being a going concern. It is illegal for the directors to continue to trade if they believe that the company is not a going concern – i.e. it is illegal for a company to enter into a contract to buy goods and services, knowing that it will be unable to pay for them.

This is of concern to us, and earns the company its first negative mark
☑ ☑ ☑ ☑ ☑ ☑ ☑ ☒

8   What is its working capital requirement?

With the information from the balance sheet and profit & loss account, we can work out the company's working capital requirement in days.

To find the figures on trade debtors, you need to look in Note 14, which provides the breakdown of the trade and other debtors figure on the face of the balance sheet.

To find the figures on trade creditors, you need to look in Note 15, which provides the breakdown of the creditors: amounts falling due within one year figure on the face of the balance sheet.

Stock Turnover

$$\frac{\text{Average Stock}}{\text{Cost of Sales}} \quad \text{x} \quad 365$$

Open Stock	£4.101	
Close Stock	£5.440	
Average Stock	£4.771	$\dfrac{£4.771}{£11.097} \quad \text{x} \quad 365$

$$= \quad 156.91 \text{ Days}$$

Debtor Turnover

$$\frac{\text{Average Trade Debtors}}{\text{Sales}} \quad \text{x} \quad 365$$

Open Debtors	£1.273	
Close Debtors	£2.144	
Average Debtors	£1.709	$\dfrac{£1.709}{£14.697} \quad \text{x} \quad 365$

$$= \quad 42.43 \text{ Days}$$

Creditor Turnover

$$\frac{\text{Average Trade Creditors}}{\text{Purchases}} \quad \text{x} \quad 365$$

Open Creditors	£1.933	
Close Creditors	£2.631	
Average Creditors	£2.282	$\dfrac{£2.282}{£12.436} \quad \text{x} \quad 365$

$$= \quad 66.98 \text{ Days}$$

How to Calculate Purchases

Open Stock	£4.101
+ Purchases	Balancing figure
- Close Stock	£5.440
= Cost of Sales	£11.097

How to Calculate Purchases

Open Stock	£4.101
+ Purchases	£12.436
- Close Stock	£5.440
= Cost of Sales	£11.097

The working capital requirement is 131 days! This is a long time! It is taking the company, on average, 157 days to sell its stock and a further 42 days to collect the money that is owed by its customers. Even by delaying payment to its suppliers for 67 days, it still has a very significant time gap for which to fund the business.

This is not good, and earns the company a second negative mark:
☑ ☑ ☑ ☑ ☑ ☑ ☑ ☒ ☒

9 Is it generating cash?

If we revisit the P&L account, we will see that IRU is a profitable business; in fact, it is generating nearly £1 million of operating profit:

Profit and loss account	Note	2009 £	2008 £
Turnover	1	14,696,742	9,037,882
Cost of sales		11,096,720	6,073,743
Gross profit		3,600,022	2,964,139
Other operating charges	2	2,610,032	2,075,380
Other operating income	3	(150)	(150)
Operating profit OPERATING PROFIT	4	990,140	888,909
Interest receivable	7	109	36
Interest payable and similar charges	8	(52,730)	(45,344)
Profit on ordinary activities before taxation		937,519	843,601
Tax on profit on ordinary activities	9	267,647	252,227
Profit for the financial year	25	669,872	591,374

But, if we now look at the cash flow statement, the top line – called 'Net cash (outflow)/inflow from operating activities' – is a negative figure of £270,135. This line is, effectively, the cash profit that the business is making (or, in this case, a cash loss).

Cash flow statement	Note	2009 £	2008 £
Net cash (outflow)/inflow from operating activities CASH PROFIT	27	(270,135)	419,139
Returns on investments and servicing of finance	27	(52,621)	(45,308)
Taxation	27	(262,297)	(56,930)
Capital expenditure and financial investment	27	(152,855)	(49,542)
Equity dividends paid		(172,794)	(128,676)
Cash (outflow)/inflow before financing		(910,702)	138,683
Financing	27	(17,147)	(14,834)
(Decrease)/increase in cash	27	(927,849)	123,849

How can a company, that appears to be making such a large profit, be making such a large loss? The answer is to be found in Note 27.

You may remember that, for National Grid, the reconciliation that turned their accounting profit into a cash profit was to be found at the top of the cash flow statement. Well, some companies – such as IRU – choose to show this reconciliation in the notes to the accounts:

27	Notes to the statement of cash flows		
	Reconciliation of operating profit to net cash (outflow)/inflow from operating activities		
		2009	2008
		£	£
	Operating profit	990,140	888,909
	Depreciation	82,028	50,716
	Loss/(Profit) on disposal of fixed assets	298	(98)
	Increase in stocks	(1,338,609)	(1,506,259)
	Increase in debtors	(949,304)	(290,569)
	Increase in creditors	945,315	1,276,440
	Net cash (outflow)/inflow from operating activities	(270,135)	419,139

(ACCOUNTING PROFIT arrow points to Operating profit 990,140; CASH PROFIT arrow points to Net cash (outflow)/inflow from operating activities)

The top line shows the £990k of operating profit. The first adjustment is to add back depreciation. This figure is quite small, which we would expect as the company has very low fixed assets (it is more of a service company – acting as the middleman – and will rent any office space or warehousing that it needs).

Then we see a negative £1.3 million, due to increase in stocks. Think about this for a minute. If you start buying lots of stock, what impact does it have on your profit? The answer is nothing. When you buy stock, you are merely transferring one form of asset (cash) into another form of asset (stock). This is known as a balance sheet transaction. But what impact does this have on your cash? Negative, of course, because you have spent all that cash buying stock. So IRU has been buying stock – and tying increasing amounts of money up in this stock.

What about the next line: 'Increase in debtors'? If you sell lots of stock (which the company has been doing), then you will recognise these sales in the P&L account. But, if you do not collect the money owed to you, then it will have a negative effect on your cash flow.

Similarly, 'Increase in creditors' is the opposite. If you buy stock, but don't pay for it, then it will have a positive effect on your cash flow.

So IRU is a profitable company, but is tying up an additional £1.3 million in stock, has failed to collect an extra £1 million from customers who owe it money, does not appear to have any cash, and so has not been paying its suppliers, so the amount owed to suppliers has risen by £1 million.

This clearly is not a good situation, and earns another negative mark ☑ ☑ ☑ ☑ ☑ ☑ ☑ ☒ ☒ ☒

10 Can you follow the accounting profit (P&L) through to the cash profit (cash flow statement) and then through to the movement in cash on the balance sheet?

Let us return to the cash flow statement again:

Cash flow statement	Note	2009 £	2008 £
Net cash (outflow)/inflow from operating activities **CASH PROFIT** →	27	(270,135)	419,139
Returns on investments and servicing of finance	27	(52,621)	(45,308)
Taxation	27	(262,297)	(56,930)
Capital expenditure and financial investment	27	(152,855)	(49,542)
Equity dividends paid		(172,794)	(128,676)
Cash (outflow)/inflow before financing		(910,702)	138,683
Financing	27	(17,147)	(14,834)
(Decrease)/increase in cash **CASH FLOW** →	27	(927,849)	123,849

IRU is making a £270k cash loss. It is paying £52k in interest; it is paying tax, because it is profitable, of £262k; it is investing in the business, because it is growing, to the tune of £153k; it is paying dividends (not sure why – it clearly cannot afford to) of £173k. All of these transactions result in a total cash outflow during the year of £928k – that is nearly £1 million!

This clearly is not sustainable!

Now return to the balance sheet. The company started the year with approximately £12,000 in cash and finished the year with £44 (yes, that is £44 – not £44,000!).

Balance sheet			
	Note	2009 £ £	2008 £ £
Fixed assets			
Tangible assets	11	**286,896**	216,367
Investments	12	**2**	2
		286,898	216,369
Current assets			
Stocks	13	**5,440,505**	4,101,896
Debtors	14	**2,330,581**	1,383,277
Cash at bank CASH ➡		**44**	11,892
		7,771,130	5,497,065
Creditors: amounts falling WHAT IS IN HERE? ➡	15	**5,210,966**	3,384,365
due within one year			
Net current assets		**2,560,164**	2,112,700
Total assets less current liabilities		**2,847,062**	2,329,069
Provisions for liabilities			
Deferred taxation	17	**20,915**	
		2,826,147	2,329,069
Capital and reserves			
Called-up equity share capital	22	**26,199**	26,199
Share premium account	23	**7,651**	7,651
Other reserves	24	**3,559**	3,559
Profit and loss account	25	**2,788,738**	2,291,660
Shareholders' funds	26	**2,826,147**	2,329,069

The company has no cash. The £44 is probably in the petty cash tin under the receptionist's desk. If you have no cash, then you probably have an overdraft at the bank. An overdraft is a liability – and is payable on demand – which makes it a current liability. This will be in the 'Creditors: amounts falling due within one year line' so let us take a closer look at what makes up the £5.211 million. We can find the breakdown in Note 15:

15	Creditors: amounts falling due within one year		
		2009	**2008**
		£	**£**
Overdrafts	NEGATIVE CASH – LOAN ➔	**1,437,505**	521,504
Trade creditors		**2,631,773**	1,932,710
Corporation tax		**244,732**	262,297
Other taxation and social security		**397,717**	170,855
Amounts due under hire purchase agreements			17,147
Proposed dividends		**172,794**	172,794
Other creditors		**36,163**	
Director's loan accounts		**39,254**	59,515
Accruals and deferred income		**251,028**	247,543
		5,210,966	3,384,365

An overdraft is like negative cash; IRU started the year with an overdraft of £0.5 million and finished the year with an overdraft of £1.4 million; the cash outflow was £0.9 million, which ties back to the cash flow statement.

11 Is there anything else that looks funny?

We observed that, while the company can meet its interest payments based on profitability, it was odd that it should be paying interest at all.

We can now conclude that this is not odd – the interest relates to the overdraft!

12 What about commitments and contingent liabilities?

16	Commitments under hire purchase agreements		
	Future commitments under hire purchase agreements net of future finance lease changes are as follows:		
		2009	**2008**
		£	**£**
	Amounts payable within 1 year	=	17,147
		=	17,147

The commitments and contingent liabilities is a form of off balance sheet finance – i.e. amounts that the company owes (because it has entered into a contract to pay these amounts over a future period), but do not appear on the balance sheet (because the company does not owe this amount today).

The above note suggests that this is not an issue for IRU.

Importers-R-Us case study – conclusions

So, what is our conclusion with regards to IRU?

The company is a perfect example of a profitable business, which is growing rapidly (its sales have increased by 60 per cent from 2008 to 2009), but is running out of cash.

At the end of each month, the managing director has to phone up the bank manager to ask permission to pay the staff. If the bank manager says no then it is game over – last one out turns off the lights.

The bank manager probably will not say this just yet (the overdraft is secured on the assets of the company – mainly the debtors and stock), but losing £1 million per year in cash clearly is unsustainable.

It would appear that the best course of action is not to use IRU as your key supplier until is has sorted out its finances.

Importers-R-Us case study – advice

So, what advice would you give IRU?

Well, the first thing to do might be to call a meeting with the sales team and the purchasing team, as they do not appear to be communicating well with each other.

Suggest to the purchasing team that they go on holiday (or at least stop buying – anything!). When they get back, they should buy only what the sales team can sell.

Now suggest to the sales team that they go into the warehouse, look at what is on the shelves, and focus their efforts on selling that stock.

And, while we are there, give the warehouse manager a clip round the ear. Someone needs to be managing the stock – looking at each line of stock and assessing how quickly it is moving. The stock controller should be using the stock turnover calculation to assess the stock on a line-by-line basis – identifying quick-moving lines (which need to be restocked) and slow moving lines (and what to do about the slow-moving items).

What else?

Perhaps you would like to speak to the credit controller (someone who makes sure the debtors pay on time). Who? Ah – so the company needs to appoint a credit controller (or two), give them a list of all the companies that owe IRU money, a baseball bat and a telephone, and tell them to get on with it.

You also need to speak to someone in Accounts Payable – they need to get on the phone and keep the suppliers sweet. If you delay paying your suppliers for long enough (and 67 days is quite a long time!), then they will stop supplying you. The wheels will come off your business model in a very short space of time if your suppliers stop supplying your business.

And, while you are in the accounts department, you might want to speak to the financial controller. While this company might be well run operationally, it does not appear to be particularly well run financially. They need to implement a comprehensive budgeting system, produce management accounts and, ultimately, undertake accurate cash flow forecasting. They will then be in a position to go and see the bank manager and negotiate the conversion of the overdraft into a long-term loan and agree the terms of repayment of this loan.

Chapter summary

So far we have been through the basic financial structure of a business and looked at the key financial statements and how they interact with each other.

We have then undertaken some key ratio analysis, to help us to become more familiar with those statements. This exercise also helped show how much and what sort of information is contained in those financial statements.

The first half of this book has been focused on building up the big picture of a business and how it works from a financial perspective. This is a key part of *How to Talk Finance* – understanding the background to the internal financial workings of a business. Remember, line managers in a business generally will be responsible just for the P&L for their department – the finance department will run the balance sheet of the business that sits behind the P&L, and the cash flow for the company, too. Understanding how these three interact is crucial in understanding the finances of a company as a whole.

So, by now, you should start to feel much more comfortable with the financial aspects of your business, particularly when talking to members of the finance department – understanding their concerns (primarily not running out of cash!).

The second half of this book now will focus on the internal finances of the business – the income and the costs that you may come across and how they are treated. When working through the following sections, try to keep in the back of your mind the big picture that we have drawn up so far. Every decision by a line manager has a financial impact; while you might see the impact in the P&L, it will also affect the balance sheet and the cash flow of the business – understanding and appreciating this inter-connectedness of the accounts will allow you to appreciate the challenges of running the business from a financial, as well as opera-tional, perspective to a much greater degree, and therefore be able to make decisions from a more financially aware perspective.

 Next steps

▶ Think about companies in the news that are in financial difficulties (hint – football clubs often are a good place to start).

▶ See if you can get hold of their accounts and marry up what is being said about them in the papers with your analysis (use the check list at the beginning of this chapter to guide you).

6

Costs

'Beware of little expenses. A small leak will sink a great ship.'

Benjamin Franklin

 ## Aim

So far in this book we have looked at the financial statements of a business, and what those statements tell us about the business.

We now turn our attention to some of the detail within the accounts. This chapter focuses on costs and other accounting concepts that you may come across in your business.

 ## Outcomes

By the end of this chapter you will be able to:

▶ identify direct and indirect costs

▶ consider how costs behave

▶ learn how to (financially) treat costs

▶ appreciate the difference between opex and capex

▶ understand accruals, prepayments, accrued income and deferred income.

What sort of costs can I expect to encounter at work?

Let us start by looking at the costs of the business. As a manager in your company, your primary focus usually will be on the costs of your team, department or business unit and how you can manage those costs.

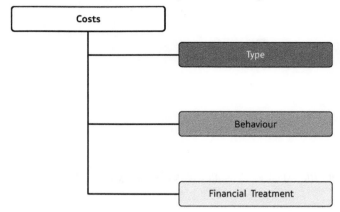

We can look at costs in terms of the type of costs that you might find in a business, how those costs behave and how they are treated financially. Let us start with the different types of cost.

What are the different types of cost?

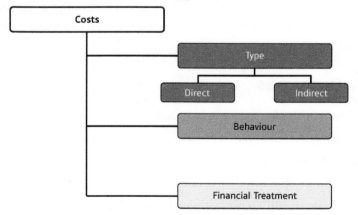

Costs can be divided into two main categories – direct costs and indirect costs.

Direct costs are those costs that can be allocated specifically to a particular product, such as a cost of sale.

Indirect costs are all other costs that cannot be allocated to a particular product. Often, these are referred to as overheads – such as rent, rates, finance (department), human resources (department), etc.

The distinction between the two types of costs is not black and white.

Let us return to A&B Ltd. Having been trading apples in Chapter 1, the company has now moved into the production of dog food.

In order to produce a tin of dog food, the company needs the following items: some dog food, a tin in which to put the food and a label for the tin. All of these items are direct costs of producing the finished product – a tin of dog food.

But, in order to produce a tin of dog food, A&B Ltd has to run a production line.

What about the costs of running the production line – the staff costs, the electricity etc? And what about the rent and rates of the warehouse in which the production line is situated?

So, you can see that some costs are very obviously direct (the dog food and tin, etc.) and some costs are very obviously indirect, such as the rent on the head office. The finance team will decide at what point to make the distinction for costs that are marginal – i.e. that could be one or the other.

Having made this distinction, the finance team have to apply this categorisation on a consistent basis. There is no point in treating the production line staff as a direct cost one month and then as an indirect cost the next month. Why do you think this is?

One of the principles of accounting is one of consistency. ('Why did the accountant cross the road?' 'Because they crossed the road last year.' Not very funny, but reflects the fact that accountants like consistency.) This consistency will enable comparability – not only between different companies, but also for your company on a month-by-month basis.

A&B Ltd will be examining its gross margin on dog food each month. If some costs are randomly being included in this calculation (i.e. classified as direct costs) in some months and then excluded (i.e. classified as indirect costs) in other months, then the analysis will, effectively, become meaningless.

What sort of costs can you find in your business? Are they direct or indirect costs? Now consider how those costs behave.

? What sort of costs in your business would be considered to be direct?

? What sort of costs would be considered to be indirect?

How do costs behave?

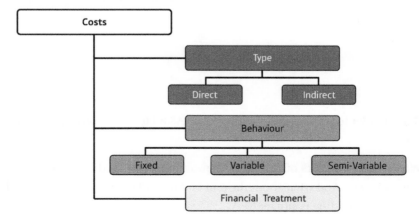

Costs generally behave in one of three ways – fixed, variable and semi variable or stepped. Let us look at each of these in turn.

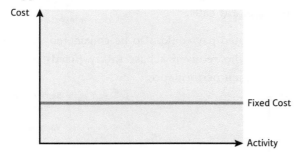

A fixed cost is one that does not change with the level of activity in a business. A typical example of this is rent or rates that are paid on a building. It does not matter how many apples or tins of dog food A&B produces or sells, the rent on their premises will remain the same. Fixed costs are more likely to be indirect costs.

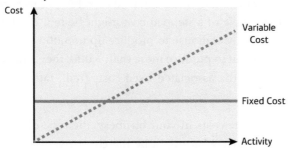

A variable cost is one that always changes with the level of activity. For A&B Ltd, the obvious example of a variable cost would be the cost of the apples or the raw materials (i.e. the inputs) for making the dog food. If A&B Ltd wants to sell more apples, then the company will have to buy more apples.

But there may be other variable costs to the business. What about electricity? Perhaps the more tins of dog food that are produced, the more electricity is required to run the machinery. Variable costs are more likely to be direct costs.

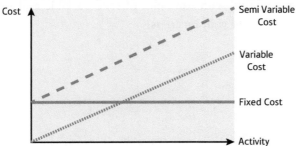

A semi variable cost is a cost that has an element of both fixed and variable. Telephone costs might be a good example of this – a fixed line rental, plus the additional cost of any calls.

Any performance-related pay could also be considered as a semi-variable cost; the salesman who received a base salary (fixed) plus commission (variable) based on their performance.

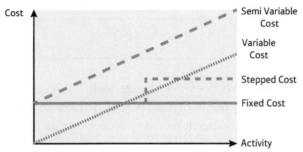

A stepped cost is one that looks like a fixed cost, but jumps at certain levels of activity. An example of a stepped cost might be rent on the warehouse. A&B Ltd can use one warehouse to produce up to 5,000 tins of dog food a year (for example), but to produce more than 5,000, they will need a second warehouse, with all the associated fixed costs (rent, rates, etc.) associated with that warehouse.

When considering the costs in your business, the type of cost and how it might behave, consider what might be the cost drivers – i.e. what are the underlying causes that make a cost go up or down?

So, we have considered the difference types of cost that you might come across in your business and how they might behave; the final consideration is how they should be treated.

? Can you identify some fixed and some variable costs in your business?

? Do they behave **exactly** in this way? Why do you think this is?

? Can you come up with examples of semi variable and stepped costs that are specific to your business?

How are costs treated financially?

```
Costs
        ┌──────────────────────────────┐
        │            Type              │
        │    ┌─────────┐  ┌─────────┐   │
        │    │ Direct  │  │ Indirect│   │
        └──────────────────────────────┘
        ┌──────────────────────────────┐
        │          Behaviour           │
        │  ┌──────┐ ┌────────┐ ┌──────────────┐
        │  │Fixed │ │Variable│ │Semi-Variable │
        └──────────────────────────────┘
        ┌──────────────────────────────┐
        │     Financial Treatment      │
        │    ┌─────────┐  ┌─────────┐   │
        │    │ Direct  │  │ Direct  │   │
        └──────────────────────────────┘
```

When considering how costs are treated, we are looking at the difference between **opex** and **capex**.

So, what is opex?

Opex stands for operational expenditure. This relates to costs that are incurred in the ongoing day-to-day running of the business (such as those we have already identified – rent, rates, salaries, etc.).

These costs will appear in the P&L account and will have a direct impact on profit – i.e. the more you spend on staff or rent, the less profit your business will make (assuming that there is no corresponding increase in sales).

So, what is capex?

Capex stands for capital expenditure. This relates to the cost of assets – such as plant and machinery – that will add value to the business, not only in this year, but also in future years. So, if A&B Ltd purchases a machine for £10,000 to put the dog food into the tin, then they will treat this purchase as capex. The machine will appear on the balance sheet under non-current assets and so, at the point of purchase, will have no impact on the P&L account (remember, when a company buys a machine, it is merely transforming one form of asset – cash – into another form of asset – machine).

The cost of the machine will be written off over the period of its lifetime, and so will have a deferred impact on profit – via depreciation.

? What sorts of costs are treated as opex in your business?

? What might be treated as capex?

? Does your business try to use capex as much as possible? Or as little as possible?

? Why do you think this is?

So, should a cost be opex or capex?

How can I tell if a cost is opex or capex?

We have established the difference between opex and capex, but is the distinction clear-cut?

Sometimes, if you ask a member of the finance department, 'Is this item of expenditure opex or capex?' they will reply, 'It depends; what would you like it to be?' (again followed by, 'Are you buying or selling?').

What do they mean? Surely it is either one or the other, and cannot be both? Well, let us look at an example.

Arthur has just purchased some office furniture for A&B Ltd. Unfortunately, Arthur has no idea how to assemble the furniture (his skills lie elsewhere), so he employs Imogen to assemble the furniture for him. Imogen suggests that she would be better off doing it by herself:

Arthur paid £200 for the furniture, and pays Imogen £50 to assemble the furniture. Once it has been assembled, Arthur speaks to his finance team and asks them how to account for these two items of expenditure.

The accountants give him two options:

▶ **Option 1** – the £200 spent on the furniture is capex (and so appears in the balance sheet) and the £50 paid to Imogen is opex (a cost of assembling the furniture). Outcome – profits are reduced by £50 in this year and the asset of £200 is depreciated over future years.

▶ **Option 2** – the £200 spent on the furniture is capex (and so appears in the balance sheet) and the £50 paid to Imogen is **also** capex, as Imogen has created an additional £50 of value. The furniture in a flat pack state is not as useful for running a business as the final assembled furniture, so Imogen must have added value. Another way of looking at this is that, if you order the furniture to be delivered ready assembled, then probably you will pay more than if it is delivered as a flat pack.

So, the outcome under option 2 is that there is **no** effect on the profit at the point of purchase, but the depreciation charge will be higher in future years (as the asset is now £250 rather than the £200 valuation under option 1).

The £50 paid to Imogen is said to have been capitalised – that is, treated as an item of capex – or capital expenditure – and therefore will appear in the balance sheet.

Which is correct? Often you will hear the finance team talking about the accounting rules (international financial reporting standards – IFRS; United Kingdom generally accepted accounting practice – UKGAAP; United States generally accepted accounting practice – USGAAP; financial reporting standards – FRS; etc.), which are guidelines as to how things can be accounted for. These provide guidance on how costs might be treated (for example, you cannot capitalise training costs, however much you might think that the company will benefit for many years to come from the time management workshop that you attended last week).

It is important to have an overall view of the objective of the company. Some companies are very much more focused on short-term profits – and there is, therefore, pressure to capitalise costs where possible; remember – capitalising a cost does not remove that cost, it merely defers it to a future period. The cost will end up hitting the P&L account at some point in the future via depreciation.

Note that, under both options, the impact on cash is the same. It is, therefore, fairly easy for the finance team to manipulate profit, but much less easy to manipulate cash!

? Think of some of the projects that are being implemented in your business. Are they opex projects?

? Or capex projects? Or a mixture of both?

What is the difference between an operating lease and a finance lease?

Imagine that you were looking to acquire a photocopier for use in your office; the company who will supply you with the photocopier gives you two options to finance the purchase:

▶ **Option 1** (finance lease or capital lease) – you could buy the copier for £6,000. They will lend you the £6,000 (interest-free), which you have to repay in £500 instalments each month for a year.

▶ **Option 2** (operating lease) – you can rent the photocopier for 11 months at a rate of £500 per month. In month 12, you have the option of buying the photocopier for a final payment of £500.

Think about the cash implications of these two options. Both options will involve paying £500 per month for a year – a total of £6,000. So, what is the difference?

In the first option, the photocopier will sit on your balance sheet as an asset. The amount that you owe the leasing company will also appear on the balance sheet as a liability. Each month, as you pay £500, the liability will reduce.

In the second option, you do not own the photocopier, and so it will not appear on your balance sheet – the only effect is the £500 rent that appears in your P&L each month (in fact, there may be no difference in the effect on profit if you choose to write off the asset under option 1 over a year).

Option 2 is a form of off balance sheet finance – where an asset is leased rather than owned. Think about the effect that this might have, for example, on the return on capital. By leasing the asset, there is less capital (no debt and no fixed asset relating to the photocopier) and so return on investment should improve.

The accountants tend to approach these two scenarios by looking at what they call **substance over form** – let us look at another example:

If you buy a car on a hire purchase (HP) agreement then it would appear that this is option 2 – you are, in effect, renting the car on a monthly basis – with the option to buy it at the end of the rental period for a specific sum of money. But the accountants would look at the contract – who is responsible for insuring the vehicle; taxing it; and sorting out any repairs? In this case it will be you – in effect, you actually own the vehicle, and so this would be accounted for under option 1 – as a finance lease.

Compare this to the car that you rent while on holiday. The car rental company is responsible for tax, insurance and repairs, and so, clearly, this is option 2 – an operating lease.

There are tax implications of finance versus operating leases – usually specific to the circumstances of the company entering into the agreement. As a general rule, though, a lease is classified as a finance lease if the contract transfers a substantial amount of the risk of running the asset from the lessor to the lessee.

Remember – an operating lease will have a direct impact on the profit that a business makes (as the rental payments are treated as an expense), while under a finance lease, the impact on profit will be though the depreciation of the asset.

? Do you make any decisions regarding leases? If so, see if you can obtain the contract. How would you treat it if you were in the finance team?

? See if you can find out exactly how it has been treated. Do you agree?

What is depreciation?

So, just what, exactly, is depreciation? Most people think that the aim of depreciation is to reflect the loss in value of an asset over time. However, depreciation is less concerned with value, and is actually focused on **matching** the cost of an asset over its useful economic life.

In Chapter 2 we introduced the concept of the accruals or matching concept – whereby we recognise a sale in the period in which it is earned and a cost in the period in which it is incurred – not when the cash was received or paid.

In exactly the same way, the cost of the office furniture for A&B Ltd is recognised over its useful economic life – in effect, for how long it is expected to be used.

Let us return to Imogen – who assembled the office furniture for Arthur. Imogen has a company car (her office furniture assembly business is clearly very successful!) – a £160,000 supercar:

Imogen intends to drive her company car for 15 years, at the end of which she will sell it for £10,000.

The aim of a company's depreciation policy is to match the cost of an asset (£160,000), less any residual value (£10,000), to its useful economic life (15 years). This can be represented on a graph as follows:

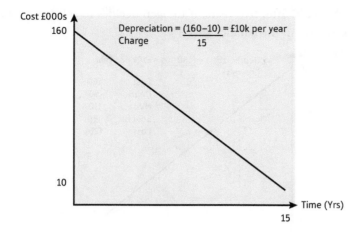

This method of depreciation is known as straight line depreciation – where the value of an asset is written off on a straight-line basis.

? What is the depreciation policy in your business?

? Does this appear reasonable to you?

So, what about the value of the car over the 15 years? A more accurate picture of the market value of the car during the time that Imogen is driving around in it might be as follows:

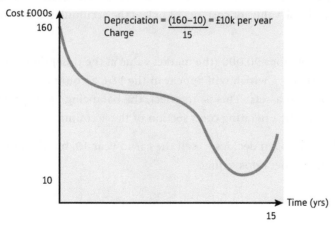

As Imogen drives it off the forecourt, the car drops significantly in value; it then levels out for a bit and, when someone crashes into her, it falls again, then gets repaired. After 15 years, it becomes a classic car and starts going up in value!

So, what happens after five years, if Imogen decides to sell the car for less than it is 'worth' in the balance sheet?

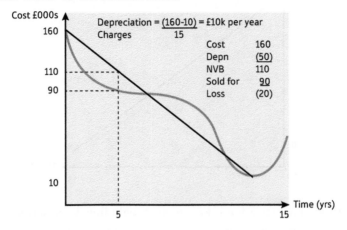

The depreciation charge of the car has been calculated as the cost, less the residual value, divided by its economic life; so, in this example, the car is depreciated at £10,000 per year.

So, after five years, the total accumulated depreciation (i.e. the total amount by which the car has been depreciated so far) is £50,000 (five years at £10,000 per year). The car is, therefore, said to have a net book value (NBV – that is the book value, or cost, net of or less the accumulated depreciation) of £110,000.

If the car is sold for £90,000 (the market value at the time) then it is sold at a loss of £20,000 – which will appear in the P&L account as a 'loss on the disposal of fixed assets'. This is, in effect, the balancing figure and usually will appear in the operating costs section of the accounts.

Now, what if Imogen decides to sell the car in year 10, but the sale price is higher than the net book value?

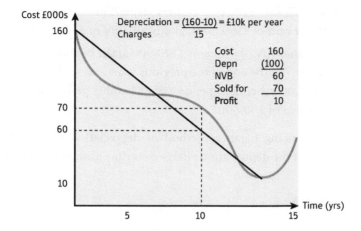

In this example, the car now has a NBV of £60,000 (that is, a cost of £160,000 less the accumulated depreciation of £100,000). If Imogen sells the car for £70,000, then she will make a profit of £10,000.

Again, this profit will appear in the P&L account (as an income this time, not an expense) within the 'other operating charges' section of the accounts.

Depreciation can be charged on a straight line or reducing balance basis.

? Are you aware of any assets that have been sold in your business?

? Did they generate a profit or a loss?

? What does this tell you about the accuracy of your depreciation policy?

What is the difference between straight line and reducing balance?

Straight-line depreciation is the method adopted above (you will notice that the depreciation line is straight).

The alternative is known as **reducing balance**. The reducing balance approach to depreciation merely reduces the NBV of the previous year by a given percentage.

So, for example, if Imogen's car was being depreciated by 25 per cent per year on a reducing balance basis, then:

▶ in year one, the NBV (which, at the time of purchase, is the same as the cost of the car) was £160,000 and the depreciation charge is £40,000 (being 25 per cent of £160,000), giving an NBV of £120,000

▶ in year two, the NBV of the car is £120,000 at the beginning of the year (being the NBV at the end of the previous year) and so the depreciation charge is £30,000 (being 25 per cent of £120,000), giving an NBV at the end of year two of £90,000.

Applying the reducing balance method of depreciation will result in a different profile of the depreciation charge over time as shown by the dotted line below:

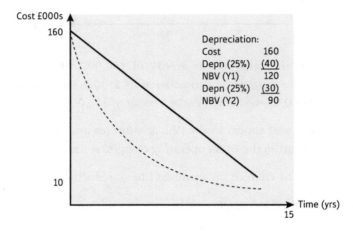

Usually, you will be able to find a note in the accounts of the company regarding their depreciation policy, and how they treat amortisation, too. Here is the note from the accounts of Tesco:

Property, plant and equipment

Property, plant and equipment is carried at cost less accumulated depreciation and any recognised impairment in value.

Property, plant and equipment is depreciated on a straight-line basis to its residual value over its anticipated useful economic life. The following depreciation rates are applied for the group:

▶ *Freehold and leasehold buildings with greater than 40 years unexpired – at 2.5 per cent of cost;*

▶ *Leasehold properties with less than 40 years unexpired period of the lease; and*

▶ *Plant, equipment, fixtures and fittings and motor vehicles – at rates varying from 9–50 per cent.*

Assets held under finance leases are depreciated over their expected useful lives on the same basis as owned assets or, when shorter, over the term of the relevant lease.

? Do you use a reducing balance depreciation policy in your business?

? Why do you think this is?

What is the difference between depreciation and amortisation?

Very simply, tangible assets are depreciated and intangible assets are amortised.

? Does your business have any intangible fixed assets?

? How are they amortised (i.e. what is the company's policy)?

? Do you think that this is reasonable?

What is impairment?

We have seen that depreciation is the writing off (or matching) of the cost of an asset to its useful economic life. An impairment charge is a one-off reduction in the value of an asset.

Imagine that A&B Ltd purchased a table 7 years ago for £100, which they intend to use for 10 years. Today the table would be worth (i.e. NBV) £30 – being the cost (£100) less total accumulated depreciation to date of £70 (7 years at £10 per year).

If Lucy then sat on the table and broke it, the table now would be deemed as worthless. Yet, the table continues to appear in the accounts with an NBV of £30. Now this is misleading, meaning A&B Ltd would have to write down – or impair – the value of the table to an NBV of nil.

So, we have seen how accountants use the accounting concepts of depreciation and amortisation to ensure that costs are correctly matched to the correct period. They also use other accounting adjustments, such as accruals, prepayments, accrued income and deferred income in order to ensure that costs and income appear in the correct accounting period to which they relate.

? Can you identify any impairment charges in your accounts?

? To what do you think they relate?

What are accruals, prepayments, accrued income and deferred income?

The **accruals** or **matching concept** states that we recognise an income or expense in the income statement (P&L account) in the period in which it is earned or incurred, not in the period in which payment is received or made.

Thus, if you consider a training course:

Jan.   PO (purchase order) is raised

Feb.   PO is approved

Mar.   Course is booked

Apr.   Invoice is received

May   Invoice is queried

Jun.   Course is attended

Jul.   Invoice is agreed

Aug.   Invoice is approved

Sep.   Invoice is paid

Oct.   Remittance advice is submitted

Nov.   Receipt is acknowledged

Dec.   Cheque clears bank

In which month does the cost of the training course hit the income statement or P&L account?

The answer is June – when you attend the course. It does not matter when it was booked or when the invoice was paid – the cost of the course was incurred when it was actually run.

In order to ensure that costs (and revenues) are allocated to the correct period, we use prepayments, accruals, accrued income and deferred income.

In order to understand these concepts, let us look at an example.

Alice has a garden with a large lawn and Kate has a lawnmower. So, Alice asks Kate if Kate will mow her lawn for £100. Kate considers the offer and accepts, but states that Alice will have to pay the full £100 in advance.

So, Alice pays Kate the £100, and then thinks to herself, 'What is the cost to me of cutting the grass?' The answer is, at the point of payment, nothing. Why? Because while Alice may have paid for the service, she has not yet received the benefit of the service; she is either owed £100 worth of lawn cutting services from Kate or she is owed a refund. Either way, she is owed something – which is an asset. Alice has prepaid – i.e. paid in advance for the service.

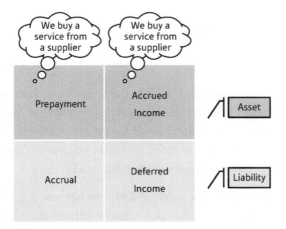

Look at the accounting table (above) as this may help you understand the concept. If you are buying a service (like Alice), then you are on the left-hand side of the table and, if you are selling a service (like Kate), then you are on the right-hand side of the table.

Alice is owed £100 of (grass cutting) service, or a refund of £100 – either way she is owed the £100, so will treat it as an asset (prepayment). Kate has received £100 but has not yet earned the money. She now owes Alice £100 of grass cutting services or a £100 refund – either way she owes £100, so will treat it as a liability (deferred income – that is, income that she has received, but must defer until she earns it).

Have a look at the balance sheets of Alice and Kate:

Balance sheets

		Alice	Kate
Assets			
	Cash	-£ 100	£ 100
	Prepayment		
	Accrued income		
		-£ 100	£ 100
Liabilities			
	Accruals		
	Deferred income		
		£	£
Net assets		-£ 100	£ 100
Shareholders' funds			
	Investment		
	Retained profit		
		£	£

After the initial transaction, Alice has paid £100 – so her cash had gone down by £100; but she has not incurred any expense (remember, the expense will reduce her retained profit figure in the balance sheet) so this must be nil. Net assets have reduced by £100 and shareholders' funds have not changed. The balance sheet does not balance!

Kate, on the other hand, has received £100, so her assets (cash) have gone up. But, again, because she has not actually earned the money (she still owes Alice the lawn mowing services, or a refund), then she cannot show this money in the P&L account, so the retained profit is still zero – and, again, Kate's balance sheet does not balance.

In order to address this, Alice posts a **prepayment** – a payment in advance of the service – which is an asset. Alice is saying that she is owed £100 of lawn mowing services.

Kate, on the other hand, posts a **deferred income** – income that has been received, but must be deferred until it is earned. This is, therefore, treated as a liability (Kate owes Alice £100 of lawn mowing services or £100 refund – either way this is a liability).

Reflecting these two transactions in their balance sheet now results in both balance sheets balancing:

Balance sheets

		Alice		Kate	
Assets					
	Cash	-£	100	£	100
	Prepayment	£	100		
	Accrued income				
		£		£	100
Liabilities					
	Accruals				
	Deferred income			-£	100
		£		-£	100
Net assets		£		£	
Shareholders' funds					
	Investment				
	Retained profit				
		£		£	

Now let us fast forward. Kate turned up at Alice's house and has now cut 25 per cent of the grass. The two ladies are sitting on the patio, enjoying a cool glass of lemonade, and considering their individual finances.

Alice is thinking to herself that she has paid for £100 of grass cutting services, but has received only £25 worth. She has, therefore, prepaid the balance of £75, and has incurred the cost of the £25 that has been cut – which must now appear in her P&L account as an expense.

Kate is thinking to herself that she has now earned £25. While she has received the full payment of £100, she has to defer only £75 of this income. The £25 that she has earned will now appear in her P&L account as a sale or income.

Balance sheets

		Alice		Kate	
Assets					
	Cash	-£	100	£	100
	Prepayment	£	75		
	Accrued income				
		-£	25	£	100
Liabilities					
	Accruals				
	Deferred income			-£	75
		£		-£	75
Net assets		-£	25	£	25
Shareholders' funds					
	Investment				
	Retained profit	-£	25	£	25
		-£	25	£	25

When Kate is halfway through the job – and has cut 50 per cent of the grass – then Alice will recognise £50 of expense and Kate will recognise £50 of income, the balance remaining as a prepayment/deferred income:

Balance sheets

		Alice		Kate	
Assets					
	Cash	-£	100	£	100
	Prepayment	£	50		
	Accrued income				
		-£	50	£	100
Liabilities					
	Accruals				
	Deferred income			-£	50
		£		-£	50
Net assets		-£	50	£	50
Shareholders' funds					
	Investment				
	Retained profit	-£	50	£	50
		-£	50	£	50

And, when the job is 75 per cent done, Alice will show expenses of £75 (with a £25 prepayment) and Kate will reflect £75 of income (with a £25 deferred income):

Balance sheets

		Alice		Kate	
Assets					
	Cash	-£	100	£	100
	Prepayment	£	25		
	Accrued income				
		-£	75	£	100
Liabilities					
	Accruals				
	Deferred income			-£	25
		£		-£	25
Net assets		-£	75	£	75
Shareholders' funds					
	Investment				
	Retained profit	-£	75	£	75
		-£	75	£	75

When Kate has finished cutting the lawn, Alice's P&L account will reflect the full cost and Kate's P&L account will show the amount earned:

Balance sheets

		Alice		Kate	
Assets					
	Cash	-£	100	£	100
	Prepayment	£			
	Accrued income				
		-£	100	£	100
Liabilities					
	Accruals				
	Deferred income			£	
		£		£	
Net assets		-£	100	£	100
Shareholders' funds					
	Investment				
	Retained profit	-£	100	£	100
		-£	100	£	100

Now let us look at this transaction again. What would have happened if Alice had agreed to pay Kate only once the work had been completed, rather than in advance?

If they had agreed to this, there would be no accounting entries, to start with. Alice has not paid for anything, and has not received any service; Kate has not been paid and has not provided any service. Remember – a future commitment is not a current period liability.

Their balance sheets would look like this:

Balance sheets

Assets		Alice	Kate
	Cash		
	Prepayment		
	Accrued income		
		£ _____	£ _____
Liabilities			
	Accruals		
	Deferred income		
		£ _____	£ _____
Net assets		£ _____	£ _____
Shareholders' funds			
	Investment		
	Retained profit		
		£ _____	£ _____

When 25 per cent of the grass had been cut, as Alice and Kate were enjoying their glasses of lemonade, they would be thinking to themselves as follows:

▶ Alice would be thinking that she has had 25 per cent of her lawn cut. She now owes Kate £25, but has not yet paid it. She therefore needs to accrue for her costs (remember, Alice is on the left-hand side of the accounting table because she is buying a service, and owes the amount to Kate, so this is treated as a liability).

▶ Meanwhile, Kate is thinking that she has earned £25 from cutting 25 per cent of the lawn. This is owed to her, so is an asset, and so will be accounted for as accrued income. Thus their two balance sheets will look like this:

Balance sheets

		Alice		Kate	
Assets					
	Cash				
	Prepayment				
	Accrued income			£	25
		£		£	25
Liabilities					
	Accruals	-£	25		
	Deferred income				
		-£	25	£	
Net assets		-£	25	£	25
Shareholders' funds					
	Investment				
	Retained profit	-£	25	£	25
		-£	25	£	25

When the lawn is half mown, their balance sheets will look like this:

Balance sheets

		Alice		Kate	
Assets					
	Cash				
	Prepayment				
	Accrued income			£	50
		£		£	50
Liabilities					
	Accruals	-£	50		
	Deferred income				
		-£	50	£	
Net assets		-£	50	£	50
Shareholders' funds					
	Investment				
	Retained profit	-£	50	£	50
		-£	50	£	50

And, when the lawn is 75 per cent cut, their balance sheets will look like this:

Balance sheets

		Alice	Kate
Assets			
	Cash		
	Prepayment		
	Accrued income		£ 75
		£	£ 75
Liabilities			
	Accruals	-£ 75	
	Deferred income		
		-£ 75	£
Net assets		-£ 75	£ 75
Shareholders' funds			
	Investment		
	Retained profit	-£ 75	£ 75
		-£ 75	£ 75

As Kate finishes the work, she will reflect that she is now owed the full £100 that she has earned and Alice now owes the full £100 having now incurred the full cost:

Balance sheets

		Alice	Kate
Assets			
	Cash		
	Prepayment		
	Accrued income		£ 100
		£	£ 100
Liabilities			
	Accruals	-£ 100	
	Deferred income		
		-£ 100	£
Net assets		-£ 100	£ 100
Shareholders' funds			
	Investment		
	Retained profit	-£ 100	£ 100
		-£ 100	£ 100

If Kate were to give an invoice to Alice, then in Alice's balance sheet the accruals (liability) would merely become a trade creditor (liability), with no effect on the P&L account. In Kate's balance sheet, the accrued income (asset) would become a trade debtor (asset), again with no effect on the P&L account.

When Alice pays Kate, this removes the liability from Alice's balance sheet and the asset from Kate's balance sheet as follows:

Balance sheets

		Alice	Kate
Assets			
	Cash	£ 100	£ 100
	Prepayment		
	Accrued income		
		£ 100	£ 100
Liabilities			
	Accruals		
	Deferred income		
		£	£
Net assets		£ 100	£ 100
Shareholders' funds			
	Investment		
	Retained profit	£ 100	£ 100
		£ 100	£ 100

Now go back over the two examples (payment in advance and payment in arrears). What you should notice is that, irrespective of when the physical payment was made, the costs (for Alice) and income (for Kate) appeared in their P&L accounts at exactly the same time.

This is the aim of using prepayments, accruals, deferred and accrued income; the finance team are trying to ensure that costs and income are matched (i.e. appear in the P&L account) in the period in which they are earned/incurred, irrespective of when the cash actually changed hands or when invoices were raised.

So, now that we understand how the finance team use accounting concepts to allocate costs (and income) into the correct period, we can examine how to mark these costs up to achieve a target margin.

? What sort of accruals and prepayments do you come across in your business?

? Is it the responsibility of the finance team to raise them, or line managers in the business?

? Does your business make adjustments for accrued and/or deferred income?

? Why do you think this is?

What is the difference between margin and mark-up?

Now assume that Kate, rather than cutting the grass herself, is going to subcontract the work to Imogen (who has already proved herself as rather adept at putting together office furniture).

Imogen will charge Kate £100 to cut the grass, and Kate decides to **mark up** the costs when pricing for Alice by 20 per cent. What will be the gross margin?

Imogen is going to charge Kate £100; Kate marks up the costs by 20 per cent and therefore will charge Alice £120 (£100 × 120%). For Kate, she will record sales of £120 and costs of £100, leaving a gross profit of £20. What will be her gross margin?

The answer is less than 20 per cent (approximately 17 per cent in this example):

Margin versus mark up

Base cost	£ 100	£ 100	
Mark up	20%	25%	
Sales price	£ 120	£ 125	

Profit & loss account

Sales	£ 120	£ 125	
Cost of sales	£ 100	£ 100	
Gross profit	£ 20	£ 25	

Gross margin

$\dfrac{\text{Gross profit}}{\text{Sales}}$	$\dfrac{£20}{£120}$	$\dfrac{£25}{£120}$
	17%	20%

Why? Because when Kate marks up by 20 per cent, she is arriving at a sales price of £120, leaving her with a gross profit of £20. But the gross margin expresses the £20 of profit as a percentage of sales (£120) and not costs (£100).

If Kate wanted to achieve a gross margin of 20 per cent, then she would have to mark up her costs by more than 20 – 25 per cent, in fact. To work this out, Kate needs to divide the original cost by (1 less the mark up) which in this case is (1–0.2) which is 0.8.

Dividing the cost (£100) by 0.8 will give a sales price of £125, which is needed to achieve a gross margin of 20 per cent.

So, we can see that, if you are working in a cost plus environment (i.e. typically you work out what it will cost you and then add a percentage when charging your clients), then you need to be careful that you do not fall short of your target margin.

When you are working out the total costs to charge the client, how do you ensure that all costs are accounted for? This is where we look at absorption costing.

? Does your business use mark up costing?

?   If so, what is the target margin?

?   By how much must costs be marked up to achieve this margin?

What is absorption costing?

When we examined direct and indirect costs, we considered the costs to A&B Ltd of making dog food. Let us revisit that example.

Here are the three main ingredients to make a tin of dog food, and their respective costs: dog food £1; tin 25p; label 5p.

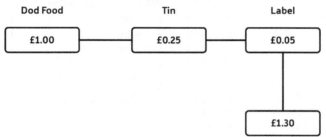

If we look at the raw materials (direct costs) we can see that it costs £1.30 to make a single tin of dog food. But what about the individual, Matt, who works on the production line? We need to **absorb** his costs into the cost of the tin of dog food, so as to reflect the **true** or **fully absorbed** cost of getting the finished tin of dog food to its final condition.

Let us assume that Matt is paid £100 per day, and can reasonably expect to produce 200 tins of dog food. This works out at 50p per tin.

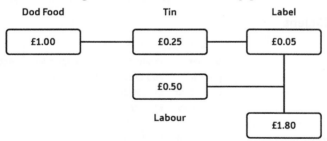

Now the cost of each tin of dog food has risen to £1.80, as the additional costs have been absorbed into the product. We do not have to stop there – we can consider Matt's boss (Sarah), rent, rates, heat, light, etc. – all of these are direct costs and can be absorbed into the cost of the business.

Now let us consider what happens when Grace works on the production line. Grace is a very efficient worker, and is able to produce 250 tins in a single day. This means that we will end up with 250 tins that are 'worth' £450 (i.e. 250 tins × £1.80 each), but we have incurred only £425 of costs (i.e. 250 tins × £1.30 each plus the £100 paid to Grace) – we have over-absorbed the costs into the product and now need to make an adjustment:

Too efficient

	Budget per tin	Product 250 tins:	(Over-)/Under-absorption		Actual costs
Dog food	£ 1.00	£ 250.00			£ 250.00
Tin	£ 0.25	£ 62.50			£ 62.50
Label	£ 0.05	£ 12.50			£ 12.50
Total raw materials	£ 1.30	£ 325.00	£		£ 325.00
Labour*	£ 0.50	£ 125.00	-£ 25.00		£ 100.00
Total cost of tin	£ 1.80	£ 450.00	-£ 25.00		£ 425.00
*Labour cost per day	£ 100.00				
Tins to be produced	£ 200.00				
Cost per tin	£ 0.50				

As a result of Grace working so efficiently, we need to make an adjustment, due to over-absorption of costs, of £25.

Now, what if Daisy is on the production line? Daisy is much less efficient than Grace, and can produce only 150 tins per day. In this case we will be showing an under-absorption – we have paid Daisy £100, but only £75 has been allocated to the product, and again we need to make an adjustment:

Too inefficient

	Budget per tin	Product 250 tins:	(Over-)/Under-absorption		Actual costs
Dog food	£ 1.00	£ 150.00			£ 150.00
Tin	£ 0.25	£ 37.50			£ 37.50
Label	£ 0.05	£ 7.50			£ 7.50
Total raw materials	£ 1.30	£ 195.00	£		£ 195.00
Labour*	£ 0.50	£ 75.00	£ 25.00		£ 100.00
Total cost of tin	£ 1.80	£ 270.00	£ 25.00		£ 295.00
*Labour cost per day	£ 100.00				
Tins to be produced	£ 200.00				
Cost per tin	£ 0.50				

So, we can see that absorption costing will give us an increasingly accurate view of the business, but will involve much more work from the finance team in making over-/under-absorption costing adjustments.

? Is absorption costing used in your business?

? What impact does it have on operational decision making?

? What do you think are the advantages and disadvantages of this approach?

What is break even analysis?

Oscar is considering employing Daisy and Grace and starting to produce tinned dog food – selling for £3 per tin.

If he treats all of the costs as variable costs, then he might conclude that he has to make (and sell) only one tin of dog food to **break even** – i.e. if he sells the tin for £3 and it costs him £1.80 to produce, then he will make a gross profit of £1.20 – a margin of 40 per cent.

Break even analysis

Number of units	1
Sales	£ 3.00
Cost of sale	£ 1.80
Gross profit	£ 1.20
Gross margin	40%

But he realises that he is paying Daisy and Grace on a daily basis – not per tin produced. While fully absorbed costing will ensure that the sale price covers all of the costs of the dog food – both direct and indirect – he also needs to make sure that he produces and sells enough to cover his fixed costs (in this case, the £100 paid to Daisy and Grace). First Oscar must ensure that he revisits his cost of sales figure to determine which costs are really variable, and which are, in actual fact, fixed costs?

Break even analysis

Number of units	1		1	
Sales	£	3.00	£	3.00
Cost of sale	£	1.80	£	1.30
Gross profit	£	1.20		£1.70
Gross margin		40%		57%
Fixed costs		———	£	0.50
Operating profit			£	1.20
Operating margin				40%

Now Oscar can perform his break even analysis. He has shown the fixed costs above as £0.50 – but this is, in fact, an estimate of the fixed cost per tin. The actual fixed costs are £200 (that is, £100 per day each for Daisy and Grace). Oscar can now work out the minimum number of tins to be produced to cover their costs:

Break even analysis

Number of units	1		1		118	
Sales	£	3.00	£	3.00	£	354.00
Cost of sale	£	1.80	£	1.30	£	520.00
Gross profit	£	1.20	£	1.70	£	680.00
Gross margin		40%		57%		57%
Fixed costs		———	£	0.50	£	200.00
Operating profit			£	1.20	£	480.00
Operating margin				40%		40%

Between them, Daisy and Grace have to produce and sell 118 tins of dog food per day in order to break even. This should be reasonably easy, as Oscar is expecting them to be able to produce 200 each per day. If they achieve this target, then Oscar will see a profit of £480 – an operating margin of 40 per cent.

Break even analysis

Number of units	1		1		118		400	
Sales	£	3.00	£	3.00	£	354.00	£	1,200.00
Cost of sale	£	1.80	£	1.30	£	520.00	£	520.00
Gross profit	£	1.20	£	1.70	£	680.00	£	680.00
Gross margin	40%		57%		57%		57%	
Fixed costs			£	0.50	£	200.00	£	200.00
Operating profit			£	1.20	£	480.00	£	480.00
Operating margin			40%		40%		40%	

Notice how the gross margin remains constant as the quantity that is produced and sold varies.

Break even analysis will enable Oscar to determine the minimum level of activity to cover all of the costs associated with his business. While full absorption costing will ensure that the sale price covers all of the costs of the business, variable costing will allow him to determine the volume of sales that he must hit to start making a profit; so both methods are relevant in allowing Oscar to make the correct decisions.

In this way, Oscar is now starting to consider the marginal costs of dog food. He may also want to consider sunk costs in the decision-making process.

? Is break even analysis relevant to your business?

? What is the minimum level of activity for your business/business unit to still remain profitable?

? How will operational gearing affect the break even analysis?

What are marginal costs and sunk costs?

A sunk cost is defined as a cost that has already been incurred, and therefore should not be included in the future decision-making process.

For example, imagine that Oscar employs Alexandra as head of sales; Alexandra is planning on selling a tin of dog food (cost as above – £1.80). She purchases a bus ticket for £0.50 and travels to see Olivia, who has expressed an interest in buying a tin. On arrival, Olivia states that she will only purchase the tin of dog food for £2.20.

Alexandra may be tempted not to undertake the transaction. After all, a tin of dog food that cost £1.80 to produce, plus a bus ticket of £0.50, gives a total cost of £2.30. If Olivia will only purchase the tin for £2.20, then Alexandra will make a loss on the transaction of 10p.

But the bus ticket should be considered a sunk cost for the purposes of making this decision. If Alexandra does not sell the tin of dog food to Olivia, then she will still have incurred a cost of £0.50, being the cost of the bus ticket; if she sells the tin to Olivia for £2.20, at least she will limit this loss to £0.10.

Going forward, it would appear that Alexandra should not continue to trade with Olivia (unless she can obtain the volume required to make it viable), but for the individual trade, she needs to ignore the sunk cost.

The marginal cost is a similar tool for decision-making purposes, and aims to look at the additional costs of producing one extra unit.

When we looked at fixed costs, we examined how stepped costs behaved. A stepped cost is where a fixed cost suddenly increases – the example we gave was of the rent on a warehouse where A&B Ltd produces 5,000 tins of dog food each year. The cost of producing the 5,001st tin of dog food includes not only the ingredients and raw materials, but also the cost of renting a second warehouse. For A&B Ltd, therefore, it would appear a better decision to make 5,000 tins rather than 5,001 tins. There will be a level of increased production (perhaps 6,000 tins) where it makes commercial sense to rent the new warehouse and expand production, but not at 5,001.

Thus, a clearer understanding of costs, how they behave and how they are financially treated will allow managers to make increasingly informed financial, as well as operational, decisions about their business units.

? What are the marginal costs associated with an additional unit of output for your business?

? What sort of sunk costs can you identify in your business?

What are provisions?

When the finance team talk about provisions, they are not referring to the provisions that you might take with you on a camping trip. This is a way of accounting for a loss.

In Chapter 1, Arthur and Ben sold some apples to Harry on credit (for £500, if you remember) on day two, and they collected this amount owed to them on day three. But, what if, on getting home at the end of day two, they were informed that Harry had skipped the country and was never to be heard of again?

To continue to show the asset (the amount that Harry owes A&B Ltd) in the balance sheet would be inaccurate, as they do not expect to get the money back from Harry. Yet, they do not want to write off the amount owed completely, as there is a chance that Harry will return to the country and come good on the amount owed.

In this case, Arthur and Ben might choose to **make a provision** (or provide) for the amount that they do not expect to receive (in this case £500). This will reduce their net assets by £500. In effect, having originally recorded a profit of £400 in day two, they are now forced to record a loss of £100 (overall reduction of £500):

	End of day 2	Provision	New end of day 2	Harry pays in day 3
Balance sheet				
Assets				
Stock	£ –		£ –	£ –
Debtors	£ 500.00	-£ 500.00	£ –	£ –
Cash	£ 500.00		£ 500.00	£ 1,000.00
	£ 1,000.00	-£ 500.00	£ 500.00	£ 1,000.00
Liabilities	£ 100.00		£ 100.00	£ 100.00
Net assets	£ 900.00	-£ 500.00	£ 400.00	£ 900.00
Shareholders' funds				
Investment	£ 100.00		£ 100.00	£ 100.00
Retained profits	£ 800.00	-£ 500.00	£ 300.00	£ 800.00
	£ 900.00	-£ 500.00	£ 400.00	£ 900.00

However, if Harry now pays during day three, then the company will show the whole £500 as a profit. Compare the balance sheet above for the end of day 2 and end of day 3 with the original ones discussed in Chapter 1.

The profits for each day are different:

Profit in day –	Chapter 1	Chapter 6
1	£400	£400
2	£400	(£100) loss
3	£nil	£500

The cash payments are the same, but the pattern of profits is very different.

Now we can see how easy it is for the finance team to 'manipulate' the accounts. 'Turn around Terry' has recently joined the company as the finance director. The first thing he does is to review the debtor book – all of the amounts owed to the company by its customers. He concludes that none of them is going to pay, and that the full amount must be provided for; this creates a big loss in the current year, which he blames on the outgoing finance director.

The next year all of the customers pay up (they were going to anyway) – causing the company to book large profits. 'Turn around Terry' takes the credit for turning a loss-making business into a profit-making business, banks his bonus and heads off to another company before anyone finds out.

If only it was that easy. One of the roles of the auditors is to ensure that this does not happen – any changes to (for example) the provisions policy must be justified clearly and backed up with hard data.

It is not only the debtor book that might be provided for. Car companies will establish a **warranty provision** – on the basis that cars sold with a warranty may need to be fixed. Or if a company is being sued, and there is a reasonable expectation that they will lose the case, they may need to raise a provision.

Remember – the provision merely books the loss in the current period (or the existence of the provision shows that the loss has been accounted for). It does not reflect whether or not any money has been set aside to pay out costs. A **provision** for non-payment of an amount owed (called a provision for bad and doubtful debts) merely reduces the asset (debtor) and appears as a loss in the P&L account – this is booked in the period in which the debtor is expected not to pay. When it becomes clear that they will definitely not pay, the amount is **written off** as a bad debt – note, it has already hit the P&L account when it was provided for, so writing off a bad debt that has already been provided for has no further impact on the P&L account.

? Can you identify any provisions in the financial statements of your business?

? Why do you think they are there?

? Can you think of any provisions that should be there but are not?

? Why do you think this is?

Chapter summary

We have examined the different types of cost that you might encounter in your business, how they might behave and how they are treated. Considering costs in different ways (marginal, sunk, absorbed etc.) will help us to make the correct decisions when pricing products or deciding on the level of production that is required.

Understanding costs and how they behave is a crucial skill in being able to manage budgets (Chapter 8) as well as being able to draw up business plans (Chapter 7). Before we tackle these two topics, it is necessary to consider how assets are valued – after all, financially the business is trying to create value (for the shareholders).

Next steps

▶ Consider the types of costs that you come across in your business or area. Are they predominantly fixed or variable?

▶ What does this say about your operational gearing (see Chapter 4)?

▶ What would be the impact of trying to turn fixed costs into variable or vice versa? Does your business require a lot of capital expenditure (capex)?

▶ Is there a drive to capitalise costs? If so, why do you think this is?

▶ Do you have to make accrual or prepayment adjustments at the end of each month? Or do the finance team do this for you?

▶ What about accrued or deferred income – are adjustments made to allocate income to the correct period? If so, by whom?

▶ A greater understanding of your cost base and how it behaves will increase your effectiveness in making informed financial decisions.

 Key learning points

▶ Direct costs are those that can be allocated to a product, indirect costs are overheads.

▶ Costs may be fixed, variable, semi variable or stepped.

▶ Some costs may be capitalised (capex) while others are operational and are treated as opex.

▶ Depreciation matches the cost of an asset to its useful economic life.

▶ Accruals, prepayments, accrued income and deferred income are all accounting adjustments made to ensure that costs (and income) appear in the correct accounting period.

▶ Costs may be classified based on the decision-making tools being applied – such as breakeven analysis or marginal decision making.

Test yourself

6.1   Costs can be categorised into two different types:

   (a)   current and non-current   ☐

   (b)   fixed and variable   ☐

   (c)   opex and capex   ☐

   (d)   direct and indirect   ☐

6.2   Direct costs are ones that:

   (a)   can be allocated specifically to a product or service   ☐

   (b)   are always variable   ☐

   (c)   are always fixed   ☐

   (d)   must be capitalised   ☐

6.3   Indirect costs are ones that:

   (a)   are allocated internally   ☐

   (b)   vary based on the level of activity   ☐

   (c)   cannot be specifically allocated to a product or service   ☐

   (d)   cannot be capitalised   ☐

6.4   Costs can be said to behave in one of three ways:

   (a)   up, down or stay the same   ☐

   (b)   fixed, variable or semi variable (or stepped)   ☐

   (c)   current, non-current and long-term   ☐

   (d)   opex, capex and depreciation   ☐

6.5   A fixed cost is one that:

   (a)   will jump, given a specific level of activity   ☐

   (b)   always changes with the level of activity   ☐

   (c)   has a fixed and a variable element   ☐

   (d)   never changes with the level of activity   ☐

6.6   A variable cost is one that:

   (a)   will jump, given a specific level of activity   ☐

   (b)   always changes with the level of activity   ☐

   (c)   has a fixed and a variable element   ☐

   (d)   never changes with the level of activity   ☐

6.7   A semi variable cost is one that:

(a)   will jump, given a specific level of activity ☐

(b)   always changes with the level of activity ☐

(c)   has a fixed and a variable element ☐

(d)   never changes with the level of activity ☐

6.8   A stepped cost is one that:

(a)   will jump, given a specific level of activity ☐

(b)   always changes with the level of activity ☐

(c)   has a fixed and a variable element ☐

(d)   never changes with the level of activity ☐

6.9   Costs can be treated financially in one of two ways:

(a)   opex and capex ☐

(b)   fixed and variable ☐

(c)   current and non-current ☐

(d)   profit and loss ☐

6.10   Opex is:

(a)   expenditure on special operations ☐

(b)   expenditure on the day-to-day running of the business ☐

(c)   expenditure on assets that will be used for more than one year ☐

(d)   expenditure that must be capitalised ☐

6.11   Capex is:

(a)   expenditure on special operations ☐

(b)   expenditure on the day-to-day running of the business ☐

(c)   expenditure on assets that will be used for more than one year ☐

(d)   expenditure that appears in the P&L account ☐

6.12   Capitalising a cost:

(a)   will have no impact on profit ☐

(b)   will have a deferred impact on profit via depreciation ☐

(c)   will appear in the P&L account ☐

(d)   is illegal under IFRS ☐

6.13   A finance lease is the same as:

(a)   buying an asset on credit ☐

(b)   renting an asset ☐

(c)   borrowing an asset ☐

(d)   selling an asset ☐

6.14   An operating lease is the same as:

   (a)   buying an asset on credit ☐

   (b)   renting an asset ☐

   (c)   borrowing an asset ☐

   (d)   selling an asset ☐

6.15   The aim of depreciation is to:

   (a)   reduce the value of an asset ☐

   (b)   reflect the market value of an asset in the balance sheet ☐

   (c)   reduce profits ☐

   (d)   match the cost of an asset to its useful economic life ☐

6.16   Amortisation is:

   (a)   allowed only under IFRS ☐

   (b)   the depreciation of intangible assets ☐

   (c)   the depreciation of tangible assets ☐

   (d)   determined by the auditors ☐

6.17   The two methods of depreciation are:

   (a)   straight line and impairment ☐

   (b)   impairment and reducing balance ☐

   (c)   straight line and reducing balance ☐

   (d)   variable and reducing balance ☐

6.18   NBV stands for:

   (a)   net book value ☐

   (b)   near book value ☐

   (c)   net balance value ☐

   (d)   near balance value ☐

6.19   An impairment is:

   (a)   an asset ☐

   (b)   a depreciation method ☐

   (c)   the write down in the value of an asset ☐

   (d)   a long-term liability ☐

6.20   An accrual is where:

   (a)   you have paid for a service, but not yet received that service ☐

   (b)   you have provided a service, but not yet been paid ☐

   (c)   you have received a service, but not yet paid ☐

   (d)   you have been paid, but have not yet provided the service ☐

6.21   A prepayment is where:

   (a)   you have paid for a service, but not yet received that service   ☐

   (b)   you have provided a service, but not yet been paid   ☐

   (c)   you have received a service, but not yet paid   ☐

   (d)   you have been paid, but have not yet provided the service   ☐

6.22   Deferred income is where:

   (a)   you have paid for a service, but not yet received that service   ☐

   (b)   you have provided a service, but not yet been paid   ☐

   (c)   you have received a service, but not yet paid   ☐

   (d)   you have been paid, but have not yet provided the service   ☐

6.23   Accrued income is where:

   (a)   you have paid for a service, but not yet received that service   ☐

   (b)   you have provided a service, but not yet been paid   ☐

   (c)   you have received a service, but not yet paid   ☐

   (d)   you have been paid, but have not yet provided the service   ☐

6.24   Accruals, prepayments, accrued and deferred income are all
        accounting adjustments that are designed to:

   (a)   keep the finance team busy   ☐

   (b)   adjust profit for movements in cash   ☐

   (c)   reverse capex decisions   ☐

   (d)   recognise costs and income in the periods in which they occur   ☐

6.25   When considering margin and mark up:

   (a)   margin is always higher   ☐

   (b)   mark up is always higher   ☐

   (c)   they are both always the same   ☐

   (d)   there is no relationship between the two   ☐

6.26   Absorption costing involves:

   (a)   a lot of complicated calculations   ☐

   (b)   allocating costs to other departments   ☐

   (c)   allocating costs to the units of output   ☐

   (d)   allocating costs to overheads   ☐

6.27   Breakeven analysis determines:

     (a)   the level of production required to cover fixed costs   ☐

     (b)   the level of production required to cover fixed and variable   ☐
           costs

     (c)   the level of production required to cover absorbed costs   ☐

     (d)   the level of production required to cover sunk costs   ☐

6.28   A marginal cost is:

     (a)   always very small   ☐

     (b)   the average cost per unit of output   ☐

     (c)   the total cost of all units of output   ☐

     (d)   the cost of an additional unit of output   ☐

6.29   A sunk cost is:

     (a)   a big cost that could sink the business   ☐

     (b)   a high-risk cost   ☐

     (c)   one that has already been incurred   ☐

     (d)   a future cost   ☐

6.30   A provision is:

     (a)   accounting for a future expected loss   ☐

     (b)   accounting for a future expected profit   ☐

     (c)   accounting for a past loss   ☐

     (d)   accounting for a past profit   ☐

7

CHAPTER 7
Building the business case

'I made my money by selling too soon.'

Bernard Baruch

 Aim

An investment by the business is usually undertaken in order to generate money value – measured based on the future income stream that the investment will generate. These assets are valued based on the future income stream that they will deliver.

The aim of this chapter is to build on this concept and examine how the use of discounted cash flow modelling will assist in building a strong business case for investment within the business.

 Outcomes

By the end of this chapter you will be able to:

▶ explain the time value of money concept

▶ understand terminology such as NPV, DCF and IRR

▶ produce a basic business case using discounted cash flows

▶ consider the WACC of your business.

What is the time value of money?

Antonia is asked the question: 'Would you rather have £100 now, or in a year's time?' What do you think will be Antonia's answer?

Hopefully, you will conclude that now is preferable to a year's time. Why? Because Antonia can buy more with £100 today than she can in a year's time (the purchasing power of £100 will be reduced due to inflation); alternatively, Antonia could invest £100 today and see it grow into more than £100 in a year's time.

The difference between the value of £100 today, and the value of £100 in a year's time, but expressed in today's prices, is known as the **time value of money**. This is an important concept in building the business case for investment.

This chapter will show you how to build a model in Excel. To gain the most benefit from this chapter, it is advisable to obtain access to a computer, and follow the steps outlined here to building your own model on your PC.

? What is your time value of money?

? Does your answer surprise you?

How are assets valued?

When we purchase an asset – or make an investment – we are, in effect, purchasing the future income stream associated with that asset.

Antonia, a manager in A&B Ltd, can now use this to good effect when preparing a business case for investment that she must put to the board of directors. She has identified an opportunity in the business, which will require an investment of £1 million. This investment is expected to generate additional cash flow (income net of expenses) of £200,000 per year for eight years. She considers year 0 to be now (when the investment is made), with the cash flows being generated at the end of each of the subsequent eight years. Note – this is examining future **cash flows**, not future **profit**!

Antonia produces the following model:

Year	0	1	2	3	4	5	6	7	8	9	10
Invest	£1,000,000										
Income		£200,000	£200,000	£200,000	£200,000	£200,000	£200,000	£200,000	£200,000		£1,600,000
Profit	£600,000										

Antonia concludes that her investment will generate £200,000 per year for eight years – or £1.6 million in total. For an investment of £1 million, this will leave her with £600,000 of straight profit – a 60 per cent return on her investment. She is feeling very pleased with this proposal and is about to make an appointment to present her case, when she considers the time value of money concept.

Working on the principles already discussed in this chapter, the £200,000 that the investment will generate in year 8 is not worth the same, in today's money, as the £200,000 that will be generated in year 1.

Somehow, she needs to translate the £200,000 in future years into today's equivalent. While thinking about how to go about this, she notices a bank outside of her office window – Bertie's Bank.

Antonia sees that Bertie has a sign in the bank's window, which offers 5 per cent interest on any money that is deposited with the bank. Antonia starts to wonder to herself – her proposed investment will generate (among other things) a sum of £200,000 in one year's time. How much must Antonia invest with Bertie today in order to be able to walk into the bank in a year's time and withdraw £200,000?

To answer this, she needs to solve the following equation:

Amount invested + interest earned on investment = amount at end of period

£[invest now] + (£[invest now] × 5%) = £200,000

This can be expressed as:

£[invest now] × 1.05 = £200,000

So:

$$£[\text{invest now}] = \frac{£200,000}{1.05}$$

Thus, the amount to be invested today is £190,476.19; we can check this by multiplying £190,476.19 by the interest rate (1.05).

So, Antonia has now worked out that she could invest £190,000 today into Bertie's Bank and withdraw £200,000 in a year's time (we are ignoring tax and risk in this example).

We can simplify the above formula to make the discount rate applicable to any investment amount:

Discount factor

$$\frac{1}{(1 + \text{rate})^2} \quad \times \quad \text{Investment amount}$$

Antonia can then express the discount factor as $1/1.05 = 0.9524$; this discount factor, when applied to the future cash flow of £200,000, gives a present day value of £190,000:

Year	0	1	2	3	4	5	6	7	8	9	10
Invest	£1,000,000										
Income		£200,000	£200,000	£200,000	£200,000	£200,000	£200,000	£200,000	£200,000		£1,600,000
Profit	£600,000										
DCF	5%	0.9524									
		£190,476									

Thus, Antonia would be **indifferent** between receiving £190,000 today, or £100,000 in a year's time, if her time value of money was 5 per cent.

Antonia then starts to consider the £200,000 that the project will deliver in year 2. How much would she have to invest in Bertie's Bank today, to be able to withdraw £200,000 in two years' time? Again, she can use the above formula, but do not forget that the money is invested for two years – so in year 2 she will not only be earning interest on the original investment, but also earning interest on the interest earned in year 1. This is known as **compounding**, and must be reflected in the calculation.

In this case, the equation will be:

Amount invested	+	Interest earned on investment	+	Interest earned on interest earned	=	Amount at end of period
£ [invest now]	+	£[invest × 5% now]	+	£[invest × 5% now]	=	£200,000

This can be expressed as:

$$\text{£[invest now]} \times 1.05 \times 1.05 = \text{£200,000}$$

So:

$$\text{£[invest now]} = \frac{\text{£200,000}}{1.05^2}$$

Again, we can simplify the equation by removing the investment element, giving us:

Discount factor

$$\frac{1}{(+\ rate)^2} \times \text{Investment amount}$$

The discount factor is $1/1.05^2$, which is 0.9070; this discount factor, when applied to the £200,000 future cash flow, gives a present day value of £181,406.

We can double-check this figure – £181,406 multiplied by 1.05 (invested for the first year at 5 per cent) and then the result multiplied again by 1.05 (invested for the second year at 5 per cent) gives £200,000.

So, Antonia can now plug the numbers into her business case model:

Year	0	1	2	3	4	5	6	7	8	9	10
Invest	£1,000,000										
Income		£200,000	£200,000	£200,000	£200,000	£200,000	£200,000	£200,000	£200,000		£1,600,000
Profit	£600,000										
DCF	5%	0.9524	0.9070								
		£190,476	£181,406								

This tells her that, if she wanted £200,000 from Bertie's Bank in one year's time, she would have to invest £190,000 today; if she wanted £200,000 from Bertie's Bank in two years' time, then she would have to invest £181,000 today. If she wanted both £200,000 in a year's time and £200,000 in two years' time, then she would have to invest £371,000 today (i.e. £190,000 + £181,000).

The formula for year 3 is exactly the same as for year 2, but rather than two lots of interest, she has to account for three lots of interest (i.e. it is £[invest now] × 1.05 × 1.05 × 1.05 = £200,000). She can, therefore, deduce that the bottom section of the discount factor formula is expressed as to the power of the year (given below as 'n'):

Discount factor

$$\frac{1}{(1 + rate)^n} \times \text{Investment amount}$$

Inputting this formula into an Excel sheet, she uses the following:

Discount factor

$$= 1/(1+rate)^{year}$$

Antonia can now calculate the present day value of all of the future cash flows associated with her project:

Year	0	1	2	3	4	5	6	7	8	9	10
Invest	£1,000,000										
Income		£200,000	£200,000	£200,000	£200,000	£200,000	£200,000	£200,000	£200,000		£1,600,000
Profit	£600,000										
DCF	5%	0.9524	0.9070	0.8638	0.8227	0.7835	0.7462	0.7107	0.6768		
		£190,476	£181,406	£172,768	£164,540	£156,705	£149,243	£142,136	£135,368		

For example, if she invested £135,000 into Bertie's Bank today, in eight years' time it would have turned into £200,000.

Adding all of these amounts up gives a total of £1,292,643; what this means is that, if Antonia walked into Bertie's Bank today and deposited exactly £1,292,643 and then returned to the bank each year, for eight years, and withdrew exactly £200,000 on each visit, on the last visit at the end of year 8, she would find that there was exactly £200,000 left which, when withdrawn, would leave the account empty.

Year	0	1	2	3	4	5	6	7	8	9	10
Invest	£1,000,000										
Income		£200,000	£200,000	£200,000	£200,000	£200,000	£200,000	£200,000	£200,000		£1,600,000
Profit	£600,000										
DCF											
	5%	0.9524	0.9070	0.8638	0.8227	0.7835	0.7462	0.7107	0.6768		
		£190,476	£181,406	£172,768	£164,540	£156,705	£149,243	£142,136	£135,368		£1,292,643
NPV	£292,643										

Armed with this information, Antonia starts to consider her project again. The original business case requires an investment of £1 million to generate £200,000 every year for eight years. To generate the same future cash flows from Bertie's Bank would require an investment today of £1,292,643. Antonia would be better off by £292,643 by opting to invest in the project rather than Bertie's Bank.

? What rate of interest can you earn in a bank today?

? Do you think that this is historically high or low?

What is the NPV?

The net present value (NPV) is the present day value of all of the future cash flows associated with a project at a given discount rate. So, for Antonia, the NPV of her project is the present day value (£293k) of receiving £200k per year for 8 years at a discount rate of 5%.

Antonia is confident that her proposal will earn the company more than could be earned in Bertie's Bank. She is about to make an appointment to put her proposal to the board, when she starts to think about the Bank – what if Bertie increases the interest rate that could be earned from 5 per cent to 10 per cent? Would A&B Ltd still be better off investing in her project, or would Bertie's Bank now be more attractive?

Having completed the spreadsheet, it is now relatively easy to rerun the figures using a discount rate of 10 per cent rather than 5 per cent:

Year	0	1	2	3	4	5	6	7	8	9	10
Invest	£1,000,000										
Income		£200,000	£200,000	£200,000	£200,000	£200,000	£200,000	£200,000	£200,000		£1,600,000
Profit	£600,000										
DCF	5%	0.9524	0.9070	0.8638	0.8227	0.7835	0.7462	0.7107	0.6768		
		£190,476	£181,406	£172,768	£164,540	£156,705	£149,243	£142,136	£135,368		£1,292,643
NPV	£292,643										
DCF	10%	0.9091	0.8264	0.7513	0.6830	0.6209	0.5645	0.5132	0.4665		
		£181,818	£165,289	£150,263	£136,603	£124,184	£122,895	£102,632	£93,301		£1,066,985
NPV	£66,985										

If Bertie's Bank offered an interest rate of 10 per cent, A&B Ltd would still be better off investing in Antonia's project. The project requires £1 million of investment, while A&B Ltd would need to invest £1,066,985 to generate the same future cash flows from the bank.

Thus, at a 10 per cent discount factor, Antonia's project will generate a NPV of £66,985. This is telling us that, if using a discount rate of 10 per cent, then Antonia's project would generate value to the tune of £67k – she is better off investing in the project than she is investing in Bertie's Bank.

What if Bertie's Bank offered a 15 per cent interest rate? If this were to happen, then the NPV would turn negative:

Year	0	1	2	3	4	5	6	7	8	9	10
Invest	£1,000,000										
Income		£200,000	£200,000	£200,000	£200,000	£200,000	£200,000	£200,000	£200,000		£1,600,000
Profit	£600,000										
DCF	5%	0.9524	0.9070	0.8638	0.8227	0.7835	0.7462	0.7107	0.6768		
		£190,476	£181,406	£172,768	£164,540	£156,705	£149,243	£142,136	£135,368		£1,292,643
NPV	£292,643										
DCF	10%	0.9091	0.8264	0.7513	0.6830	0.6209	0.5645	0.5132	0.4665		
		£181,818	£165,289	£150,263	£136,603	£124,184	£122,895	£102,632	£93,301		£1,066,985
NPV	£66,985										
DCF	15%	0.8698	0.7561	0.6575	0.5718	0.4972	0.4323	0.3759	0.3269		
		£173,913	£151,229	£131,503	£114,351	£99,435	£86,466	£75,187	£65,380		£897,464
NPV	-£102,536										

In effect, A&B Ltd needs to invest only £897,464 in Bertie's Bank in order to generate the same future cash flows (£200,000 per year for eight years) as opposed to Antonia's £1 million investment proposal. A negative NPV suggests that A&B Ltd would be better off not pursuing Antonia's project proposal.

So, what would be the rate that Bertie's Bank must offer for the board of directors of A&B Ltd to be indifferent between investing in Bertie's Bank and investing in Antonia's project? We can calculate this using the goal seek function in Excel. We need to change the value of the discount rate in order to result in a nil value for the NPV. In Excel, the 'set cell' should contain the NPV; the 'to value' should be zero; and the 'by changing cell' should be the cell with the discount factor number.

Using this method, we can calculate a discount factor of 12 per cent (or 11.8145 per cent, to be exact), which gives a NPV of zero:

Year	0	1	2	3	4	5	6	7	8	9	10
Invest	£1,000,000										
Income		£200,000	£200,000	£200,000	£200,000	£200,000	£200,000	£200,000	£200,000		£1,600,000
Profit	£600,000										
DCF	5%	0.9524	0.9070	0.8638	0.8227	0.7835	0.7462	0.7107	0.6768		
		£190,476	£181,406	£172,768	£164,540	£156,705	£149,243	£142,136	£135,368		£1,292,643
NPV	£292,643										
DCF	10%	0.9091	0.8264	0.7513	0.6830	0.6209	0.5645	0.5132	0.4665		
		£181,818	£165,289	£150,263	£136,603	£124,184	£122,895	£102,632	£93,301		£1,066,985
NPV	£66,985										
DCF	15%	0.8698	0.7561	0.6575	0.5718	0.4972	0.4323	0.3759	0.3269		
		£173,913	£151,229	£131,503	£114,351	£99,435	£86,466	£75,187	£65,380		£897,464
NPV	-£102,536										
DCF	12%	0.8943	0.7998	0.7153	0.6397	0.5721	0.5117	0.4576	0.4093		
		£178,868	£159,968	£143,066	£127,949	£114,430	£102,339	£91,526	£81,855		£1,000,000
NPV	£0										

So, if Bertie's Bank offered an interest rate of 12 per cent (or exactly 11.8145 per cent!), then the board of directors would be **indifferent** between investing in the bank and investing in Antonia's project. In effect, Antonia's project is the **equivalent** of investing in a bank that has an annual interest rate of 12 per cent. So Antonia's project is said to have an annualised return of 12 per cent (not quite the 60 per cent return that Antonia initially thought she had achieved).

? See if you can build an NPV model in Excel on your PC.

? Once calculated, use the NPV function to see if you get the same result.

? What discount rate should you use in your business?

? How might you adjust this discount rate to reflect the additional risk in, for example, IT projects?

What is the IRR?

Antonia's project shows a return that is the equivalent of investing in Bertie's Bank when the bank pays a 12 per cent rate of interest.

This annualised return is known as the internal rate of return (IRR). It is, in effect, the annualised equivalent of the rate of return achieved by an internal project.

You can work out the IRR of a project by calculating the NPV for a variety of discount rates and then using interpolation (i.e. working out where the line crosses the x-axis) or by using the goal seek method in Excel.

If you were to plot the NPV (y-axis) for each discount rate (5 per cent, 10 per cent and 15 per cent on the x-axis), then you would have a graph as follows:

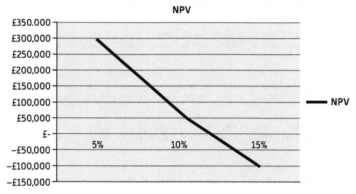

The internal rate of return is where the line crosses the x-axis (12 per cent).

The internal rate of return is the discount rate that returns a net present value of nil. (Try saying: 'The IRR is the DCF that returns a NPV of nil' – now you sound like a fully fledged member of the finance team!)

? What do you think is the target IRR in your business?

? Do you think this is high or low?

What discount rate should we use?

Antonia has examined her business proposal using three different discount rates – 5 per cent, 10 per cent and 15 per cent. She has concluded that, by using a rate of under 12 per cent, her project returns a positive net present value (NPV). The project has an internal rate of return (IRR) of 12 per cent – which means that it is the equivalent of investing £1 million in a bank that has a rate of interest of 12 per cent.

But the project is clearly not the same as investing in a bank. Banks will pay much less interest than the project, but provide a more secure cash flow (i.e. it is easier to predict the future interest that Antonia will receive on her bank deposit than it is to predict the future income that Antonia will receive on her project) – the bank is lower risk than the project.

In Chapter 2 we were introduced to the relationship between risk and reward. As Antonia's project is higher risk than a deposit in the bank, she must expect a higher rate of return. So, is 12 per cent high enough?

Consider the £1 million that Antonia is looking to invest. From where do you think she will get the money? In Chapter 2 we examined the source of funding available to business – debt and equity.

Businesses that are funded by debt need to pay interest on that debt. Providers of equity also require a return on their investment (through both dividend income and capital appreciation in the value of their shares – known as total shareholder return, TSR). Thus, capital (debt and equity) comes at a cost. This cost could be considered to be an opportunity cost – the £1 million that is invested in Antonia's project cannot be invested elsewhere in the business; the investment that could have been made instead of Antonia's project is known as the opportunity cost.

Companies will use an internal cost of capital when calculating the net present value. This can be viewed either as an internal opportunity cost or as an internal charge to Antonia's project of investing £1 million – i.e. just as it costs the business to borrow money, so it should also cost Antonia's project to borrow that money for investment.

The investment in Antonia's project is going to require a mix of both debt and equity (she will not be able to identify, for each £1 invested, whether it came from debt or equity), so she will need some way of calculating the cost to her project of borrowing the £1 million. One way of assessing this cost is to calculate the **weighted average cost of capital** (WACC).

What is the WACC?

The WACC represents the cost to a company of raising the funds for investment. However, the WACC recognises that the capital has been provided from two different sources – debt and equity – and the returns that each of the two providers of capital require are different, because the risks associated with debt are different than those of equity.

In Chapter 3 we examined the accounts of a number of different businesses, including National Grid. National Grid's balance sheet looked like this:

Balance sheet analysis

	National Grid **£bn**				
Non-current assets	£ 45.1	Investment capital	£ 45.1		
Current assets	£ 9.6	Working			
Current liabilities	£ 7.5	Capital	£ 2.1		
Non-current liabilities	£ 37.0	Debt		Capital	
Net assets/shareholders' funds	£ 10.2	Equity			£ 47.2

We concluded that National Grid has £47.2 billion of capital invested, sourced from debt (£37 billion) and equity (£10.2 billion).

Let us convert these into round numbers, which are easier to work with. Let us assume that the company has £40 billion of debt and £10 billion of equity – giving £50 billion of capital in total (this is very close to National Grid's actual figures).

Now let us assume that the cost of borrowing is 5 per cent. The equity investors in National Grid are taking a greater risk, and therefore will demand a higher return. Let us assume that they require a 10 per cent return on their investment.

We can present the two sources of funding and their required return in a table thus:

Weighted average cost of capital

Source of funds	Amount £bn	Return required
Debt	£40	5%
Equity	£10	10%
Total	£50	

The debt makes up approximately 80 per cent of National Grid's capital (£40 billion of debt out of total capital of £50 billion), and 80 per cent of the 5 per cent return required by debt investors is 4 per cent.

The equity makes up approximately 20 per cent of National Grid's capital (£10 billion of equity out of total capital of £50 billion), and 20 per cent of the 10 per cent return required by equity investors is 2 per cent.

Weighted average cost of capital

Source of funds	Amount £bn	Return required	Weighted return
Debt	£40	5%	4%
Equity	£10	10%	2%
Total	£50		6%

So, on a weighted basis, the providers of capital to National Grid – i.e. the investors – require a 6 per cent return on their investment – the WACC.

If Antonia's project is for National Grid, then she must ensure that her project has an IRR of at least 6 per cent – or, put another way, using a discount rate of 6 per cent, Antonia must ensure that her project returns a positive NPV. In this case, she is creating value for the business.

? What is the WACC for your business?

? How would you go about calculating it?

What is the difference between the WACC and ROCE?

In Chapter 4 we undertook some analysis of various accounts, and calculated that the return on capital employed (ROCE), or return on investment, for National Grid, was 11 per cent.

If National Grid has a WACC of 6 per cent and a ROCE of 11 per cent, then it means that National Grid is creating value for its shareholders. The investors require a minimum return of 6 per cent, but National Grid is actually returning 11 per cent.

Does this mean that Antonia's project, which shows a return of 12 per cent, will get the green light? Not necessarily. There are other factors to consider, such as:

▶ What is the internal target cost of capital for National Grid? The company is returning 11 per cent, but some projects may fall short of the original budget; in order to compensate, other projects will have to over deliver. National Grid may, therefore, set a target cost of capital of, say, 15 per cent in order to ensure that they continue to achieve the 11 per cent. If this is the case, then Antonia's project may not get the go ahead.

▶ What is the risk associated with Antonia's project? The investment may be in new and untried technology – which carries greater than normal risk (you only have to look as far as the experience of the UK Government in implementing new technologies to understand the risk and implications of cost overruns). If Antonia's project carries a higher than normal degree of risk, then National Grid may demand a higher rate of return (to compensate the company for taking on that risk) and, again, the project may not get the go ahead.

▶ What is the business strategy? Is the project aligned with the business strategy or is it taking the business in an entirely different direction? If Antonia's project is for a new flavour of crisps, for example, then National Grid may want to think twice before committing to something that is not part of its core competencies (i.e. what it is good at).

How can we use discounted cash flow analysis to compare various projects?

While Antonia was putting together the business case for her project, three members of her team – Nicky, Christopher and Julia – were also putting together business cases for three alternative projects.

They meet to compare the future cash flows on each of their projects, which are as follows:

Year	0	1	2	3	4	5	6	7	8	9	10
Antonia's Project											
Invest	£1,000,000										
Income		£200,000	£200,000	£200,000	£200,000	£200,000	£200,000	£200,000	£200,000	£0	£0	£1,600,000
Profit	£600,000										
Nicky's Project											
Invest	£500,000										
Income		£0	£5,000	£5,000	£10,000	£10,000	£10,000	£10,000	£200,000	£350,000	£600,000	£1,200,000
Profit	£700,000										
Julia's Project											
Invest	£750,000										
Income		£2,500	£7,500	£250,000	£100,000	£350,000	£75,000	£350,000	£150,000	£10,000	£5,000	£1,300,000
Profit	£550,000										
Christopher's Project											
Invest	£100,000										
Income		£75,000	£75,000	£75,000	£0	£0	£0	£0	£0	£0	£0	£225,000
Profit	£125,000										

You will notice that they are all generating future incomes, but at different times. If we were to rank the three projects based purely on profit, we would conclude that Nicky's project is the most profitable, followed by Antonia's project and then Julia's project. Christopher's project is the least profitable:

Project comparison

Project	Profit	Ranking
Antonia	£ 600,000	[2]
Nicky	£ 700,000	[1]
Julia	£ 550,000	[3]
Christopher	£ 125,000	[4]

Assume that they all work for National Grid, and that the finance team have informed them that the company's cost of capital is 8 per cent. What is the NPV on each of the projects? What impact does this have on the ranking?

See if you can work out the answers yourself in a spreadsheet before comparing with the table below:

Year	0	1	2	3	4	5	6	7	8	9	10	Total
Antonia's Project												
Invest	£1,000,000											
Income		£200,000	£200,000	£200,000	£200,000	£200,000	£200,000	£200,000	£200,000	£0	£0	£1,600,000
Profit	£600,000											
DCF	8%	0.9259	0.8573	0.7938	0.7350	0.6806	0.6302	0.5835	0.5403	0.5002	0.4632	
		£185,185	£171,468	£158,766	£147,006	£136,117	£126,034	£116,698	£108,054	£0	£0	£1,149,328
NPV	£149,328											
Nicky's Project												
Invest	£500,000											
Income		£0	£5,000	£5,000	£10,000	£10,000	£10,000	£10,000	£200,000	£350,000	£600,000	£1,200,000
Profit	£700,000											
DCF	8%	0.9259	0.8573	0.7938	0.7350	0.6806	0.6302	0.5835	0.5403	0.5002	0.4632	
		£0	£4,287	£3,969	£7,350	£6,806	£6,302	£5,835	£108,054	£175,087	£277,916	£595,606
NPV	£95,606											
Julia's Project												
Invest	£750,000											
Income		£2,500	£7,500	£250,000	£100,000	£350,000	£75,000	£350,000	£150,000	£10,000	£5,000	£1,300,000
Profit	£550,000											
DCF	8%	0.9259	0.8573	0.7938	0.7350	0.6806	0.6302	0.5835	0.5403	0.5002	0.4632	
		£2,315	£6,430	£198,458	£73,503	£238,204	£47,263	£204,222	£81,040	£5,002	£2,316	£858,753
NPV	£108,753											
Christopher's Project												
Invest	£100,000											
Income		£75,000	£75,000	£75,000	£0	£0	£0	£0	£0	£0	£0	£225,000
Profit	£125,000											
DCF	8%	0.9259	0.8573	0.7938	0.7350	0.6806	0.6302	0.5835	0.5403	0.5002	0.4632	
		£69,444	£64,300	£59,537	£0	£0	£0	£0	£0	£0	£0	£193,282
NPV	£93,282											

The ranking has thus changed:

Project comparison

Project	Profit	Ranking	NPV	Ranking
Antonia	£ 600,000	[2]	£ 149,328	[1]
Nicky	£ 700,000	[1]	£ 95,606	[3]
Julia	£ 550,000	[3]	£ 108,753	[2]
Christopher	£ 125,000	[4]	£ 93,282	[4]

Now Antonia's project is the most desirable, as it creates the most value, assuming the cost of capital is 8 per cent, while Nicky's project falls to ranking 3. How does this ranking change as the cost of capital changes (you will have to work this out in a spreadsheet)? The reason for this change in ranking is that the cash flows for each of the three projects are not only different, but they happen at different times (for example, Antonia's project is £200,000 per year constantly, but Nicky's project generates most of its cash at the end of the project timeline).

What is the IRR for each of the projects?

Year	0	1	2	3	4	5	6	7	8	9	10
Antonia's Project											
Invest	£1,000,000										
Income		£200,000	£200,000	£200,000	£200,000	£200,000	£200,000	£200,000	£200,000	£0	£0	£1,600,000
Profit	£600,000										
DCF	12%	0.8943	0.7998	0.7153	0.6397	0.5721	0.5117	0.4576	0.4093	0.3660	0.3274	
		£178,868	£159,968	£143,066	£127,949	£114,430	£102,339	£91,526	£81,855	£0	£0	£1,000,000
NPV	£0										
Nicky's Project											
Invest	£500,000										
Income		£0	£5,000	£5,000	£10,000	£10,000	£10,000	£10,000	£200,000	£350,000	£600,000	£1,200,000
Profit	£700,000										
DCF	10%	0.9081	0.8247	0.7489	0.6801	0.6177	0.5609	0.5094	0.4626	0.4201	0.3815	
		£0	£4,124	£3,745	£6,801	£6,177	£5,609	£5,094	£92,518	£147,033	£228,900	£500,000
NPV	£0										
Julia's Project											
Invest	£750,000										
Income		£2,500	£7,500	£250,000	£100,000	£350,000	£75,000	£350,000	£150,000	£10,000	£5,000	£1,300,000
Profit	£550,000										
DCF	11%	0.9023	0.8141	0.7345	0.6627	0.5979	0.5395	0.4868	0.4392	0.3963	0.3575	
		£2,256	£6,106	£183,627	£66,272	£209,280	£40,462	£170,369	£65,879	£3,963	£1,788	£750,000
NPV	£0										
Christopher's Project											
Invest	£100,000										
Income		£75,000	£75,000	£75,000	£0	£0	£0	£0	£0	£0	£0	£225,000
Profit	£125,000										
DCF	55%	0.6461	0.4175	0.2697	0.1743	0.1126	0.0728	0.0470	0.0304	0.0196	0.0127	
		£48,459	£31,310	£20,230	£0	£0	£0	£0	£0	£0	£0	£100,000
NPV	£0										

Project Comparison

Project	'Profit'	Ranking	NPV	Ranking	IRR	Ranking
Antonia	£600,000	[2]	£149,328	[1]	12%	[2]
Nicky	£700,000	[1]	£95,606	[3]	10%	[4]
Julia	£550,000	[3]	£108,753	[2]	11%	[3]
Christopher	£125,000	[4]	£93,282	[4]	55%	[1]

Christopher's project returns the highest rate of return (it required a very low initial investment and so was low in the NPV calculation).

Our conclusion? All four projects return a positive rate of return, so will get the go ahead (subject to some of the concerns mentioned earlier). If funds are limited, then investment should be made in the order of the IRR ranking – i.e. Christopher's project should be given priority, followed by Antonia's project and then Julia's. If there are any funds still available then they can be allocated to Nicky's project.

? What is the cost of capital for your business

? If there is not one, why do you think this is?

How is pay back analysis used to assess projects?

Pay back analysis examines the cash flow associated with each project. Imagine that each of the project managers had to borrow (i.e. create an overdraft at the bank) the amount to be invested. In which year would they clear the overdraft and actually see money in the bank? Again, we get a different ranking of the projects:

Year	0	1	2	3	4	5	6	7	8	9	10	
Antonia's Project												
Invest	£1,000,000											
Income		£200,000	£200,000	£200,000	£200,000	£200,000	£200,000	£200,000	£200,000	£0	£0	£1,600,000
Profit	£600,000											
Cumulative Cash Flow	−£800,000	−£600,000	−£600,000	−£400,000	−£200,000	£0 (circled)	£200,000	£400,000	£600,000	£600,000	£600,000	
Nicky's Project												
Invest	£500,000											
Income		£0	£5,000	£5,000	£10,000	£10,000	£10,000	£10,000	£200,000	£350,000	£600,000	£1,200,000
Profit	£700,000											
Cumulative Cash Flow	−£500,000	£495,000	−£490,000	−£480,000	−£470,000	−£460,000	−£450,000	−£250,000	£100,000 (circled)	£700,000		
Julia's Project												
Invest	£750,000											
Income		£2,500	£7,500	£250,000	£100,000	£350,000	£75,000	£350,000	£150,000	£10,000	£5,000	£1,300,000
Profit	£											
Cumulative Cash Flow	−£747,500	−£740,000	−£490,000	−£390,000	−£40,000	£35,000 (circled)	£385,000	£535,000	£545,000	£550,000		
Christopher's Project												
Invest	£100,000											
Income		£75,000	£75,000	£75,000	£0	£0	£0	£0	£0	£0	£0	£225,000
Profit	£125,000											
Cumulative Cash Flow	−£25,000	£50,000 (circled)	£125,000	£125,000	£125,000	£125,000	£125,000	£125,000	£125,000	£125,000		

Christopher's project is still the preferred as it breaks even in the second year; Nicky's project does not break even until the very last year – it is therefore much higher risk as it depends heavily on the ability to accurately predict a significant cash flow in 10 years' time.

While a business might not use this method for ranking projects, it may use it for selecting which projects are considered. Projects that do not pay back until after, for example, seven years may be deemed too risky – in this case, Nicky's project would not be considered for investment.

? What is the maximum pay back for a project in your business?

? Why?

How is the accounting rate of return (ARR) used for investment appraisal?

The accounting rate of return (ARR) is a simplified method of assessing two or more projects. It does not take into account the time value of money, but is a quicker and easier method of analysing the return expected from an investment.

The ARR formula is:

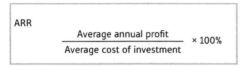

$$\text{ARR} = \frac{\text{Average annual profit}}{\text{Average cost of investment}} \times 100\%$$

Where:

▶ the average annual profit is the total profit (after deducting depreciation) for the project divided by the number of years; and

▶ the average cost of investment is the total investment, plus any residual value of the investment, divided by two.

Let us apply the formula to the figures in Antonia's project:

	Antonia's project
Investment	£ 1,000,000
Residual value	£ -
Life time (years)	8
Average cost of investment	£ 500,000
Total profit before depreciation	£ 1,600,000
Total depreciation	£ 1,000,000
Total profit after depreciation	£ 600,000
Average annual profit	£ 75,000
Average annual profit	£ 75,000
Average cost of investment	£ 500,000
ARR	15%

The original investment is £1,000,000 and, for the time being, we will assume that there is no residual value for the investment (the residual value is the value of the investment – for example the machinery purchased – at the end of the project). Thus the average cost of investment is £500,000.

The total cash flows for the project are projected to be £1.6 million, which – after deducting the depreciation of £1 million (that is, the investment of £1 million that is written off in totality over the duration of the project) – result in a total profit for the project of £600,000, an average of £75,000 for each of the eight years.

£75,000 average profit divided by £500,000 of average investment gives an ARR of 15 per cent.

Now let us run these figures in respect of each of the other three projects being run by Nicky, Julia and Christopher. In all cases, we will assume that there is no residual value for the investments:

	Antonia's Project	Nicky's Project	Julia's Project	Christopher's Project
Investment	£ 1,000,000	£ 500,000	£ 750,000	£ 100,000
Residual Value	£ –	£ –	£ –	£ –
Life Time (years)	8	10	10	3
Average Cost of Investment	£ 500,000	£ 250,000	£ 375,000	£ 50,000
Total Profit before Depreciation	£ 1,600,000	£ 1,200,000	£ 1,300,000	£ 225,000
Total Depreciation	£ 1,000,000	£ 500,000	£ 750,000	£ 100,000
Total Profit after Depreciation	£ 600,000	£ 700,000	£ 550,000	£ 125,000
Average Annual Profit	£ 75,000	£ 70,000	£ 55,000	£ 41,667
Average annual profit	£75,000	£70,000	£55,000	£41,667
Average cost of investment	£500,000	£250,000	£375,000	£50,000
ARR	**15%**	**28%**	**15%**	**83%**

The ARR now gives us a new ranking of the projects, with Christopher's project coming out on top:

Project Comparison										
Project	'Profit'	Ranking	NPV	Ranking	IRR	Ranking	PB	Ranking	ARR	Ranking
Antonia	£600,000	[2]	£149,328	[1]	12%	[2]	Year 5	[2]	15%	[3]=
Nicky	£700,000	[1]	£ 95,606	[3]	10%	[4]	Year 9	[4]	28%	[2]
Julia	£550,000	[3]	£108,753	[2]	11%	[3]	Year 6	[3]	15%	[3]=
Christopher	£125,000	[4]	£ 93,282	[4]	55%	[1]	Year 2	[1]	83%	[1]

? What do you think are the advantages and disadvantages of using the ARR method for investment appraisal?

We assumed that there was no residual value to the investments in the above example, but this is often not the case. A piece of machinery or software may well have value beyond the lifetime of the project. How would the above analysis change if, for example, the residual value of each project were £50,000? Let us start off by applying this to the figures for Antonia's project:

New residual values Of £50,000 each	Antonia's project	
Investment	£	1,000,000
Residual value	£	50,000
Life time (years)		8
Average cost of investment	£	525,000
Total profit before depreciation	£	1,600,000
Total depreciation	£	950,000
Total profit after depreciation	£	650,000
Average annual profit	£	81,250
Average annual profit	£	81,250
Average cost of investment	£	525,000
ARR		**15%**

With a residual value of £50,000, Antonia's new average cost of investment is now £525,000 (that is, £1 million plus the £50,000, divided by 2). The average annual profit has risen to £81,000 (remember, depreciation is the cost of an asset, **less its residual value**, divided by its useful economic life). The ARR remains at 15 per cent.

Let us see if there is any effect on the other three projects, if we assume that each has a residual value of £50,000:

New Residual Values of £50,000 each	Antonia's Project	Nicky's Project	Julia's Project	Christopher's Project
Investment	£ 1,000,000	£ 500,000	£ 750,000	£ 100,000
Residual Value	£ 50,000	£ 50,000	£ 50,000	£ 50,000
Life Time (years)	8	10	10	3
Average Cost of Investment	£ 525,000	£ 275,000	£ 400,000	£ 75,000
Total Profit before Depreciation	£ 1,600,000	£ 1,200,000	£ 1,300,000	£ 225,000
Total Depreciation	£ 950,000	£ 450,000	£ 700,000	£ 50,000
Total Profit after Depreciation	£ 650,000	£ 750,000	£ 600,000	£ 175,000
Average Annual Profit	£ 81,250	£ 75,000	£ 60,000	£ 58,333
Average annual profit	£81,250	£75,000	£60,000	£58,333
Average cost of investment	£525,000	£275,000	£400,000	£75,000
ARR	**15%**	**27%**	**15%**	**78%**

For each of the projects, there is no material change in the results (in this instance, material means significant). The ranking will remain the same as before.

? How much must the residual value be on Nicky's project to give it a higher ARR than Christopher's project?

? How relevant is this technique, given your understanding of the IRR analysis?

Chapter summary

On a fundamental basis, assets are valued based on the future income that they produce; but there is a time value of money when considering this future income.

In this chapter, we have seen how we can use discounted cash flow (DCF) techniques to address this issue and allow us to calculate the value of various projects. As well as DCF, there are other methods of creating a business case for investment. No single technique is right – each has its advantages and disadvantages. Using one or more of these techniques to analyse the financials of any proposal will enhance the financial credibility of that idea.

Next steps

▶ Does your business undertake projects?

▶ If so, what are the acceptance criteria?

▶ See if you can get hold of the DCF models from the finance team (if they use them).

▶ Is there any subsequent analysis on how accurate these historical DCF models were?

▶ What is the cost of capital in use in your business?

▶ Why is it set at this level?

▶ Do you agree with this level?

▶ What other criteria would you set for selecting which projects are given the green light in your business?

Key learning points

▶ Money has a time value, whereby £100 received today is worth more than £100 received in a year's time.

▶ Discounted cash flow models future cash flows and discounts them back into today's equivalent.

▶ The net present value (NPV) is the present day value of all of the future cash flows of an investment.

▶ The internal rate of return (IRR) is the discount rate that returns a NPV of nil.

▶ The weighted average cost of capital (WACC) is the cost to the business of raising investment, given that the providers of debt and equity require differing yields (due to the differences in the risks associated).

▶ Breakeven analysis examines when an investment becomes net cash positive.

▶ The annual accounting return (ARR) is the average profit after depreciation of a project expressed as a percentage of the average investment.

Test yourself

7.1   The time value of money states that:

   (a)   £100 today is worth less than £100 in a year's time   ☐

   (b)   £100 today is worth more than £100 in a year's time   ☐

   (c)   £100 today is worth the same as £100 in a year's time   ☐

   (d)   time is money   ☐

7.2   The discount rate is the rate at which:

   (a)   interest is earned on money in the bank   ☐

   (b)   the business rates paid are discounted by the local authority
to encourage enterprise   ☐

   (c)   a business must offer a discount to increase sales   ☐

   (d)   the future cash flows of a project are discounted   ☐

7.3   The formula for the discount rate in Excel is:

   (a) $=1/(1-r)^\wedge n$; where r = discount rate and n = the year   ☐

   (b) $=1/(1\times r)^\wedge n$; where r = discount rate and n = the year   ☐

   (c) $=1/(1+r)^\wedge n$; where r = discount rate and n = the year   ☐

   (d) $=1/(1/r)^\wedge n$; where r = discount rate and n = the year   ☐

7.4   NPV stands for:

   (a)   new present value   ☐

   (b)   net purchasing value   ☐

   (c)   new purchasing value   ☐

   (d)   net present value   ☐

7.5   The NPV of a project is defined as:

   (a)   the present day value of the future cash flows associated with
that project   ☐

   (b)   the future day value of the present cash flows associated with
that project   ☐

   (c)   the present day value of the present cash flows associated
with that project   ☐

   (d)   the future day value of the future cash flows associated with
that project   ☐

7.6 IRR stands for:

    (a) international rate of return ☐

    (b) internal real return ☐

    (c) internal rate of return ☐

    (d) internal rate of refund ☐

7.7 Which of these statements is true?

    (a) The NPV is the discount rate that gives an IRR of nil ☐

    (b) The IRR is the discount rate that gives an NPV of nil ☐

    (c) The discount rate is the IRR that gives an NPV of nil ☐

    (d) The discount rate is the NPV that gives an IRR of nil ☐

7.8 WACC stands for:

    (a) the weighted absolute cost of capital ☐

    (b) the weighted average cost of capex ☐

    (c) the working average cost of capital ☐

    (d) the weighted average cost of capital ☐

7.9 The WACC is the:

    (a) average return that debt and equity investors require ☐

    (b) total return that debt and equity investors require ☐

    (c) mean return that debt and equity investors require ☐

    (d) normal return that debt and equity investors require ☐

7.10 The payback on a project determines:

    (a) its profitability ☐

    (b) when it becomes cash positive ☐

    (c) its alignment with business strategy ☐

    (d) how successful the project will be ☐

CHAPTER 8

Budgeting and forecasts

'A budget tells us what we cannot afford, but it does not keep us from buying it.'

William Feather

 ## Aim

In Chapter 7, we looked at how businesses build their business case from a financial perspective – in effect, examining the future cash flows on a discounted basis.

In this chapter, we aim to pull together everything that has been covered in this book and examine what budgets are, how they are prepared and how they are used to control the business.

Outcomes

By the end of this chapter you will be able to:

▶ understand how budgets are used to control the business

▶ discuss the various types of budgets and how they are compiled

▶ learn how to manage the actual figures against the budgeted figures

▶ implement forecasting based on actual figures

▶ undertake flexed budget analysis

What is a budget?

Benjamin Franklin is credited with having said: 'If you fail to plan, plan to fail.' A company that fails to prepare budgets and then to use those budgets to control the business runs a high risk of failing.

Importers-R-Us, which was used as a case study in Chapter 5, is based on a real business (which, incidentally, is continuing to trade!). This case study is a good example of a company that is well run operationally, but is not so well run financially. As a company grows, the importance of good financial management, alongside operational management, cannot be over-estimated. Companies use budgets and other similar tools to financially manage their business.

So what, exactly, is a budget?

Some people might tell you that a budget is a financial picture of the future (perhaps on a short-, medium- or long-term basis); others may see a budget as more of a forecast or plan to which you add (or take away) money; it could be just a future P&L account; a benchmark or baseline. Either way, a budget is crucial to managing the business.

? Are budgets used in the financial running of your business?

? Who is responsible for preparing them? The finance team or line managers?

? Are they prepared and signed off before the beginning of the year (ideal) or is there a delay?

? What is the process for preparing, submitting and authorising the budgets in your business?

How is a budget prepared?

The business plan usually will start with an off-site meeting. The board of directors may head to the Maldives for a two-week session of blue-sky thinking, or the reality may be more along the lines of an afternoon in a hotel on the outskirts of Croydon.

Either way, their aim is to establish the overall strategy of the business.

This strategy is then translated into the operating plan – in effect who is going to do what in order to achieve the overall business strategy.

The budget then becomes the financial implications of what you intend to do. Your business might want to gain a high-level overview of the next 10 years – a long-term forecast; or a more detailed view of the next 3 years – perhaps on a rolling basis.

A budget is the financial plan for the next financial year. Once a budget has been set, it cannot (or should not) be altered; any updates are known as forecasts.

So, if that is the theory, what is the reality? The board of directors work out what they are trying to achieve and produce their key performance indicators (KPIs) and key financial indicators (KFIs) that will be used to manage the business. The front line managers compile their budgets based on what they think that they can achieve in the way of resources (i.e. sales targets and cost implications); once compiled, these are sent upstairs to the senior management. The senior management start tearing their hair out and demanding higher sales and lower costs – and the front line managers feel squeezed between the demands of their bosses and what can actually be achieved within the given resources. It is the same the world over!

What are the good reasons for budgeting?

There are many good reasons for budgeting; here are some of them:

Planning

Budgets help businesses plan in line with a long-term strategy. They ensure that the operational plans are consistent with the overall direction of the business and that those plans will deliver the expected value through total shareholder return (TSR) – that is, the dividends to be paid and the increase in the value of the shares.

Coordination

Budgets increase the need for various departments or business units in an organisation to coordinate their activities. The sales team must speak to the purchasing team (the purchasing team need to buy what the sales team can sell); the human resources team must ensure that any costs of recruitment sit in the correct budget (do HR pay for recruitment or the business unit?); IT need to understand the planned initiatives for the following year – what are the implications? Are expansion plans going to need additional hardware or software? If so, in whose budget will these costs appear? Will they be capitalised?

Communication

In a similar way to coordination, budgets help with the communication within the business. Not only must various business units communicate with each other, across the organisation, budgets also assist with the communication up and down an organisation. The senior management of the business communicate the strategy down to the business units, and the business units indicate back up the chain of command as to how they will implement that strategy through the compilation of the budgets.

Motivation

Budgets can be used as a way of motivating employees. They give budget managers something to aim for personally and also create targets for the organisation as a whole.

Control

By monitoring the actual costs and income against the original budget, managers can exercise a degree of control over the business units. This allows them to examine how the costs are changing compared with what was originally expected, and to adjust the forecast as necessary.

Evaluation

A manager's performance can be assessed against the original budget, as a budget can also be used as a target against which to benchmark the performance of individuals and teams within the business, as well as the business as a whole.

What are the different types of budgets?

Budgets can be prepared on an incremental or zero-based basis. Let us look at the difference between these two methods.

Incremental budgeting

Imagine that James is planning his holiday. One way of looking at how much the holiday will cost is to look at how much it cost James to go on holiday last year and use that as a benchmark. This is an incremental approach to budgeting. Incremental budgeting involves examining the actual spend in a previous period and then adjusting up or down to budget for the spend in a future period.

Zero-based budgeting

An alternative way for James to budget for his holiday is on a zero-based basis, which is similar to starting with a blank sheet of paper. This involves James working out exactly what he intends to do on holiday and then working out the cost implications of each of those activities. So James works out the cost of getting to the airport; the cost of the flights to Dubai; the cost of the transfers; the cost of the hotel; the cost of eating out for three nights; the cost of renting a boat for a day; the cost of lunch; and so on. He is then able to provide a fairly accurate picture of how much the holiday is going to cost him (and may decide that a week's camping in the West Country is a cheaper alternative).

So, what are the advantages and disadvantages of these two methods?

Incremental budgeting is a much quicker and easier way of compiling a budget. If James' holiday this year is going to be almost exactly the same as a previous year, then there is no point in his reinventing the wheel each time he goes on holiday; last year's actual expenditure will give a fairly accurate indication of this year's expected expenditure or budget. However, if James needs to save some money or incurs an unexpected item of expenditure, then there is no indication of where that money can be saved.

Zero-based budgeting will take a lot longer to compile. James will have to have an accurate idea of what he is going to do on holiday when compiling his budget, and he may not know exactly how much each of the activities will cost – therefore, he will have to make assumptions. The advantage of zero-based budgeting is that, if James incurs an item of unexpected expenditure during the holiday, for example he eats out for four nights rather than three, then he can quickly identify where he might be able to make the savings, for example by not renting the boat for a day.

In reality, budgets usually are a combination of the two approaches. New business plans and projects usually follow a more zero-based approach while business-as-usual activities are usually more incremental.

If James is compiling the budget for the training department for next year, he may use both incremental and zero-based budgeting. Probably, he will use incremental budgeting for the business-as-usual activities, such as salaries; and he could use incremental budgeting for the actual costs of training – for example, he spent £100,000 last year and so he intends to spend a similar amount this year. But he could use zero-based budgeting for the actual costs of training. After analysing the training needs of the business, he has established that he needs to run a graduate training programme; negotiation skills programme for the procurement team; and financial training for the senior management team. He is able to put together a training programme for the forthcoming year and look at the costs associated with each of those workshops. This will give him a clear and accurate picture of the training costs for the next year, when those costs will be incurred, and this effectively becomes his budget.

If he needs to reduce his budget for whatever reason, James is now in a position to identify where he can reduce the budget and the implications for the business. He could cut the graduate training programme and end up with a bunch of graduates who have no idea about the business in which they are working. He could cut the negotiation skills programme, which may cause costs to increase (as the procurement team are unable to negotiate better prices). Clearly he does not want to cut the financial training programme!

? Does your department prepare zero-based or incremental budgets?

? Is there a culture of 'use it or lose it' with regard to budgets in your business?

? Why do you think this is?

? What might you do to change this culture (should you wish to)?

How should budgets be phased?

When compiling his budget, James must consider the phasing or profile of the budget. It would be rational to take the total salary bill for his department and divide by 12 when allocating on a monthly basis. But, if he is intending to attend an HR conference, then this cost should be allocated to the month in which it was incurred (remember – incurred, not paid or booked!) and not spread over 12 months. Thus, some costs will be allocated across the months and some costs will be allocated to specific months.

When compiling his budget, James will focus on his P&L account. If he is running a cost centre, this will involve the costs of running his business unit. If he is running a profit centre, then it will also include sales and other income.

James also needs to consider the capex budget for his department. Perhaps he is planning to recruit a new member of his team; the costs associated with this recruitment will appear in his P&L account, but what about the new laptop for the new employee? This is an item of capital expenditure and must also be budgeted for.

As James is able to produce his sales budget, so the finance team, working on how long it will take to collect the money from the customer, will be able to budget the trade debtors. And, as James is able to produce this costs budget, so the finance team, working on how long it will take to pay suppliers, will be able to budget trade creditors. The finance team are also able to model the stock turnover – that is how long it takes from the purchase of a raw material to the sale of a finished good.

By ensuring that costs for specific items – such as the HR conference – are allocated to the correct period (and not just allocated as 1/12th into each month), James is now allowing the finance team to build up a picture of the cash flow implications of his budget.

With the capex budget and working capital budget, the finance team are able to produce a cash flow forecast – a crucial forecast for any business. This will enable the finance team to identify any future periods when funds may be tight and take the necessary action sufficiently in advance. This may involve cutting costs or it may involve going to the banks or shareholders to raise additional finance.

The finance team will also consolidate the budget produced by James and his business unit, with the budgets produced by James's colleagues and all of their respective business units, in order to provide an overall picture of the business. This budget is then used to monitor the business on an ongoing basis by the board of directors.

? What costs and incomes are seasonal in your business?

? How do you think that this affects cash flow?

How are budgets prepared?

To summarise, in order to prepare his budget, James first must define the objectives of his business unit. He must then work out who is responsible for which area of the budget – for example, does the new laptop sit in his budget or in the budget of the IT department? He must then gather all of the facts and information available and make assumptions, where necessary. Once he has gathered all of the information, he must decide what to submit, test and check this with his manager, and then agree to the final budget. This is then used to monitor and control the business on an ongoing basis.

Why should we monitor actual figures against the budget?

By regular monitoring of the actual figures against the original budget, James is able to understand what is happening within his business unit. How are costs changing? Why are they changing? How is the year likely to turn out? Has he accounted for the likelihood of unforeseen financial outcomes? What does it mean when he is re-forecasting? What has he learned?

Monitoring actual expenditure against the original budget is an ongoing learning process. The budget will never be 100 per cent accurate; James is aiming to create as accurate a picture of the future as possible in order to enable him to manage his business unit both financially as well as operationally.

What happens at month end?

At the end of each month, the finance team close the books – which means that no new invoices can be posted into the month that has just been closed. The timetable for this exercise will differ from business to business, but below is a typical month-end timetable:

Days 1–4

The first step is for the finance team to extract the raw financial information from the management information systems, and send this information to the business unit managers.

Days 5–6

The business unit managers will review this information and identify costs that have not been included and must be accrued for, and costs that have been included and should be removed through prepayment. They should also identify any items of expenditure that have been posted incorrectly to their cost code.

Day 7

The finance team post these adjustments and then produce the final management figures. The business unit managers write their commentary, based on the actual figures, in comparison with the budget and justify areas of over-expenditure or under-expenditure.

Days 8–9

The finance team collate the submissions from the various business units and produce a draft board pack, which is then reviewed.

Days 10–12

The final board pack is then submitted to the board of directors, who use the information to run the business.

Days 13–14

Usually, there is then some form of review and feedback loop, for the business to learn how to improve process. At the end of the month, the finance team get ready to close the books again for that month. In fact, life in the finance team is a little bit like life in the movie *Groundhog Day*.

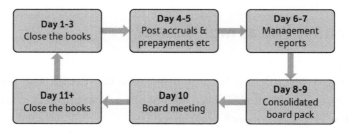

? What is the month end process in your business?

? How does this affect your department?

What is involved in the management information review?

When undertaking his management information review, James will compare his actual expenditure against his budgeted expenditure. He will do this for the months under review and may also do it on a year-to-date basis. He may also compare this month's actual expenditure with the actual expenditure from the same month in the previous year; and perhaps on a year-to-date basis – how much he has spent so far this year compared with how much had been spent this far in the previous year. He may review the original budget for the full year, and may feel the need to update the forecast for the full year. He may also compare the full-year forecast and the original budget with the total actual expenditure from the previous year.

So, James has a large amount of data to analyse. He needs to consider the level of detail into which he will go when comparing the numbers – if the figures are too high level he will not have sufficient information to allow him to manage his business unit; however, too much detail and he will drown in information overload.

James needs to consider how costs have been allocated. What degree of control does James have over the costs, which are allocated centrally to his business unit? If James has no control over costs (such as centrally allocated rent, or depreciation charges), he should not worry about them when compiling his management report.

Finally, James should undertake some variance analysis. Is the variance an underspend or an overspend? Is it due to budgeting error or to an unexpected event? Is it a controllable cost that James can influence? Why is he looking at this variance? Is it likely to reoccur? How much will it cost to investigate? Does James need to adjust the forecast? Does the variance impact another department? All of these questions should be answered in his management report and submitted as part of the board pack.

One way for James to gain a good understanding of the underlying causes of a variance is to undertake a flexed budget analysis.

? Do you receive monthly management information (MI)?

? What do you do with it?

? Are you responsible for writing reports and commentary on the figures?

? What happens to these reports?

? Why?

What is flexing the budget?

In Chapter 6, when looking at costs, we considered the costs associated with the production of dog food.

Oscar has expanded his business and is now running an operation with 20 members of staff. He has the following additional information:

▶ He expects to sell each tin for £3. There are 22 working days in the month and, with 20 staff working for 7 hours per day, he is budgeting for a total of 3,080 hours – at a rate of £7 per hour.

▶ The cost of the inputs is £1.30 as per the breakdown in Chapter 6 (£1.00 for the dog food, £0.25 for the tin and £0.05 for the label).

▶ With 20 staff working for 22 days, and each able to produce 200 tins per day, total production is expected to be 88,000 tins. He expects to sell every tin that is produced – he does not hold stock!

Additional information		Budget
Sales price:	£	3.00
Raw materials:		
Cost of inputs per output	£	1.30
Units used		88,000
Labour:		
Number of production line staff		20
Number of working days in month		22
Tins/day per member of working staff		200
No. of hours per day worked		7
No. of hours worked		3,080
Rate per hour	£	7.00

Based on a month with 22 working days, and the assumption that every unit he produces is sold, his budget looks like this:

	Budget
Number of workers	20
Output	80,000
[produced and sold]	
Sales £3.00	£ 240,000
Raw materials	-£ 104,000
Labour	-£ 19,600
Total cost of sales	**-£ 123,600**
Gross profit	£ 116,400
Margin	49%
Fixed overheads	£ 83,000
Contribution	£ 33,400
	14%

At the end of the month, Oscar receives the actual figures from his accountant, with which he is to perform his variance analysis:

	Budget		**Actual**	
Output	80,000		78,800 units	
[produced and sold]				
Sales £3.00	£	264,000	£	237,976
Raw materials	-£	114,400	£	102,555
Labour	-£	21,560	£	19,875
Total cost of sales	-£	**135,960**	-£	**122,430**
Gross profit	£	**128,040**	£	115,546
Margin		49%		49%
Fixed overheads	-£	83,000	-£	79,850
Contribution	£	**45,040**	£	35,696
		17%		15%

When examining his sales, he notices that actual sales – of £237,976 – is lower than the budgeted sales of £264,000. This he puts down to the fact that he originally budgeted to make and sell 88,000 units, but actually made and sold only 78,800 units.

But, in actual fact, on closer examination, Oscar identifies two drivers of the sales variance – the number of units that have been sold and the price at which they were sold. In order to examine this variance in more detail, Oscar decides to flex the budget. The original budget was based on producing and selling 88,000 units. Oscar managed to produce and sell only 78,800; so what would the original budget have looked like, if he had known that he was going to make and sell 78,800? This is called flexing the budget, and produces the following analysis:

	Budget	Actual	Flex Bud	Variance
Output [produced & sold]	88,000	78,800 units	78,800 units	9,200 units
Sales	£ 264,000	£ 237,976	£ 236,400	£ 26,024
Raw Materials	−£ 114,400	−£ 102,555	−£ 102,440	£ 11,845
Labour	−£ 21,560	−£ 19,875	−£ 19,306	£ 1,685
Total Cost of Sales	−£ 135,960	−£ 122,430	−£ 121,746	£ 13,530
Gross Profit	£ 128,040	£ 115,546	£ 114,654	−£ 12,494
Margin	49%	49%	49%	
Fixed Overheads	−£ 83,000	−£ 79,850	−£ 83,000	£ 3,150
Contribution	£ 45,040	£ 35,696	£ 31,654	−£ 9,344
	17%	15%	13%	

The total variance on the sales is £26,024 (right-hand column – column 4 – above). The original budgeted sales were £264,000 (column 1), but, if Oscar had prepared the budget based on sales of 78,800 units, then the budgeted sales figure would have been £236,400 (column 3).

So, Oscar concludes that sales were down by £27,600 because he made and sold fewer units. However, the total variance is £26,024 (column 4), which suggests that those units that were sold were sold at a higher price. While the budgeted price was £3.00 per tin, the actual average price was £3.02 (that is, £237,976 of actual sales divided by 78,800 of actual units sold)

Flexed budget sales variance analysis

Budgeted sales			£ 264,000	
Increase in sales price	£	1,576		
Decrease in sales vol.	−£	27,600		
Total variance			−£	26,024
Actual sales			£	237,976

So, while sales were down due to the volume produced and sold, there was a small positive compensation, as the price was slightly higher than anticipated. Why were sales down? Is it because not so many units were produced? Or perhaps Oscar increased the price and found that his customers were very price sensitive (Company A – see 'operational gearing' in Chapter 4). Either way, Oscar is now armed with much more of an insight into his business and can use this information when putting together his forecast (should he forecast lower sales volume going forward? Higher price? Or both?).

What about the costs of the business? We are now supplied with additional data – the actual amount of raw materials (inputs) used and the actual number of hours worked:

	Budget	Actual
Sales price:	£ 3.00	
Raw materials:		
Cost of inputs per output	£ 1.30	
Units used	88,000	79,500
Labour:		
Number of production line staff	20	20
Number of working days per month	22	22
Tins/day per member of staff	200	
No. of hours per day worked	7	7
No. of hours worked	3,080	2,650
Rates per hour	£ 7.00	

What about the costs of the raw materials? There is a £11,845 (circled above) positive variance; Oscar expects this, as fewer units were sold. But can Oscar undertake more detailed analysis, especially if he is told that the actual number of units used was 79,500?

He now has three different factors, which contribute to the £11,845 positive variance: the number of units sold; the efficiency in using the units of input to make the units of output; and the price per unit of output. Follow through the thinking process carefully using the table below:

Flexed budget sales raw materials variance analysis

		Units	Cost	£/unit
Original budget		88,000	£ 114,400	£ 1.30
Flexed budget	Based on lower expected volume	78,800	£ 102,440	£ 1.30
Flexed budget	Based on actual number of units of input used	79,500	£ 103,350	£ 1.30
Actual cost incurred		79,500	£ 102,555	£ 1.29

▶ **Top line – Original budget:** the original budget was to use 88,000 units of raw material at a cost of £1.30 per unit, giving a total cost of £144,400.

▶ **Second line – Flexed budget (based on lower expected volume):** the flexed budget (based on actual number of units sold) would have been to use 78,800 units of input, which at a cost of £1.30 would have cost a total of £102,440. Thus, there was a saving of £11,960 due to lower sales volume.

▶ **Third line – Flexed budget (based on actual units of raw material used):** the actual number of units of input used was 79,500 – so the production line was less efficient than expected (perhaps some tins were damaged); at a cost of £1.30 per tin, this results in an adverse variance of £910.

▶ **Fourth line – Actual cost incurred:** the actual cost was £102,555 – so each tin must have cost £1.29 rather than £1.30; this gives a positive variance of £795.

The three variances added together give the full picture of the £11,845 overall variance:

Variance due to lower sales	£	11,960
Variance due to more units used	-£	910
Variance due to lower price paid	£	795
Total variance	**£**	**11,845**

Now Oscar can undertake some detailed analysis. Was it a good idea to pay a lower price? Did this result in lower quality? Did this mean that some tins were easily damaged and had to be thrown away? Or were some tins stolen? Or lost? Undertaking a flexed budget analysis gives Oscar much more information on how the costs are changing – and much more information that he can use in the forecasting to produce an accurate picture of how the year is expected to turn out.

Now let us turn to the labour.

Oscar is told that the actual hours worked during the month were 2,650. See if you can perform the same analysis as for the raw material input above. Use the thought process that Oscar went through and then compare your answer to Oscar's analysis.

	Budget	Actual	Flex Bud	Variance
Output [produced & sold]	88,000	78,800 units	78,800 units	9,200 units
Sales	£ 264,000	£ 237,976	£ 236,400	£ 26,024
Raw Materials	–£ 114,400	–£ 102,555	–£ 102,440	£ 11,845
Labour	–£ 21,560	–£ 19,875	–£ 19,306	£ (1,685)
Total Cost of Sales	–£ 135,960	–£ 122,430	–£ 121,746	£ 13,530
Gross Profit	£ 128,040	£ 115,546	£ 114,654	–£ 12,494
Margin	49%	49%	49%	
Fixed Overheads	–£ 83,000	–£ 79,850	–£ 83,000	£ 3,150
Contribution	£ 45,040	£ 35,696	£ 31,654	–£ 9,344
	17%	15%	13%	

With regards to labour costs, there is a £1,685 (circled above) positive variance; Oscar expects this, as fewer units were made and fewer hours worked, but he now wants to examine the three different factors which contribute to the £1,685 positive variance: the number of units sold; the efficiency of the workers to make the units of output; and the price per hour of labour. Follow through the thinking process carefully using the table below:

Flexed budget labour variance analysis

		Hours	Cost	£/unit
Original budget		3,080	£ 21,560	£ 7.00
Flexed budget	Based on lower expected volume	2,758	£ 19,306	£ 7.00
Flexed budget	Based on actual units used	2,650	£ 18,550	£ 7.00
Actual cost incurred		2,650	£ 19,875	£ 7.50

▶ **Top line – Original budget:** the original budget was to use 3,080 hours of labour at a cost of £7.00 per hour, giving a total cost of £21,560.

▶ **Second line – Flexed budget (based on lower expected volume):** the flexed budget (based on actual number of units sold) would have been to use 2,758 of labour hours, which at a cost of £7.00 would have cost a total of £19,306. Thus, there was a saving of £2,254, due to lower sales volume.

▶ **Third line – Flexed budget (based on actual hours worked):** the actual number of hours worked was 2,650 – so the production line staff members were more efficient than expected; at a cost of £7.00 per hour, this results in a positive variance of £756.

▶ **Fourth line – Actual cost incurred:** the actual cost of labour was £19,875 – so each worker must have been paid £7.50 per hour rather than £7.00 per hour resulting in an adverse variance of £1,325.

The three variances added together give the full picture of the £1,685 overall variance:

Variance due to lower sales	£ 2,254
Variance due to more units used	£ 756
Variance due to lower price paid	-£ 1,325
Total variance	**£ 1,685**

Once again, Oscar is able to undertake some detailed analysis – why were the members of staff paid more? Was this due to overtime as fewer hours were worked? Or did Oscar employ higher calibre staff to try to improve efficiency?

Once again, Oscar is armed with additional information that can be used when revisiting his forecast.

? Is flexed budget analysis applicable in your business?

? Do you already do it?

? If not, how easy would it be to undertake such analysis?

What is forecasting?

Having prepared the budget and undertaken detailed analysis of the actual figures and how they compare to the original budget, managers can then prepare or update their forecasts.

? How often are forecasts prepared in your business?

? What is the process?

Why forecast?

Forecasting is a crucial element in the financial management of the business. The budget for the last month of the year may have been prepared and submitted up to 18 months previously – the figures will, therefore, be based on assumptions.

The forecast aims to update these figures with more accurate information – providing a clearer and more accurate picture of how the year is expected to turn out for the business.

Just as the finance team were able to prepare the balance sheet and the cash flow forecast from the consolidated (P&L account and capex) budgets from the various business units, so they can prepare these statements from the forecasts provided by the business units. While a small increase in costs in one part of the business may not appear to be an issue, when consolidated and fed into the forecasts, they may have a very material (i.e. significant) impact.

As Oscar undertook his flexed budget analysis, he was able to gain greater insight into how his costs were changing and why. By feeding this information into his forecast, he can create a more accurate picture of how the year will turn out for his business unit. If this is being done for all of the business units, then the board of directors will not only see how the business is performing compared with the budget, but also they will be provided with an increasingly accurate picture of how the business will develop in the future – and in particular the cash implications.

In Chapter 5 we examined the accounts of IRU. If the business had been running a detailed budgeting and forecasting process, then it is unlikely that the business would have run into such difficulties. Sometimes the answer to cash flow issues is not to sell more!

Chapter summary

In this chapter, we have pulled together all of the topics covered so far to demonstrate how they are all important to the modern-day manager. An understanding of how a company is structured and how it trades – in particular the balance sheet and cash flow statement – that sit behind the P&L account for which a manager is responsible, will provide a greater appreciation of the implications of financial decisions.

The ability to determine the KFIs and KPIs to measure and monitor on an ongoing basis; the understanding of how to create (shareholder) value in the business; and the ability to grasp the concepts of how business plans are created are all crucial skills to assist the business in achieving its financial, as well as strategic, objectives.

An appreciation of the finances of a business will allow today's manager to add value to the budgeting and forecasting process. These are not designed merely to keep the finance team busy (despite what you might think) but are crucial in allowing the board of directors to effectively manage the business.

Next steps

▶ How involved are you in the preparation and ongoing management of budgets?

▶ How might you change the process of preparation now that you have finished this chapter?

▶ Is incremental or zero-based budgeting the preferred methodology?

▶ Is there a 'use it or lose it' mentality in your business?

▶ Why do you think this is?

▶ How would you go about changing it?

▶ Can you?

▶ What is the month end process for closing the books in your organisation?

▶ Is the production of the monthly figures driven by the finance team or by the various business units?

▶ See if you can get hold of the final version of the board pack – the report to the board of directors.

▶ What sort of information is in there?

▶ Do you think that anything is missing (either financial or non-financial data)?

▶ How accurate a picture do you think the report paints of what is happening in the organisation?

Key learning points

▶ A budget represents the financial implications of future operational activities.

▶ The budget for the forthcoming year, once set, should not be amended.

▶ Variance analysis is the comparison of actual figures against the budget.

▶ Forecasting involves updating the budget to gain an increasingly accurate picture of how the year is expected to turn out.

▶ Flexing the budget will assist in breaking down a variance into its constituent elements.

Test yourself

8.1 A budget might be described as:

(a) something to keep the finance team busy ☐

(b) a reflection of what happened in the past ☐

(c) a plan of what you intend to do in the future ☐

(d) a waste of time ☐

8.2 The relationship between the budget and the strategy is:

(a) irrelevant ☐

(b) the strategy reflects the impact of delivering on the budget ☐

(c) the budget reflects the financial implications of delivering on the strategy ☐

(d) the more time spent on one, the less time is spent on the other ☐

8.3 Good reasons for budgeting include:

(a) planning, coordination, consistency motivation, control and evaluation ☐

(b) planning, coordination, communication, justification, control and evaluation ☐

(c) planning, coordination, communication, motivation, control and evaluation ☐

(d) profit setting, coordination, communication, motivation, control and evaluation ☐

8.4   An incremental budget is one that is:

(a)   phased correctly over the various months   ☐

(b)   based on what happened in previous periods   ☐

(c)   flexed, based on actual volume achieved   ☐

(d)   started from a blank sheet of paper   ☐

8.5   A zero-based budget is one that is:

(a)   phased correctly over the various months   ☐

(b)   based on what happened in previous periods   ☐

(c)   flexed, based on actual volume achieved   ☐

(d)   started from a blank sheet of paper   ☐

8.6   Month end involves

(a)   stressing out the finance team   ☐

(b)   hiding unspent budget   ☐

(c)   closing the books and preparing management reports   ☐

(d)   allocating costs to other departments   ☐

8.7   Variance analysis examines:

(a)   the difference between actual and budget   ☐

(b)   the difference between budget and forecast   ☐

(c)   the difference between actual and prior year   ☐

(d)   all of the above   ☐

8.8   Flexing the budget involves:

(a)   adjusting the actual level of output achieved to the budgeted   ☐
       amount

(b)   adjusting the budget for the actual level of output achieved   ☐

(c)   adjusting the actual costs to come into line with the original   ☐
       budget

(d)   updating the forecast   ☐

8.9   Forecasting involves:

(a)   projecting the budget forward   ☐

(b)   guessing how the year will turn out   ☐

(c)   using formulae in spreadsheets   ☐

(d)   updating the budget based on more up-to-date actual figures   ☐

CHAPTER 9
Commercial awareness

'If all the economists were laid end to end, they would never reach a conclusion.'

George Bernard Shaw

Aim

This final chapter aims to translate much of the theoretical concepts covered in this book into the day-to-day reality of working in a business.

Outcomes

By the end of this chapter you will be able to:

▶ define commercial awareness and how finance plays a core role in the development of a company's business strategy

▶ understand how finance is applied in the delivery of strategic goals.

What is commercial awareness?

In business, commercial awareness has many different interpretations, from understanding the commercials of a contract to how a business is run.

The *Cambridge Business English Dictionary* defines commercial awareness as: 'the knowledge of how businesses make money; what customers want and what problems there are in a particular area of business.'

In this book, we will consider commercial awareness to be the application of financial theory to real life business challenges. The chapters in this book have dealt, where possible, with real life companies and situations, rather than theoretical concepts. But the challenge still exists in applying this knowledge into the workplace on a day-to-day basis.

And so, this final chapter aims to give some guidance on how to leverage the knowledge gained in this book and apply it to your business in a commercial manner.

Most of the concepts covered have focused on the operational application of finance to the day-to-day running of a business. But, just as the day-to-day operations must be aligned to the overall strategic goals of the business, so the application of the financial concepts – or commercial awareness – must also consider the context of the strategy of the business. The first challenge, therefore, is to define what that strategy is.

? Take time to reflect on what we have covered so far in this book. How has it changed your understanding of your business?

What is strategy?

Capitalism involves the allocation of a scarce resource – in this case capital (or investment). In order to maximise their chances of success, it is important that companies have a clear vision of what they are trying to achieve – defined as their strategic intent – and are confident that this goal is based on sound financial or commercial principles.

There are many different definitions of strategy, but one of the best is from Johnson and Scholes (Johnson, G., Scholes, K. and Whittington, R. (2007) *Exploring Corporate Strategy: Text and Cases*. UK: Financial Times/Prentice Hall):

'Strategy is the **direction** and **scope** of an organisation over the **long term** that achieves an **advantage** for the organisation through the **configuration of its resources** within a **changing environment** to meet the **needs of the customers** and to **fulfil stakeholder expectations**.'

This is a long definition, but the highlighted phrases demonstrate how this definition provides a comprehensive understanding of strategy and how the finances of the business contribute towards this strategy:

▶ Determining the **direction** of the business involves setting the vision of the organisation – i.e. where it is hoping to end up (number one by sales; rated top for customer service; or 80 per cent of the domestic market share, for example). The budget of a company provides the short-term financial implications of this direction and the 5–10-year forecast gives a picture of how the company will look financially over the longer term.

▶ Whilst **direction** is concerned with what the company wants to do and where it wants to go, **scope** is concerned with what the company should not do. It is all too easy for a businesses to branch out into all sorts of new products, new services and new markets; successful business are ones that are good at identifying their core competencies – i.e. what they are really good at – and focusing on these. Sound financial analysis (i.e. accurate cost allocation models and realistic business cases) will enable a business to make the correct trade-offs and focus on the more profitable areas of the business.

▶ Whilst the company may engage in short-term tactics, the overall strategy of the business is focused on the **long-term**. It is not about next week, but the next three to five years (or longer). Thus the need for long-term financial forecasting is important to avoid short-term financial mistakes that can prevent a business from continuing as a going concern.

▶ Any strategy that does not create an **advantage** for an organisation is not really a strategy. The strategy must be aimed at creating a competitive advantage that has the potential to be translated into increased profitability.

▶ A company must create an organisational structure to deliver the strategy – in effect the **configuration of its resources**. While companies may compete in the same market place, they will be structured in different ways. This structure creates what Michael Porter called the value chain. The stronger this value chain (i.e. the greater the degree to which the various functions of the business are integrated), the more difficult it will be for competitors to replicate and, hence, a business can build barriers to entry that prevent other companies competing effectively. This, in turn, creates a **sustained** competitive advantage – ongoing profitability. The finance team form part of this value chain but more importantly, so does the culture of an organisation. A business that has a culture of financial discipline, with managers taking responsibility for their budgets and having an appreciation of the financial implications of their operational decisions, will have a greater chance of strategic success.

▶ The world is a constantly changing place – new technologies, changes in economic circumstances (both domestically and internationally) – and a constantly changing geopolitical world means that companies must recognise that they operate in a **changing environment**. They must adapt constantly and innovate just to survive – standing still is not an option. Thus strategy becomes an ever-evolving process – not something that is undertaken once. The financial analysis of a business will help to highlight some of these trends and how they are affecting the business; being able to spot trends in financial data will enable managers to take corrective action sooner rather than later.

▶ Companies must remain focused on meeting the **needs of their customers** and clients. And, just as the company's environment is changing, so is the environment of your customers. Companies must, therefore, recognise that the needs of their customers will change over time – successful companies are those that are good at recognising this change and anticipating future requirements.

▶ Finally, the strategy must be able to secure the future of the business and to **fulfil stakeholder expectations** – to ensure that the company is a going concern – and it will deliver the profits for the shareholders as well as long-term employment for employees. There are multiple other stakeholders – from the government and regulators to suppliers and financers; all have a vested interest in a successful company that continues to trade profitably long into the future. Techniques such as investment appraisal will assist the company in its ultimate financial aim – to maximise the wealth of the owners (through a combination of dividend income and/or capital growth).

? What is the strategy of your organisation?

? Where will you find it? (Look on your website or in your annual accounts.)

? Do you share your strategy with your stakeholders?

? How important is finance to delivering this strategy?

So, now we understand what strategy is, we need to examine how the board of directors determines the strategy. In this section, we will consider how strategy is determined with a focus on the financial aspects.

How is the strategic direction of a business determined?

There is no hard and fast rule in terms of how the business establishes the overall strategy. Some companies may try a two-week blue-sky thinking executive retreat in Barbados, while others may have to settle for a rain-filled couple of days at a small pub somewhere in the West Country.

The process of establishing the strategic direction might involve addressing some of the following questions.

Where are we now?

Before trying to determine the strategy of an organisation (where do we want to be), a business first should examine where it is right now. This involves examining the current position of the business in relation to the environment in which it operates, and identifying the trends that are taking place. Identifying the trends will help determine where the world is going and will allow the business to make an informed decision on where it wants to be in that new world (i.e. determining the strategy). Remember, the balance sheet provides the 'where are we now?' view of the world, while identifying trends in the P&L account and cash flow will help the board to determine how the changes will affect the business in the future.

There are two ways of looking at the business and the world in which it operates – **inside out strategic thinking** and **outside in strategic thinking**.

What is inside out strategic thinking?

Inside out refers to the process of standing inside the company and looking out at the changing environment in which the business is operating. The aim is to identify the trends that are affecting the world in which your business is operating and then trying to pull those trends together into a multi-dimensional vivid picture of what the future will look like.

A technique for shaping your thinking is to use STEEPLE analysis. STEEPLE stands for:

- Social: what are the social trends affecting, for example, your clients? Individuals are more accepting of the collection of data on their habits, for example, or are changing the way that they communicate through the use of social media. What will be the social norms of the future?

- Technical – the rapid development of technology, from the PC to the smart phone and beyond, has changed the world dramatically. What did people do in an elevator before the advent of the smart phone?

- Economic – the economy moves in cycles and, once in a while, experiences a significant upheaval (such as the financial crisis of 2007–8). Where are we in that economic cycle and what does the future hold?

- Environmental – global warming and increased awareness of pollution issues have given rise for the need for companies to demonstrate their green credentials. How might these environmental concerns develop in the future?

- Political – changes in the political landscape can have far-reaching consequences (both good and bad). Companies that operate in countries with less stable governments run an increased risk in choosing to do business there. Where are your key markets and what political changes are taking place there?

- Legal – changes in legislation will affect companies; particularly those that operate in highly regulated environments (such as banks and utility companies). How are regulations affecting your business? Are laws becoming tighter or more light touch?

- Ethical – just as society is changing socially, so its ethical values are changing. What might have been considered ethically acceptable in the past may no longer be so. What effect do changes, which are considered ethically acceptable, have on your business?

So, inside out strategic thinking involves looking at the world in which a business is operating and trying to determine what that world is going to look like.

This will allow a business to identify the **opportunities** as well as the **threats** that the company might face.

? Conduct a STEEPLE analysis for your business. Where do you think your world is heading?

? What opportunities can you see?

? What are the threats of which you need to be aware?

? Now apply this methodology to your personal situation. How does this framework help you think about your career?

What is outside in strategic thinking?

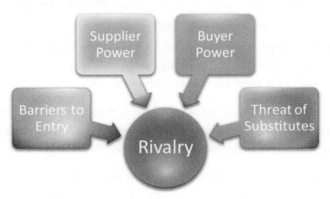

Having looked at the world in which a company is operating and identified what that world might look like in the future, a company might then turn to look inwards at itself. A common framework for undertaking this analysis is the use of Porter's Five Forces:

▶ **Supplier power** – is the business dependent on one or two companies to supply a particular product or component? If there is lack of competition – i.e. alternative suppliers – then a company may be held to ransom. Companies who deal with strong suppliers often see their margins eroded as they have little bargaining power to drive down costs. Trying to 'commoditise' the input will encourage competition from suppliers and thus ensure that your company can gain the best price.

▶ **Buyer power** – is the business dependent on one or two customers? Again, if so, then they may be able to dictate the terms of business and push (sale) prices down. A business that is overly dependent on one or two customers should look to diversify in order to reduce this dependency. Not only will your customer be able to dictate terms to you, the success of your business will be heavily dependent on their business. If your customers run into financial difficulties, then you could easily see this being passed on to your business.

▶ **Threat of new entrants** – what is the likelihood that new (or existing) companies will enter the market? Markets with high barriers to entry – such as requiring significant infrastructure investment or brand awareness – are much more difficult to penetrate.

▶ **Threat of substitute products** – if a customer does not use your product, or a similar product from a competitor, do they have an alternative? If so, what is that alternative?

▶ **Existing competition** – what is the competition like at the moment in the market place in which you are operating? Do you have an effective monopoly or is there fierce price competition?

Outside in strategic thinking will allow a company to understand its **strengths** and **weaknesses**. Remember – what is considered to be a strength or weakness today may not be so in the future.

Thus, the two frameworks should be used in conjunction with one another to produce a SWOT analysis that identifies the strengths (S) and weaknesses (W) of the company and also the opportunities (O) and threats (T) that the future holds.

? Use Porter's Five Forces to analyse your business. Where do the strengths and weaknesses of the business lie? Consider what you think are your own personal S & W in the light of your personal O & T identified above.

An understanding of the finances of a business is crucial in performing an outside in analysis. Understanding the accounts of a supplier will enable you as the buyer to determine whether this is a company with which you want to do business (remember IRU in Chapter 5?). It will also enable you to determine whether they are very price sensitive (see operational gearing in Chapter 4) or can offer a big discount, or perhaps whether or not they have cash flow issues (see liquidity in Chapter 4) and perhaps you can negotiate a discount for early payment of invoices (but only if your own cash flow will allow for this).

Similarly, a sound understanding of your customers' accounts will increase your confidence to extend credit without having to write off bad debts when it becomes clear that they cannot pay. Where their credit rating may look suspect, you might wish to request payment in advance (remember to treat it as deferred income) or request some other security to minimise the risk of default.

What is the vision of a business?

The senior management of the organisation can then pull these concepts together to determine the vision of the business – in effect, answering the question, 'Where do I want to be?' in, say, five to ten years' time. The vision of the business might be to become the preferred supplier, or achieve a specific level of turnover or market share. A vision should be both ambitious, but also clearly defined, so that the company knows when it has been achieved.

By projecting the finances forward, using the forecasting techniques discussed in Chapter 8, businesses – can build a financial picture of where they hope to be – both in terms of the financial position (shown in the balance sheet) as well as in terms of profitability and cash flow.

Remember – the quality of the decisions will be only as good as the data on which they are based. A sound understanding of the business from a financial perspective will provide a good idea of what activities are or are not profitable. In Chapter 6 we covered the subject of costs in some detail – the accuracy with which these costs are accounted for (into the correct periods, and into the correct cost centres with the right cost codes) and the methodology by which they are allocated to the various activities will provide a clear picture of which areas of the business are operating profitably.

The finance team can achieve only so much in ensuring that the financial data is accurate. Line managers in the business have a greater understanding of what is actually happening at the 'coal face' and it is important that this is reflected accurately in the financial data that is provided to the strategic decision makers in the organisation.

?   What is the vision of your business?

?   What about your personal vision?

What is the difference between the mission and vision of a business?

If the **vision** determines where a company wants to be in the future, the **mission** identifies what the company does. The distinction is important – the mission (what we do) will stay the same, while the vision (where we want to be) will change.

An effective mission statement is one that stakeholders (employees, but also external stakeholders such as suppliers and clients) can buy into. It should be a reflection of the core values of the business.

?   What are the core competencies of your organisation?

?   How are they leveraged to create advantage?

?   How do you leverage what you are good at to your advantage?

What is the role of commercial awareness in delivering the strategy?

Once a business has determined where it is and where it wants to be, it can perform a gap analysis to determine the best way to deliver on that strategy. This will involve breaking down the objectives into long- and short-term goals and working out how to deliver on each milestone – in effect, determining the operational decisions that must be made to move the business forward towards the long-term goals.

As we have seen during the course of this book, every decision by a manager will have a financial implication on the organisation and an appreciation of these financial implications will enable managers to identify areas of concern at an early stage and take corrective action where necessary.

Preparing the budget to achieve each objective and analysing progress against this budget will help to ensure that the business remains on track to deliver the strategy.

A comprehensive budgeting and forecasting process will ensure that managers are able to monitor progress towards the delivery of the organisational strategy. It is also a method of effectively communicating that strategy throughout the business.

Accurate forecasting, based on the historical data, will help the business project into the future and determine whether it is still on track to deliver the financial benefits of the strategy.

Armed with the knowledge of how assets are valued and the various investment appraisal techniques, the identification of additional investment opportunities – from purchasing new machinery to buying a company or expanding overseas – can now be presented in a manner that is both operationally and financially viable. Using discounted cash flow analysis, referring to the company's cost of capital and comparing the results from various appraisal concepts will demonstrate that operational and strategic proposals have undergone a sound commercial analysis before being proposed.

A thorough understanding of the costs of the business, how they behave and how they are accounted for will increase the accuracy of the decision-making process – allowing visibility of more profitable areas of activity compared with those that are less profitable. Armed with this information, it is possible to weigh up the advantages and disadvantages of expanding a business following a high operational gearing model (for example, by buying in additional staff) or a lower operational gearing model (by hiring contract workers to begin with). Both will have different impacts on the risk and return of delivering the strategy.

Additional investment will have an adverse impact on cash flow – an understanding of the pressures currently on the cash flow of the business will allow the business to make informed decisions. How will the additional investment be funded? If there are insufficient retained earnings, perhaps there is the capacity for additional debt to be taken on. Remembering that, as demonstrated by the WACC (see Chapter 7), there is no such thing as free money. Investment made in one area of the business is investment that cannot be made in another area of the business. An appreciation and acknowledgement of this opportunity cost will again bring commercial weight to any proposal.

Being able to build an effective business model and study the future cash flows associated with the investment will allow managers to assess the risk – or sensitivity – of the plan to changes in assumptions. Again, this will allow for a greater understanding of the risks associated with delivering on the strategy and thereby increase the chances that proposals that demonstrate commercial rigour will be accepted.

How else can commercial awareness be applied in the workplace?

So far, we have talked about the internal delivery of your business strategy. What about your suppliers? Have you negotiated the best terms? How sensitive are they to changes in price? How reliant are they on future cash flows? Might they offer a discount on price in exchange for earlier payment? We can use the knowledge gained in this book to improve commercial dealings with our suppliers. The checklist in Chapter 5 is a good place to start when considering your suppliers from a financial perspective.

And how about our clients? What additional information can we gain about them from their financial reports? Are their profitability margins increasing or decreasing? How secure are they as a business? And how strained is their cash flow? Do we want to align ourselves more closely with them – in terms of a strategic partnership, for example, or does it make more commercial sense to keep them at arm's length?

Applying commercial logic, based on the financial knowledge gained in this book, will allow us to make increasingly commercially informed decisions.

What are the implications of getting it wrong?

As we saw in Chapter 5, a company that is expanding rapidly will place additional strain on its cash flow. We often hear of successful businesses that expand too quickly and go bust as a result. Commercial awareness will allow us to reduce the risk of this happening in our business – to apply sound financial logic to the commercial realities that exist in a business.

Chapter summary

Commercial awareness involves the application of financial theory to real life business decisions. Being able to think in terms of finance as well as operational terms allows us to make increasingly informed, commercially aware decisions.

 ## Next steps

▶ Try to start (if you are not already) thinking about your business strategically.

▶ If you were running it, what would be your strategic goals and why?

▶ See if you can understand the strategic context of some of the tactical decisions made by the senior management – do you agree with these decisions and why?

 ## Key learning points

▶ Commercial awareness is concerned with the application of financial knowledge to the practical operations of the business.

▶ Strategy involves determining the direction of the business.

▶ STEEPLE analysis is an inside out strategic thinking tool, while Porter's Five Forces is an outside in strategic thinking tool.

▶ The mission of the business (what we do) stays constant, while the vision (where we want to be) will change.

▶ The mission will be a reflection of the core competencies of the business (i.e. what the business is good at) and the values or culture of the organisation.

Test yourself

9.1 Commercial awareness might be:

    (a)   an awareness of finance ☐

    (b)   knowing how to get the best out of others ☐

    (c)   managing the business both financially and operationally ☐

    (d)   being able to cover for members of the finance team when they are away ☐

9.2 Strategy involves:

    (a)   formulating the direction of the business ☐

    (b)   learning from past mistakes ☐

    (c)   guessing what the future might hold ☐

    (d)   two weeks in Barbados ☐

9.3 STEEPLE analysis is:

    (a)   an accounting methodology ☐

    (b)   an inside out strategic thinking tool ☐

    (c)   an outside in strategic thinking tool ☐

    (d)   used to determine a core competence ☐

9.4 Porter's Five Forces include:

    (a)   a SWOT analysis ☐

    (b)   identifying buyer and supplier power ☐

    (c)   setting the direction of the business ☐

    (d)   conducting online surveys ☐

9.5 The vision of the business is:

    (a)   what it does ☐

    (b)   what it did ☐

    (c)   where it has been ☐

    (d)   where it wants to go ☐

9.6 The mission of the business is:

    (a)   what it does ☐

    (b)   what it did ☐

    (c)   where it has been ☐

    (d)   where it wants to go ☐

9.7   Commercial awareness is important because:

    (a)   you might get a job in the finance team   ☐

    (b)   you will learn to develop complicated spreadsheets   ☐

    (c)   you will be able to negotiate a higher salary   ☐

    (d)   it helps to make informed business decisions based on sound   ☐
        financial analysis

10

Conclusion

In this book, I have tried to paint the big picture for you, the reader – to help you understand the backdrop against which key financial, commercial (and operational) decisions are made.

We started by looking at how a company is structured and how it trades, before moving on to how a company is funded. Using this knowledge, we were able to examine the three main trading statements and to consider some of the key financial indicators (KFIs) that might be used in running our business or when examining another business. We consolidated this knowledge with a case study – IRU.

In the second half of the book, we started to examine the business in more detail – understanding the different types of costs that you might encounter, how they behave and how they are treated financially. We considered how to build a business case using discounted cash flow.

We finished by pulling together all the information contained in this book and examining what a budget is, how it is put together, and the importance of budgeting and forecasting in running the business. As a final reflection, we considered the concept of commercial awareness and looked at how you can apply what you have learned from this book in your place of work.

In the introduction to this book, I likened the learning of finance to the learning of a new language. If you have got this far (and are still awake!), then congratulations – you have completed the first step towards your fluency in finance. But, remember – it does not stop here!

You should treat your reading so far as a first step, not conclusive in itself. Unless you work in the finance department, or in senior management, finance is unlikely to be part of your day-to-day life – and it is, therefore, very easy to forget the lessons that you have (hopefully) learnt so far in this book.

Use this book as a starting point; obtain copies of the statutory accounts of your own business, your competitors, your suppliers, your clients, etc. See if you can undertake the same analysis that we have done here. What conclusions can you draw?

It is worth making friends with someone in the finance department who can sense check your conclusions – some kind of mentor will be of great assistance.

Finally, remember – finance is not everyone's favourite discipline. But do not be afraid of the numbers, do not be afraid to ask for help, do not be afraid to say that you do not understand something. Finance is a key skill for anyone looking to develop their career – either with their current organisation or a new one. The financial skills that you pick up will set you in very good stead for the future.

Good luck!

Ted Wainman
ted@wainman.net
www.wainman.net
March 2015

Answers

0.1   Finance is:

    (a)   not important in a business

    (b)   the domain of the finance team only

    (c)   crucial to managing a business effectively

    (d)   the only thing that managers should consider when running a business

0.2   Accounting is about:

    (a)   making sure that the business is profitable

    (b)   providing financial information to assist with running the business

    (c)   keeping the finance department busy

    (d)   telling sales people what they cannot do

Answers – Chapter 1

1.1   A sole trader is someone who:

    (a)   works for themselves

    (b)   buys and sells fish – specialising in Dover Sole

    (c)   is the sole owner of a company

    (d)   trades goods but not services

1.2   A partnership is one where:

    (a)   profits are shared equally between the partners

    (b)   profits are shared equitably between the partners

    (c)   profits are distributed to the shareholders before the partners get paid

    (d)   the company cannot make a loss

1.3   A company is best described as:
        (a)   the same as a sole trader
        (b)   the same as a partnership
        (c)   a separate legal entity
        (d)   an organisation with employees

1.4   The veil of incorporation:
        (a)   limits the liabilities of the shareholders to their investment
        (b)   limits the liabilities of the debt providers to their investment
        (c)   separates the executive from the non-executive
        (d)   separates assets and liabilities

1.5   The role of the executive board is to:
        (a)   work on a part-time basis
        (b)   maximise their share options
        (c)   formulate and implement strategy
        (d)   formulate strategy and hold the non-executive to account

1.6   The role of the non-executive board is to:
        (a)   work on a part-time basis
        (b)   maximise their share options
        (c)   formulate and implement strategy
        (d)   formulate strategy and hold the executive to account

1.7   The statutory accounts:
        (a)   show only the balance sheet
        (b)   show only the P&L account
        (c)   show only the cah flow statement
        (d)   are a legal requirement of all limited companies

1.8   The role of the auditors is to:
        (a)   do what the directors ask them to do
        (b)   prepare the accounts
        (c)   check the accounts and sign them off as true and fair
        (d)   minimise the tax of the company

1.9   The accounting equation states that:

   (a)   assets must be greater than liabilities

   (b)   assets will always be equal to liabilities

   (c)   the difference between assets and liabilities is profit

   (d)   shareholders' funds will always be an asset

1.10   The balance sheet contains:

   (a)   assets and liabilities

   (b)   assets and expenses

   (c)   income and liabilities

   (d)   income and expenses

1.11   If a company makes a profit it can either:

   (a)   spend it or reinvest it

   (b)   reinvest it or return it to shareholders

   (c)   return it to shareholders or pay a dividend

   (d)   pay a dividend or spend it

1.12   Who appoints the auditors of a company?

   (a)   the directors

   (b)   the non-executive directors

   (c)   the shareholders

   (d)   the bankers

1.13   Shareholders' funds are:

   (a)   an asset

   (b)   a liability

   (c)   an income

   (d)   an expense

1.14   The matching concept ensures that:
   (a)   income and expenses are recognised in the period ordered
   (b)   income and expenses are recognised in the period invoiced
   (c)   income and expenses are recognised in the period paid
   (d)   income and expenses are recognised in the period earned/ incurred

1.15   Profit and cash are:
   (a)   always the same
   (b)   sometimes the same
   (c)   never the same
   (d)   inversely related

Answers – Chapter 2

2.1   The business cycle shows:
   (a)   how cash flows within a business
   (b)   how goods and services flow within a business
   (c)   the role of employees in a business
   (d)   how a business responds to the global economic climate

2.2   A business can raise investment/cash from:
   (a)   equity and shareholders
   (b)   debt and equity
   (c)   shareholders and employees
   (d)   debt and banks/loans

2.3   Debt is:
   (a)   riskier than equity
   (b)   unlikely to be repaid
   (c)   a loan, usually bearing interest
   (d)   probably interest-free

2.4   Equity is:

(a)   a combination of retained profit and dividends

(b)   the shareholders' stake in the business

(c)   the concept of all shareholders being treated equally

(d)   an investment that will attract interest

2.5   The primary market is where:

(a)   companies raise money from investors

(b)   investors trade shares that they own

(c)   companies trade goods and services

(d)   companies resell goods and services

2.6   The secondary market is where:

(a)   companies raise money from investors

(b)   investors trade shares that they own

(c)   companies trade goods and services

(d)   companies resell goods and services

2.7   Capital is a combination of:

(a)   debt and equity

(b)   debt and dividends

(c)   dividends and equity

(d)   debt, equity and dividends

2.8   A derivative is:

(a)   something only bankers know about

(b)   a trade between two parties where neither owns the underlying asset

(c)   a trade between two parties where both own the underlying asset

(d)   a swap

2.9   An option is:

     (a)   the right to buy an asset at a future point in time

     (b)   the obligation to buy an asset at a future point in time

     (c)   a swap

     (d)   a derivative product that is traded only in the USA

2.10   Companies usually use derivatives to:

     (a)   bet on markets going up

     (b)   bet on markets going down

     (c)   bet on markets going up and down

     (d)   hedge risk

Answers – Chapter 3

3.1   The financial objective of a business might include:

     (a)   maximising the wealth of the shareholders

     (b)   paying creditors early

     (c)   maximising staff bonuses

     (d)   tax evasion

3.2   Who of the following might be interested in a company's annual report?

     (a)   suppliers to competitors

     (b)   suppliers

     (c)   the general public

     (d)   ex-employees

3.3   In which month must I show the cost of a service?

     (a)   purchase order raised in February

     (b)   invoice received in March

     (c)   service delivered in April

     (d)   invoice paid in May

3.4   The financial statements are:

(a)   always correct

(b)   a clear picture of the future of a company

(c)   a clear picture of the past of a company

(d)   never to be relied upon, due to accounting manipulation techniques

3.5   The balance sheet contains:

(a)   assets and liabilities

(b)   assets and expenses

(c)   income and liabilities

(d)   income and expenses

3.6   Assets are categorised as:

(a)   fixed and non-current

(b)   fixed, non-current and current

(c)   non-current and current

(d)   long-term and current

3.7   Cash will appear in:

(a)   non-current assets

(b)   current assets

(c)   current liabilities

(d)   non-current liabilities

3.8   Plant and machinery will appear in:

(a)   non-current assets

(b)   current assets

(c)   current liabilities

(d)   non-current liabilities

3.9   Current assets are:

(a)   assets that the business needs to keep to do business

(b)   assets that the business is trying to sell

(c)   assets that the business is trying to turn into cash

(d)   not really assets at all

3.10 Non-Current (or fixed) assets are:

(a) assets that the business needs to keep to do business

(b) assets that the business is trying to sell

(c) assets that the business is trying to turn into cash

(d) not really assets at all

3.11 Liabilities are categorised as:

(a) current and fixed

(b) non-current and fixed

(c) current, non-current and shareholders' funds

(d) current, short-term, non-current and long-term

3.12 An overdraft is most likely to appear in:

(a) non-current assets

(b) current assets

(c) current liabilities

(d) non-current liabilities

3.13 An interest-only mortgage is most likely to appear in:

(a) non-current assets

(b) current assets

(c) current liabilities

(d) non-current liabilities

3.14 Current liabilities are:

(a) liabilities that need to be repaid soon

(b) liabilities that do not need to be repaid soon

(c) amounts owed to shareholders

(d) dividends payable

3.15 Non-current (or long-term) liabilities are:

(a) liabilities that need to be repaid soon

(b) liabilities that do not need to be repaid soon

(c) amounts owed to shareholders

(d) dividends payable

3.16 Equity is:
- (a) liabilities that need to be repaid soon
- (b) liabilities that do not need to be repaid soon
- **(c) amounts owed to shareholders**
- (d) dividends payable

3.17 Share capital is:
- (a) the initial investment in the business by shareholders
- **(b) the nominal value of all investments in the business by shareholders**
- (c) debt and equity
- (d) reinvested profits

3.18 Capital is:
- (a) debt and current assets
- **(b) total assets and current liabilities**
- (c) total liabilities and current assets
- (d) equity and current liabilities

3.19 Capital is used for:
- (a) investment capital and equity
- (b) debt and equity
- (c) debt and working capital
- **(d) investment capital and working capital**

3.20 Capital comes from:
- (a) investment capital and equity
- **(b) debt and equity**
- (c) debt and working capital
- (d) investment capital and working capital

3.21 The income statements contains:
- (a) assets and liabilities
- (b) assets and expenses
- (c) income and liabilities
- **(d) income and expenses**

3.22 Turnover is **not** also known as:

(a) sales

(b) deferred income

(c) income

(d) revenue

3.23 Cost of sales usually contains:

(a) fixed costs

(b) sunk costs

(c) variable costs

(d) marginal costs

3.24 Gross profit is sales less:

(a) turnover

(b) administration costs

(c) cost of sales

(d) cost of sales and administration costs

3.25 Administration costs usually contain:

(a) fixed costs

(b) sunk costs

(c) variable costs

(d) marginal costs

3.26 Operating profit is sales less:

(a) turnover

(b) administration costs

(c) cost of sales

(d) cost of sales and administration costs

3.27 Interest costs are:

(a) the costs of servicing the equity investment

(b) the costs of servicing the debt investment

(c) the costs of servicing both debt and equity investments

(d) included only on the balance sheet

3.28 Profit before tax is sales less:

(a) cost of sales

(b) cost of sales and administration costs

(c) cost of sales, administration costs and dividends

(d) cost of sales, administration costs and interest

3.29 Dividends are paid out of:

(a) gross profit

(b) net profit

(c) operating profit

(d) retained profit

3.30 Retained earnings appears:

(a) in the balance sheet

(b) in the cash flow statement

(c) in the income statement

(d) in the balance sheet and the income statement

3.31 The difference between brought forward and carried forward retained earnings is:

(a) operating profit less interest

(b) operating profit less dividends

(c) net profit less interest

(d) net profit less dividends

3.32 A retained loss is:

(a) an asset

(b) a liability

(c) an income

(d) an expense

3.33 The reason for a difference in accrual and cash profit will **not** be due to:

(a) a sales invoice that has been paid

(b) amortisation

(c) a supplier's invoice that has not yet been settled

(d) rent that has been paid in advance   303

3.34   The cash flow statement will include:

   (a)   a reconciliation between accrual profit and cash profit

   (b)   a cash flow forecast

   (c)   a reconciliation between actual and budgeted cash

   (d)   a reconciliation between cash and overdraft balances

3.35   Depreciation will appear in the cash flow reconciliation because:

   (a)   it is always a big figure

   (b)   it affects cash profit but not accrual profit

   (c)   it affects accrual profit but not cash profit

   (d)   it affects both accrual and cash profit

3.36   The cash flow statement will also include sections covering:

   (a)   cash from sales and investments

   (b)   how cash was invested and cash from sales

   (c)   cash from sales and cash from financing activities

   (d)   how cash was invested and cash from financing activities

Answers – Chapter 4

4.1   Return on investment gives an indication of:

   (a)   profitability compared to the cash flow

   (b)   cash generated compared to the capital invested

   (c)   profitability compared to the capital investment

   (d)   cash generated compared to profitability

4.2   Capital is a combination of:

   (a)   debt and working capital

   (b)   equity and investment capital

   (c)   debt, equity and working capital

   (d)   debt and equity

4.3　The return on capital employed compares:

(a)　net profit with debt

(b)　net profit with equity

(c)　net profit with investment and working capital

(d)　net profit with debt, equity, investment and working capital

4.4　EBITDA stands for:

(a)　earnings between interest, taxation, depreciation and amortisation

(b)　excess before income, taxation, depreciation and amortisation

(c)　earnings before interest, taxation, depreciation and amortisation

(d)　earnings before income, taxation, depreciation and amortisation

4.5　Gross margin is:

(a)　sales expressed as a percentage of cost of sales

(b)　gross profit expressed as a percentage of sales

(c)　sales expressed as a percentage of gross profit

(d)　gross profit expressed as a percentage of cost of sales

4.6　As a company increases turnover, the gross margin is expected to:

(a)　increase

(b)　decrease

(c)　stay the same

(d)　it is impossible to say

4.7　Operating margin is:

(a)　administration costs expressed as a percentage of sales

(b)　operating profit expressed as a percentage of administration costs

(c)　sales expressed as a percentage of operating profit

(d)　operating profit expressed as a percentage of sales

4.8   As a company increases turnover, the operating margin is expected to:

(a)   increase

(b)   decrease

(c)   stay the same

(d)   it is impossible to say

4.9   Net profit is:

(a)   sales less all costs

(b)   sales less all costs and interest

(c)   sales less all costs and interest and tax

(d)   sales less all costs and interest and tax and dividends

4.10   Net margin is:

(a)   EBITDA expressed as a percentage of net profit

(b)   net profit expressed as a percentage of sales

(c)   dividends expressed as a percentage of net profit

(d)   sales expressed as a percentage of net profit

4.11   As a company increases turnover, the net margin is expected to:

(a)   increase

(b)   decrease

(c)   stay the same

(d)   it is impossible to say

4.12   Operational gearing is reflected in the relationship between:

(a)   sales and fixed costs

(b)   fixed costs and variable costs

(c)   variable costs and operating profit

(d)   operating profit and sales

4.13   A company with high operational gearing will have:

(a)   high variable costs and high fixed costs

(b)   high variable costs and low fixed costs

(c)   low variable costs and high fixed costs

(d)   low variable costs and low fixed costs

4.14   A company with low operational gearing will have:

   (a)   high variable costs and high fixed costs

   (b)   high variable costs and low fixed costs

   (c)   low variable costs and high fixed costs

   (d)   low variable costs and low fixed costs

4.15   We should take on additional debt only if:

   (a)   interest rates are high

   (b)   things are going badly

   (c)   things are going well

   (d)   things are going well and we can afford the interest payments

4.16   Financial gearing is:

   (a)   debt expressed as a percentage of equity

   (b)   debt expressed as a percentage of capital

   (c)   capital expressed as a percentage of debt

   (d)   capital expressed as a percentage of debt and equity

4.17   Financial gearing shows:

   (a)   whether a company is insolvent

   (b)   the proportion of funding coming from employees

   (c)   the proportion of funding coming from the banks and loans

   (d)   whether a company can meet its interest payments

4.18   The interest cover ratio shows:

   (a)   how much interest a company pays compared to dividends

   (b)   how much interest a company pays compared to net profit

   (c)   how much interest a company pays compared to operating profit

   (d)   how much interest a company pays compared to gross profit

4.19   The tax shield means that:

   (a)   debt is more tax efficient than equity as a source of funding

   (b)   equity is more tax efficient than debt as a source of funding

   (c)   debt and equity are both as tax efficient as each other

   (d)   companies are not obliged to pay interest if they do not want to

4.20   Leverage shows:

(a)   how equity multiplies the return on equity

(b)   how debt multiplies the return on equity

(c)   how equity multiplies the return on debt

(d)   how debt multiplies the return on debt

4.21   Working capital is:

(a)   fixed assets and current assets

(b)   current assets and current liabilities

(c)   current liabilities and non-current liabilities

(d)   non-current liabilities and non-current assets

4.22   Working capital is used to:

(a)   fund the long-term investment of the business

(b)   fund the repayment of debt

(c)   fund the day-to-day trading operations of the business

(d)   fund the payment of dividends

4.23   Stock turnover measures the number of days:

(a)   from buying an item of stock to selling it

(b)   from buying an item of stock to paying for it

(c)   from buying an item of stock to returning it

(d)   from buying an item of stock to receiving the invoice for it

4.24   Debtor turnover measures the number of days:

(a)   from selling an item of stock to invoicing for it

(b)   from selling an item of stock to having it returned

(c)   from selling an item of stock to receiving payment for it

(d)   from selling an item of stock to paying for it

4.25   Creditor turnover measures the number of days:

(a)   from buying an item of stock to selling it

(b)   from buying an item of stock to paying for it

(c)   from buying an item of stock to returning it

(d)   from buying an item of stock to receiving the invoice for it

4.26   Cost of sales reconciles:

   (a)   goods purchased with goods on order

   (b)   goods purchased with goods held in stock offsite

   (c)   goods purchased with goods returned

   (d)   goods purchased with goods sold

4.27   A company's working capital requirement is the difference between:

   (a)   when it sells a good and when it receives payment for that good

   (b)   when it buys a good and when it sells a good

   (c)   when it pays for a good and when it receives payment for that good

   (d)   when it buys a good and when it pays for that good

4.28   The liquidity ratio compares:

   (a)   current assets with current liabilities

   (b)   current assets with non-current liabilities

   (c)   non-current assets with current liabilities

   (d)   non-current assets with non-current liabilities

4.29   The liquidity ratio:

   (a)   must always be more than 1.0

   (b)   must never be more than 1.0

   (c)   shows whether a business is insolvent or not

   (d)   indicates potential areas of concern for further investigation

4.30   A liquidity ratio of 8.0:

   (a)   is very desirable – the company is very liquid

   (b)   is very undesirable – the company is insolvent

   (c)   indicates potential inefficient allocation of capital

   (d)   indicates highly efficient allocation of capital

4.31   The acid test is the same as the liquidity ratio but without stock because:

(a)   stock is the most difficult to turn into cash quickly

(b)   stock costs extra to store

(c)   stock can be sold quickly in a sale

(d)   stock may become obsolete

4.32   A lot of cash held on the balance sheet may indicate:

(a)   an insolvent company

(b)   inefficient allocation of capital

(c)   a company struggling to make payments to suppliers

(d)   a company has just made a significant dividend payment

Answers – Chapter 6

6.1   Costs can be categorised into two different types:

(a)   current and non-current

(b)   fixed and variable

(c)   opex and capex

(d)   direct and indirect

6.2   Direct costs are ones that:

(a)   can be allocated specifically to a product or service

(b)   are always variable

(c)   are always fixed

(d)   must be capitalised

6.3   Indirect costs are ones that:

(a)   can be allocated internally

(b)   vary based on the level of activity

(c)   cannot be specifically allocated to a product or service

(d)   cannot be capitalised

6.4   Costs can be said to behave in one of three ways:

    (a)   up, down or stay the same

    (b)   fixed, variable or semi variable (or stepped)

    (c)   current, non-current and long-term

    (d)   opex, capex and depreciation

6.5   A fixed cost is one that:

    (a)   will jump, given a specific level of activity

    (b)   always changes with the level of activity

    (c)   has a fixed and a variable element

    (d)   never changes with the level of activity

6.6   A variable cost is one that:

    (a)   will jump, given a specific level of activity

    (b)   always changes with the level of activity

    (c)   has a fixed and a variable element

    (d)   never changes with the level of activity

6.7   A semi variable cost is one that:

    (a)   will jump, given a specific level of activity

    (b)   always changes with the level of activity

    (c)   has a fixed and a variable element

    (d)   never changes with the level of activity

6.8   A stepped cost is one that:

    (a)   will jump, given a specific level of activity

    (b)   always changes with the level of activity

    (c)   has a fixed and a variable element

    (d)   never changes with the level of activity

6.9   Costs can be treated financially in one of two ways:

    (a)   opex and capex

    (b)   fixed and variable

    (c)   current and non-current

    (d)   profit and loss

6.10 Opex is:
  (a) expenditure on special operations
  (b) expenditure on the day-to-day running of the business
  (c) expenditure on assets that will be used for more than one year
  (d) expenditure that must be capitalised

6.11 Capex is:
  (a) expenditure on special operations
  (b) expenditure on the day-to-day running of the business
  (c) expenditure on assets that will be used for more than one year
  (d) expenditure that appears in the P&L account

6.12 Capitalising a cost will have:
  (a) no impact on profit
  (b) a deferred impact on profit via depreciation
  (c) will appear in the P&L account
  (d) is illegal under IFRS

6.13 A finance lease is the same as:
  (a) buying an asset on credit
  (b) renting an asset
  (c) borrowing an asset
  (d) selling an asset

6.14 An operating lease is the same as:
  (a) buying an asset on credit
  (b) renting an asset
  (c) borrowing an asset
  (d) selling an asset

6.15 The aim of depreciation is to:
  (a) reduce the value of an asset
  (b) reflect the market value of an asset in the balance sheet
  (c) reduce profits
  (d) match the cost of an asset to its useful economic life

6.16 Amortisation is:
  (a) allowed only under IFRS
  (b) the depreciation of intangible assets
  (c) the depreciation of tangible assets
  (d) determined by the auditors

6.17 The two methods of depreciation are:
  (a) straight line and impairment
  (b) impairment and reducing balance
  (c) straight line and reducing balance
  (d) variable and reducing balance

6.18 NBV stands for:
  (a) net book value
  (b) near book value
  (c) net balance value
  (d) near balance value

6.19 An impairment is:
  (a) an asset
  (b) a depreciation method
  (c) the write down in the value of an asset
  (d) a long-term liability

6.20 An accrual is where:
  (a) you have paid for a service, but not yet received that service
  (b) you have provided a service, but not yet been paid
  (c) you have received a service, but not yet paid
  (d) you have been paid, but have not yet provided the service

6.21 A prepayment is where:
  (a) you have paid for a service, but not yet received that service
  (b) you have provided a service, but not yet been paid
  (c) you have received a service, but not yet paid
  (d) you have been paid, but have not yet provided the service

6.22   Deferred income is where:

(a)   you have paid for a service, but not yet received that service

(b)   you have provided a service, but not yet been paid

(c)   you have received a service, but not yet paid

(d)   you have been paid, but have not yet provided the service

6.23   Accrued income is where:

(a)   you have paid for a service, but not yet received that service

(b)   you have provided a service, but not yet been paid

(c)   you have received a service, but not yet paid

(d)   you have been paid, but have not yet provided the service

6.24   Accruals, prepayments, accrued and deferred income are all accounting adjustments that are designed to:

(a)   keep the finance team busy

(b)   adjust profit for movements in cash

(c)   reverse capex decisions

(d)   recognise costs and income in the periods in which they occur

6.25   When considering margin and mark-up:

(a)   margin is always higher

(b)   mark up is always higher

(c)   they are both always the same

(d)   there is no relationship between the two

6.26   Absorption costing involves:

(a)   a lot of complicated calculations

(b)   allocating costs to other departments

(c)   allocating costs to the units of output

(d)   allocating costs to overheads

6.27   Breakeven analysis determines:

(a)   the level of production required to cover fixed costs

(b)   the level of production required to cover fixed and variable costs

(c)   the level of production required to cover absorbed costs

(d)   the level of production required to cover sunk costs

6.28   A marginal cost is:

    (a)   always very small

    (b)   the average cost per unit of output

    (c)   the total cost of all units of output

    (d)   the cost of an additional unit of output

6.29   A sunk cost is:

    (a)   a big cost that could sink the business

    (b)   a high-risk cost

    (c)   one that has already been incurred

    (d)   a future cost

6.30   A provision is:

    (a)   accounting for a future expected loss

    (b)   accounting for a future expected profit

    (c)   accounting for a past loss

    (d)   accounting for a past profit

Answers – Chapter 7

7.1   The time value of money states that:

    (a) £100 today is worth less than £100 in a year's time

    (b) £100 today is worth more than £100 in a year's time

    (c) £100 today is worth the same as £100 in a year's time

    (d) time is money

7.2   The discount rate is the rate at which:

    (a) interest is earned on money in the bank

    (b) the business rates paid are discounted by the local authority to encourage enterprise

    (c) the business must offer a discount to increase sales

    (d) the future cash flows of a project are discounted

7.3   The formula for the discount rate in Excel is:

    (a) =1/(1-r)^n; where r = discount rate and n = the year

    (b) =1/(1xr)^n; where r = discount rate and n = the year

    (c) =1/(1+r)^n; where r = discount rate and n = the year

    (d) =1/(1/r)^n; where r = discount rate and n = the year

7.4   NPV stands for:

    (a) new present value

    (b) net purchasing value

    (c) new purchasing value

    (d) net present value

7.5   The NPV of a project is defined as:

    (a) the present day value of the future cash flows associated with that project

    (b) the future day value of the present cash flows associated with that project

    (c) the present day value of the present cash flows associated with that project

    (d) the future day value of the future cash flows associated with that project

7.6   IRR stands for:

    (a) international rate of return

    (b) internal real return

    (c) internal rate of return

    (d) internal rate of refund

7.7   Which of these statements is true?

    (a) the NPV is the discount rate that gives an IRR of nil

    (b) the IRR is the discount rate that gives an NPV of nil

    (c) the discount rate is the IRR that gives an NPV of nil

    (d) the discount rate is the NPV that gives an IRR of nil

7.8   WACC stands for:

    (a)   the weighted absolute cost of capital

    (b)   the weighted average cost of capex

    (c)   the working average cost of capital

    (d)   the weighted average cost of capital

7.9   The WACC is the:

    (a)   average return that debt and equity investors require

    (b)   total return that debt and equity investors require

    (c)   mean return that debt and equity investors require

    (d)   normal return that debt and equity investors require

7.10   The payback on a project determines:

    (a)   its profitability

    (b)   when it becomes cash positive

    (c)   its alignment with business strategy

    (d)   how successful the project will be

Answers – Chapter 8

8.1   A budget might be described as:

    (a)   something to keep the finance team busy

    (b)   a reflection of what happened in the past

    (c)   a plan of what you intend to do in the future

    (d)   a waste of time

8.2   The relationship between the budget and the strategy is:

    (a)   irrelevant

    (b)   the strategy reflects the impact of delivering on the budget

    (c)   the budget reflects the financial implications of delivering on
        the strategy

    (d)   the more time spent on one, the less time is spent on the other

8.3 Good reasons for budgeting include:
- **(a)** planning, coordination, consistency motivation, control and evaluation
- **(b)** planning, coordination, communication, justification, control and evaluation
- **(c)** planning, coordination, communication, motivation, control and evaluation
- **(d)** profit setting, coordination, communication, motivation, control and evaluation

8.4 An incremental budget is one that is:
- **(a)** phased correctly over the various months
- **(b)** based on what happened in previous periods
- **(c)** flexed, based on actual volume achieved
- **(d)** started from a blank sheet of paper

8.5 A zero-based budget is one that is:
- **(a)** phased correctly over the various months
- **(b)** based on what happened in previous periods
- **(c)** flexed, based on actual volume achieved
- **(d)** started from a blank sheet of paper

8.6 Month end involves
- **(a)** stressing out the finance team
- **(b)** hiding unspent budget
- **(c)** closing the books and preparing management reports
- **(d)** allocating costs to other departments

8.7 Variance analysis examines:
- **(a)** the difference between actual and budget
- **(b)** the difference between budget and forecast
- **(c)** the difference between actual and prior year
- **(d)** all of the above

8.8   Flexing the budget involves:

    (a)   adjusting the actual level of output achieved to the budgeted amount

    (b)   adjusting the budget for the actual level of output achieved

    (c)   adjusting the actual costs to come into line with the original budget

    (d)   updating the forecast

8.9   Forecasting involves:

    (a)   projecting the budget forward

    (b)   guessing how the year will turn out

    (c)   using formulae in spreadsheets

    (d)   updating the budget based on more up-to-date actual figures

Answers – Chapter 9

9.1   Commercial awareness might be:

    (a)   an awareness of finance

    (b)   knowing how to get the best out of others

    (c)   managing the business both financially and operationally

    (d)   being able to cover for members of the finance team when they are away

9.2   Strategy involves:

    (a)   formulating the direction of the business

    (b)   learning from past mistakes

    (c)   guessing what the future might hold

    (d)   two weeks in Barbados

9.3   STEEPLE analysis is:

    (a)   an accounting methodology

    (b)   an inside out strategic thinking tool

    (c)   an outside in strategic thinking tool

    (d)   used to determine a core competence

9.4 Porter's Five Forces include:

(a) a SWOT analysis

(b) identifying buyer and supplier power

(c) setting the direction of the business

(d) conducting online surveys

9.5 The vision of the business is:

(a) what it does

(b) what it did

(c) where it has been

(d) where it wants to go

9.6 The mission of the business is:

(a) what it does

(b) what it did

(c) where it has been

(d) where it wants to go

9.7 Commercial awareness is important because:

(a) you might get a job in the finance team

(b) you will learn to develop complicated spreadsheets

(c) you will be able to negotiate a higher salary

(d) it helps to make informed business decisions based on sound financial analysis

What did you think of this book?

We're really keen to hear from you about this book, so that we can make our publishing even better.

Please log on to the following website and leave us your feedback.

It will only take a few minutes and your thoughts are invaluable to us.

www.pearsoned.co.uk/bookfeedback

Glossary

Absorption costing   The act of allocating all costs (variable and fixed) to each unit of output.

Accounting equation   States that assets less liabilities is equal to the shareholders' funds of a business.

Accounts payable   *See* **Creditor**

Accounts receivable   *See* **Debtor**

Accrual   A cost that has been incurred but is not yet reflected in the accounts; an accrual is a liability.

Accrual accounting   Recognising income when it is earned and costs when they are incurred.

Accrued income   Income that has been earned but is not yet reflected in the accounts; accrued income is an asset.

Accumulated depreciation   The total amount of depreciation already charged to the P&L account.

Acid test   Similar to the liquidity ratio, but ignoring the need to sell stock.

AGM   See **annual general meeting**.

Amortisation   Matching the cost of an intangible asset to its useful economic life.

Annual accounting return (ARR)   The ARR is the average profit (after depreciation) of a project, divided by the average investment).

Annual general meeting   The annual meeting of the company and the shareholders – where the results are presented and the shareholders are asked to vote on various resolutions.

Annual report and accounts   The accounts that are required to be prepared by law and sent to each shareholder.

Asset   Something that is owned.

Auditor   Someone who performs an independent check on the figures.

Balance sheet   The position of a company at a particular point in time – contains only assets and liabilities.

Basic   In relation to EPS – the basic EPS is the net profit of a company divided by the number of shares in issue.

Board   The group of directors of the business.

Bond   A form of loan that can be traded.

Budget   The financial implications of the future operational plans of a business.

Capex   Capital expenditure; as opposed to opex.

Capital   The total investment in a business – made up of debt and equity.

Capital and reserves   See **shareholders' funds**.

Cash   Cash in hand (bank notes) plus money in the current and deposit bank accounts of a business.

Cash flow forecast   A forecast of the future cash flows – usually on a month-by-month basis – of the business.

Cash flow statement   Statement showing the cash profit of a business and how that cash was invested and the effects of financing.

Comparable   National and international rules and guidelines exist to allow the accounts of one company to be compared to another.

Consistent   The directors determine the policy as to how transactions should be accounted for – these policies must then be applied on a consistent basis to aid comparability (between, for example, different years).

Cost   An expense to the business.

Coupon   The equivalent of interest on a bond.

Creditor   A person or company to whom the business owes money. Also known as **accounts payable**.

Current assets Assets that are expected to be turned into cash within 12 months from the balance sheet date.

Current liabilities Liabilities that are due to be repaid within 12 months from the balance sheet date.

Current ratio *See* **liquidity ratio**.

Debt A form of investment – the debt usually will attract interest and must be repaid.

Debtor A person or company who owes the business money. Also known as **accounts receivable**.

Deferred income Income received but not yet earned – it must be deferred until the period in which it is earned; deferred income is a liability.

Deflation A deflationary environment is one where prices are falling.

Depreciation Matching the cost of a tangible asset (less any residual value) to its useful economic life.

Derivative A contract between two parties where neither party owns the thing being bought or sold; a derivative derives its value from an underlying asset class.

Diluted In relation to EPS – the diluted EPS is the net profit of a company divided by the number of shares potentially in issue – that is, if all share options were exercised.

Direct cost A cost that can be allocated to a product; as opposed to an indirect cost.

Directors Individuals who run the business; directors have additional legal responsibilities. May be executive or non-executive.

Discount rate The rate at which future cash flows are discounted, reflecting the time value of money.

Discounted cash flow The process of applying a discount factor to the future cash flows associated with an investment.

Dividend A distribution of profit to the shareholders of the business.

Earnings   *See* **profit**.

Earnings per share   The earnings (or net profit) of a company divided by the number of shares in issue.

EBIT   Earnings before interest and taxation; also known as operating profit.

EBITDA   Earnings before interest, taxation, depreciation and amortisation.

EPS   *See* **earnings per share**.

Equity   A form of investment – the equity investment is not repayable, and any dividend is determined by the directors of the business.

Executive director   A director with day-to-day responsibility for running the business; as opposed to a non-executive director.

Expense   *See* **cost**.

Fair value   Similar to market value, the fair value of an asset is what it would cost to replace.

Finance lease   A lease where the lessor lends the money to the lessee to purchase an asset.

Financial gearing   Similar to leverage, a measure of the extent to which a company's operations are funded by debt as opposed to equity.

Fixed assets   *See* **non-current assets**.

Fixed cost (F/C)   A fixed cost is one that does not vary with the level of activity; as opposed to variable cost.

Flexed budget   Restating the budget to show what it would have been for the actual level of, for example, output.

Forecast   An update to the budget, providing an increasingly accurate picture of how the year is likely to turn out.

Future   A form of derivative, a future is the obligation to buy or sell at a future point in time.

Gilt   A bond issued by the UK Government.

Going concern   A company is described as a going concern if it is trading and is expected to continue to trade for the foreseeable future; a company is a going concern if it can meet its obligations as they fall due.

Goodwill   The difference between the price paid to buy a company and the fair value of its net assets.

Hedge   The offsetting of one risk against another (for example, leaving home with sun glasses and an umbrella).

Hyperinflation   A hyper inflationary environment is one where prices are rising very rapidly and spiralling out of control.

Impairment   The writing down in the value of an asset (usually a one-off charge).

Income   *See* **sale**.

Income statement   *See* **profit & loss account**.

Incremental budget   A budget that is based on last year plus or minus – i.e. based on what was spent in a previous period; as opposed to zero-based budget.

Indirect cost   An overhead; as opposed to a direct cost.

Inflation   An inflationary environment is one where prices are rising.

Intangible   A non-physical asset – that cannot be touched – such as a licence or patent; as opposed to a tangible asset.

Interest   The reward or income to the lender of funds.

Interest cover   Measures the ability of a company to meet its interest payments.

Internal rate of return   The discount rate that produces an NPV of zero.

Inventory   *See* **stock**.

Investment capital   Fixed or non-current assets; investment capital is capital that is invested into assets that are used to run the business.

IRR   *See* **internal rate of return**.

Key financial indicator A financial measure of business performance considered as important to assisting in managing the business.

Key performance indicator A non-financial measure of business performance considered as important to assisting in managing the business.

KFI *See* **key financial indicator**.

KPI *See* **key performance indicator**.

Legal entity A company is described as a separate legal entity – it can enter into contracts in its own name; the company is run by the directors.

Leverage The use of debt to increase the return on an equity investment.

Liability An amount that is owed (or potentially owed) to a third party.

Liquidation Closing down a company – when a company's assets are sold and the liabilities are settled, with any remaining amount distributed to the shareholders. As opposed to receivership.

Liquidity ratio Measures the ability of a company to meet its obligations as they fall due.

Loan An amount lent to the company.

Long-term liabilities *See* **non-current liabilities**.

Loss When costs exceed sales – the opposite of profit.

Marginal cost The additional costs associated with an extra unit of output.

Market value The value that an asset can be sold for.

Matching concept *See* **accrual accounting**.

Material significant A material impact is one that will change the user's view of the accounts or company.

Maturity The date on which a loan is due to be repaid.

NBV *See* **net book value**.

NCA Either non-current assets or net current assets.

Net assets   Assets less liabilities – also known as shareholders' funds.

Net book value (NBV)   The cost (book value) less any depreciation already charged in previous periods to the P&L account.

Net current assets   Current assets less current liabilities – also known as working capital.

Net present value   The present day value of all of the future cash flows associated with an investment, discounted back to today's value.

Net yield   The difference between the cost of borrowing funds and the return on investing those funds.

Non-current assets   Assets that are used to run the business; as opposed to current assets.

Non-current liabilities   Liabilities that are due to be repaid more than 12 months from the balance sheet date.

Non-executive director   A director who does not have day-to-day responsibility for running the business, but ensures that the business is run in the best interests of the shareholders, with consideration for other stakeholders (such as employees and suppliers); as opposed to an executive director.

NPV   *See* **net present value**.

Operating lease   A lease where the lessor rents the asset to the lessee.

Operational gearing   The relationship between the fixed and variable costs of a company; measures the sensitivity of a company's profit to changes in price.

Opex   Operational expenditure; as opposed to capex.

Opportunity cost   The benefit forgone by making one investment and thus not being able to use the capital elsewhere in the business.

Option   A form of derivative, an option is the right to buy or sell at a future point in time.

Outgoing   *See* **cost**.

Partnership   When two or more individuals agree to pool their income, deduct the costs and share the remainder on a predetermined or equitable basis.

Payable   *See* **creditor**.

PE ratio   The ratio of the price to earnings of a company.

Phasing   The allocation of items of budgeted expenditure into the relevant periods.

Plan   *See* **budget**.

PLC   Public limited company; see **public company**.

Prepayment   An amount paid in advance of receipt of the goods or services; a prepayment is an asset.

Price   The amount that you pay for an asset.

Primary market   When a company floats in an initial public offering, the shares are purchased from the company by the investors – as opposed to a secondary market transaction.

Private company   A company that is not listed (on a stock exchange), so the shares are not publicly traded – as opposed to public company.

Profit   When sales exceed costs – the opposite of loss.

Profit & loss account (P&L a/c)   Also known as the income statement, the P&L account is the trading account of the business – showing sales and costs – for a specified duration.

Provision   The recognition of a liability or the fall in the value of an asset before the event occurs.

Prudence   Accountants err on the side of caution, so financial statements are prepared generally with an air of prudence – if it can go wrong, then it might happen; but if it can go right, then it might not happen.

Public company   A company that is listed (on a stock exchange), so the shares are available for members of the public to buy and sell – as opposed to a private company.

QE   *See* **quantitative easing**.

Quantitative easing The printing of additional money by a country's central bank. In the UK, QE was used to buy UK Government Bonds (gilts).

Receivable *See* **debtor**.

Receivership When a company is run for the benefit of the creditors rather than the shareholders; a company that is no longer a going concern may be placed into receivership before being placed into liquidation.

Refinancing Where a company rolls over its debt – in effect taking out a loan to repay a loan.

Report and accounts (R&A) The report to the shareholders of a business by the directors, plus the financial statements showing how the business has performed financially.

Retained earnings Profits that have not been distributed as a dividend but have been reinvested back into the business.

Retained profit *See* **retained earnings**.

Return The income to an investor – often compared to the original amount invested.

Return on assets The profit generated by a business expressed as a percentage of its total assets (non-current assets plus current assets); this is similar to the ROCE, but not exactly the same.

Return on capital employed The profit generated by a business expressed as a percentage of the capital invested (through debt and equity).

Return on investment The income of an investment expressed as a percentage of the amount invested; this reflects the yield of the investment.

Revenue *See* **sale**.

Rights issue A rights issue gives existing shareholders the right to purchase additional shares that are issued to maintain their proportion of ownership of a business.

Risk Defined as probability × impact of an event; risk is also used as a measure of volatility.

ROA *See* **return on assets**.

ROCE   *See* **return on capital employed.**

ROI   *See* **return on investment.**

Roll over   *See* **refinancing.**

Sale   Also known as income, turnover or revenue, a sale is recognised when legal title of the goods or services is transferred to the customer.

Secondary market   Where the shares (or bonds) of a company are bought and sold between investors independently of the company – as opposed to the primary market.

Secured   A loan might be secured against an asset – if the company cannot repay the loan, then ownership of the asset transfers to the lender.

Security   A security is a stock, share or bond that can be traded.

Semi variable cost   A cost that has an element of fixed and an element of variable cost – behaving like a combination of the two.

Share capital   The nominal or face value of the shares that have been issued.

Share premium   An additional amount, over and above the share capital, that a share has been sold for by the company.

Shareholder   An equity investor – someone who owns a share in the business.

Shareholders' funds   The shareholders' investment in the business – usually initial investment and profits reinvested.

Sole trader   An individual who works for themselves – and does not trade through a company.

Spread   The difference between the yield on two investments; the spread will reflect the difference in the risk associated with the two investments (all other things being equal).

Statutory accounts   *See* **annual report and accounts**; the financial statements are required to be prepared legally by every company and are therefore referred to as statutory accounts.

Stepped cost   A fixed cost that jumps at a specified level of activity.

Stock   Items purchased or made by a company for sale; also known as inventory.

Stock exchange   A market place (now electronic) where shares in public companies can be bought and sold.

Sunk cost   A cost that has already been incurred and should not be included in any future decision making.

Swap   A form of derivative, a swap is where one income stream is swapped for another (e.g. a fixed rate of interest is swapped for a variable rate).

Tangible   A physical asset – that can be touched – such as a building or computer; as opposed to an intangible asset.

Time value of money   The concept that £100 today is worth more than £100 in a year's time.

Timely   The financial accounts of a company must be produced as soon as possible – the older the information, the less relevant – and hence the less use – it is.

Total assets   Non-current (or fixed) assets plus current assets.

Total assets less current liabilities   Another way of expressing total capital employed.

Total liabilities   Non-current (or long-term) liabilities plus current liabilities.

Total shareholder return (TSR)   A combination of dividend income and capital growth associated with a share.

Trade   The buying and selling of goods and services.

Treasury   A bond issued by the US Government.

Treasury shares   A company that has purchased its own shares and has not cancelled them will hold them on the balance sheet as treasury shares – they will be found in the shareholders' funds section.

TSR   *See* **total shareholder return**.

Turnover   *See* **sale**.

Useful economic life   The period of time over which an asset is expected to be used.

Variable cost (V/C)   A variable cost is one that varies with the level of activity; as opposed to fixed cost.

Variance   The difference between (for example) the actual figures and the budget; can be expressed as an absolute amount or as a percentage.

Veil of incorporation   What separates the shareholders in a company from the company itself; limited refers to the limited liability of the shareholders of a business.

Volatility   The extent to which a price deviates from its mean; stock prices are more volatile than bond prices.

WACC   *See* **weighted average cost of capital**.

WCR   *See* **working capital requirement**.

Weighted average cost of capital   The returns that the providers of debt and equity to the business demand, weighted to reflect the mix of debt and equity.

WIP   *See* **work in progress**.

Work in progress (WIP)   Work in progress – stock that is in the process of being converted from raw materials into finished goods.

Working capital   Also known as net current assets, the working capital is used by the business to ensure that it can meet its obligations as they fall due.

Working capital requirement   The number of days between when a company has to pay for a good or service, and when it receives the cash from its customers in payment for a good or service.

Yield   The return on an investment, expressed as a percentage.

Zero-based budget   A budget that is created from scratch – where every item of expenditure is justified; as opposed to incremental budget.

Index

Note: Glossary page numbers appear in **bold**